MONTANA: *An Uncommon Land*

MONTANA

An Un

Common Land

K. ROSS TOOLE

NORMAN : UNIVERSITY OF OKLAHOMA PRESS

BY K. ROSS TOOLE

History of Montana (editor, with Merrill Burlingame)
(New York, 1957)
Essays on the History of Montana and the Northwest (editor,
with J. W. Smurr) (Helena, Montana, 1957)
Montana: An Uncommon Land (Norman, 1959)

International Standard Book Number: 0–8061–0427–9

Copyright 1959 by the University of Oklahoma Press,
Publishing Division of the University. Manufactured in
the U.S.A. First edition, 1959; second printing, 1959;
third printing, 1964; fourth printing, 1968; fifth printing, 1970;
sixth printing, 1973.

ACKNOWLEDGMENTS

I AM INDEBTED to the contributors to the recent two-volume history of Montana, edited by Merrill Burlingame and myself, for the new material contained in those volumes which has enabled me to interpret events with some confidence that the interpretation will stand up.

To Joan and John Marchi, Mrs. Howard Toole, John Hakola, Michael Kennedy, John C. Ewers, Mrs. Shirley Coggeshall, Vivian Paladin, and John T. Vance I am indebted for contributory services which made the writing of this book possible.

Miss Virginia Walton, chief librarian of the Historical Society of Montana, has been particularly helpful in pointing the way to new and significant material.

This volume is essentially an interpretive study and, as such, owes much of whatever merit it may have to the basic work of others. To the authors of the several histories and the many monographs and manuscripts which I have used, I can only give thanks collectively.

v

All but three of the illustrations used in this book were provided through the courtesy of my good friends of the Historical Society of Montana, Helena. Therefore, unless otherwise credited, illustrations are from this source.

Notwithstanding all the help I have received, errors of fact or interpretation are exclusively my own.

K. Ross Toole

New York City

CONTENTS

ILLUSTRATIONS

MAPS

MONTANA: *An Uncommon Land*

THE MONTANA PATTERN

Professor Walter Prescott Webb in a
recent article in *Harper's* magazine[1] had some penetrating
things to say about what he called the eight desert states,
of which Montana is one. Among other things, Mr. Webb
asked how the historians dealing with these states could make
"thick" history out of such "thin" material. They must "write
of cowboys as if they were noble knights, and the cowmen
kings." They "had few men of distinction," and the historian
must deal "with a country almost without chronology or
important battles or great victories or places where armies
have surrendered or dead soldiers were buried."

In many ways Mr. Webb is right. Yet somehow we got
where we are, and there is some explanation for our being
what we are. In Montana we are only 660,000 strong, and we
inhabit the Union's third largest state. We do not, indeed,
fill it very full. There are only 4.1 of us per square mile, and
there are 146,000 square miles. But still, here we are, and it
is the business of historians not to make something of nothing

[1] "The American West: Perpetual Mirage," *Harper's*, May, 1957.

but to offer explanations based on fact—explanations either implicit or explicit since facts never speak for themselves.

It is a little misleading to say, as I have just said, that it is the business of historians not to make something of nothing, because (and this would seem to sustain Mr. Webb's thesis) "nothing" is very important in Montana in many ways. What we are *not* is often more compelling than what we are. The fact of our emptiness is in itself immensely significant.

These studies in the history of Montana take the direction its author sets them upon. The only way finally to avoid interpretation in history is to avoid history, to settle for the compilation of limmu lists, or, like the antiquarians, to fondle facts for facts' sake. I do not mean to imply that this book is neither chronological nor factual. It consists of a series of roughly chronological essays which point up the themes that course through the years. Enough ponderous and unselective compilation has taken place in Montana, and it is time for historians to deal selectively and interpretively with this material.

Effective state history is difficult to write. States, after all, are political entities, not sensible economic units. Often the destiny of a state lies neither in its stars nor in itself but in far-removed and rather obscure events. Montana is particularly notable for having had little to do with how it developed and what it became. Yet its history has almost always been set down as if such were not the case, and the consequence is that most histories of the state have a kind of vacuum-like quality. One cannot set the lens so narrowly and write meaningful history. The rivers and roads that lead outward must be followed to see what is at the other end. The movements and events that wash over and through the area from outside must be traced back to their origins; other-

4

wise, what they alter and what they produce locally cannot be made sensible.

And, it seems to me, one must recognize four elements as compounding the history of any state. First, there are those things about it that are essentially national in character—national attitudes and characteristics which constitute a common heritage. Then there are those developments we share with the region but not with the nation. Then there are those events which are common only to us and to our immediate neighbors; and, last, there are those things about us and about what has happened to us that are unique. One cannot hazard an evaluation of the given proportion of these elements because the proportion varies from time to time and from place to place. But one cannot write good state history without a consciousness of this depth and breadth.

Communities evolve like human beings. Like human beings, also, they can be warped by the external problems that beset them, they can suffer from chronic afflictions, and they can develop distinct character from the crucibles in which they are formed.

The Montana pattern has been brief, explosive, frenetic, and often tragic. The economic picture has often been one of exploitation, overexpansion, boom, and bust. The political scene has been equally extreme—from fiery, wide-open violence to apathetic resignation.

The land itself is at once mountainous and flat, hot and cold, beautiful and terrible, and benign and malevolent. And the land has profoundly influenced events. There is little or nothing moderate about the story of Montana. It has ricocheted violently down the corridor of possibilities. What is good in reasonable measure is often bad in full measure, and Montana has been a place of full measure.

Present-day Montana.

West of the 100th meridian the frontiersmen encountered a new land. Here was no humid, gently rolling forested area but a place of vastness, semiaridity, and implacably unpredictable weather. Laws designed both to help the pioneer and protect the public domain were devised by humid-area people. They were anachronistic in the West because they failed in both their salient purposes, and they exacerbated the century-old suspicion of the Westerner toward the Easterner.

For many years, while immigrants rushed to the West Coast, the facts of geography sealed off a great northern pocket. When at last it was probed, civilization came all at once. It came too fast. There was no ebb to the flow. The plains had sustained millions of buffalo. The sea of grass was endless. To the cattlemen who poured from the South and the West onto this great area in the early eighties, it was inconceivable that the plains could not sustain their great herds forever. Tough and resourceful as they were, their days on the open range were tragically numbered. In less than a decade their empire had crumbled and the grass was gone.

Then it was the "honyocker," who, like the cattlemen, moved onto the land with quick profit as a basic motive. There were a few good years, but then nature struck again. The mass exodus of people from the plains left whole communities empty. Eleven thousand farms were abandoned in eastern Montana in the late teens and early twenties. The boom had been great; so was the bust. The promoters and the ebullient honyockers did not know the land. And they left behind them mute towns with tumbleweeds banked high on the windward side of leaning buildings. They also left behind a sorely wounded country.

In 1880, Nate Levengood's meadow, where Anaconda now stands, was a lush and quiet place. As far as the eye could see in all directions there was nothing but the valley, the swelling foothills, and the mountain ramparts.

Four years later the meadow was gone, blighted by arsenic fumes from the largest copper smelter in the world. There had been no gradual encroachment of civilization, no creeping in of small farms and little stores. There was no village. First there was nothing, and then all of a sudden there was the world's largest smelter and around it a raw new city.

Politically Montana did not evolve by trial and error. Politics sprang forth the handmaiden of men battling both the wilderness and each other. And the combat was ruthless. These men, too, were literally wresting wealth from the earth. There were no theorists among them. And so, almost before it had begun, Montana's political story was characterized by violent feuds, open corruption, and personal schisms among the "copper kings" which shook the very foundations of the new land and set the course of political events for many years to come.

Nature, not the evil designs of men, decreed that Montana be a place with a colonial economy. The object of men had to be to trap it, mine it, shoot it, and get out. Every one of the salient industries has been extractive, from beaver through beef to copper. The capital required for frantic exploitation, whether of furs, cattle, silver, lumber, or copper, had to come from the East. And as Eastern capital flowed westward, control and the bulk of the wealth flowed eastward.

Montana's growth, in one sense, has been a series of traumas. There has been a strikingly consistent pattern which, appropriately enough, conforms to the pattern of the land itself. For every pinnacle there is an equally impressive declivity. For every sudden rise, a sudden fall. Optimism has alternated almost monotonously with despair.

Yet there has been genuine heroism in all this—and progress. Montana has been a state only since 1889. Its entire effective history could have been encompassed in one lifetime. It is simple in retrospect to point out the profligate waste of natural resources, the crashing blunders of haste, the blindness and shortsightedness of businessmen, and the venality of politicians. Upon reflection, however, it is not so simple to point out alternative routes that would have been more practical.

In a formidable land more than one thousand miles from the centers of trade and commerce, resources such as timber and copper could hardly have been utilized slowly and without waste. It was not a time for contemplation nor a place for the fainthearted. Those who invested in the ventures that made Montana what it is took great risks. There is no list of the thousands who lost. It is sometimes too easy to criticize the methods of those who won.

Mr. Webb calls our history "thin." It would be better to call it brief. In truth, considering the time elapsed, the history of Montana is startlingly provocative and quite thick.

II

THE LAND
AND ITS FIRST PENETRATION

WEST OF THE 100TH MERIDIAN the traveler came upon a land that required of him new skills to traverse it and different techniques to conquer it. Indeed, so formidable was this land that in a sense it was never conquered at all. In the beginning the region today known as the Great Plains—that vast, flat midriff of the country that stretches from Southern Alberta to Mexico—was a barrier to cross, a desert to be traversed with all haste. The traveler was bound for the verdant Northwest Coast or sun-drenched California.

Once he had crossed the plains, he found himself in the towering mountains, the sharp spine of America. Here the mighty gorges, swift rivers, and heaving forest land challenged his wagons. And if he was delayed in his passage, he could be caught in snowfall so deep that his animals foundered and in cold so bitter that it seared his lungs.

The plains and the mountains together, regardless of whether the traveler sought to penetrate them north or south, stood as a perpetual challenge. They defeated the weak and the unwise. They defied the builder and the farmer. They gave more than momentary pause to the compelling force of manifest destiny. Thus the westward movement was a leapfrog movement.

Long after the coastal area was settled and maturing, the mountains and the plains still bore no mark of man except perhaps for the faint track of his wagons in the grass.

Civilization and culture have never quite caught up in this great region. Over the years oases appeared on the desert, and the mountains yielded slowly to towns. The rivers were bridged in strategic places, and the soil felt the plow. But wilderness was never really far from the windowpane, and the implacable country seemed to retreat only to advance.

Far to the north in this region lay what is today Montana. Its western quarter was in the fold of the Rockies. To the east it stretched more than five hundred miles onto the plains. High, wide, handsome, and remote, this area resisted penetration longer, perhaps, than any other.

I F YOU WERE to fly in a small plane from Missoula in the west to Glendive in the east, it would take you the better part of a day, and you would pass over country spectacularly different. You would be impressed by the fact that from only three thousand feet in the air civilization seems to be largely swallowed up by the immense country. There is suddenly something very pretentious about man. There is also something wonderful about his pretensions.

Montana can be divided into several seemingly logical regions. One frequently sees historical reference to northwestern Montana, southwestern Montana, central Montana, and eastern Montana. For some purposes this regional division is useful. In fact, however, the sectionalization is arbitrary and quickly proves synthetic in an economic sense. But the state is logically divisible into two regions: the mountainous western area and the eastern plains area. Indeed, the division is actual, clear-cut, and significant. If state boundaries had been more logically drawn, Montana might have emerged less a geographical schizophrenic. For the western region has a coastal orientation (especially west of the Continental Divide), and the eastern region looks to the Middle West. Accordingly, regional historians do not know quite what to do with Montana. Western Montana is sometimes treated in general works on the Pacific Northwest, and eastern Montana gets into general works on the Great Plains. In both cases the state appears as a kind of exclave.

Roughly, the western quarter of the state is ruggedly mountainous. The eastern three-quarters is plains country. This must be qualified by pointing out that mountains do exist in central Montana. There are the Little Rockies, the Bear Paws, the Big and Little Belts, the Crazy Mountains, and lesser ranges that rise in rather isolated fashion from the prairie floor. But traveling eastward you have left the real mountain country when you leave Livingston behind in the south, Great Falls in the central portion, or Browning in the north. The country east of that line is not conditioned by mountains but is rather what Walter Prescott Webb terms the "Great Plains Environment." In short, it possesses all three characteristics of the true plains: it is treeless, level, and semi-arid. There are variations in this picture, but the generalization holds true.

This eastern section of the country is a land of extremes. It gets less than twenty inches of rainfall a year. It can get bitterly cold in the winter and desert-hot in the summer. Its winds are ocean-like in character, just as the plains themselves are ocean-like in their sweep to the horizon. Over this vast, treeless country the winds are little retarded by friction, and hence they blow with remarkable uniformity and relatively high velocity. "Does the wind blow this way here all the time?" asked the eastern visitor. "No, Mister," replied the cowboy, "it'll maybe blow this way for a week or ten days, and then it'll take a change and blow like hell for a while." In winter the combination of wind and snow sometimes results in blizzards of blinding fury. In summer, periodically, wind, heat, and dryness combine to produce real drought. Droughts in this area are cyclical and inevitable. The old-timers know it, and the newcomers invariably find it out. Such weather phenomena—hot winds and chinooks, blizzards and hailstorms—can bring great distress and economic ruin to man. They frequently do.

Most of eastern Montana is covered with what is technically called "short grass." This grass forms a sod, a heavy carpet, although its roots do not penetrate deeply. Interspersed in the drier areas are stretches of sagebrush. This short grass is nutritious, and even though it fights an apparently losing battle in some areas against Russian thistle, its rich proteins, mineral salts, and carbohydrates keep grazing cattle in excellent condition whenever there is sufficient moisture for the grass to thrive. There was a day when eastern Montana's grass "rolled in the wind like a sea," and it carpeted the plains as far as the eye could reach—sometimes a foot or two in height. But sheep, cattle, overgrazing, and, above all, the plow, put an end to such lushness. The picture should not be painted so positively, however. There were droughts then as well as now. There were more fires then. There were lean or devastating periods for the plains' animals and Indians, and there were doubtless mass migrations of game and men to better grass elsewhere. Still, the grass grew again. The seeds survived. One wet season and the sea of grass rolled again—until the plow put an end to it forever.

The rivers of eastern Montana when seen on a map seem to form an impressive water network. The great Missouri, "a little too thick for a beverage and a little too thin to cultivate," courses for two-thirds the length of the state. Of its two principal southern tributaries, the Musselshell and Yellowstone, the latter has its own tributary system—an impressive number of streams, including the Big Horn, the Tongue, and the Powder. Into the Missouri from the north flow the Sun, the Teton, the Marias, and the Milk.

In the general economy of the region, however, it is important to note that these rivers are what might be called "aggraded," that is, they are shallow, silt- and debris-bearing streams which constantly build up their own beds and hence frequently spill over into new channels. Although the Missouri and the Yellowstone were vital in that they were navigable, the other waterways were not, except for small craft during the fur trade era. The land through which these streams cut is so basically porous and dry that it remains without significant vegetation right to the water's edge. The settlers in eastern Montana turned not to irrigation as a remedy but to dry-land farming. The Missouri was not like the Nile, requiring only diversion to make the desert bloom.

If this eastern section of Montana, with its monotonous plains, it aridity, its badlands and mineral-laden waters, its blizzards and wind, seems inhospitable, the paucity of population per square mile would seem to support the contention. But there is more to it than that.

This is the land "where the sky comes down the same distance all around" and those who live in it love it—most of the time. Again, like the sea there is something compelling about its distances and sweep. Here there is elbowroom. The land is only monotonous to those who do not know it. It is, in fact, ever changing. When there is moisture it can get incredibly green. In the autumn it gets tawny, and swift-moving cloud shadows give it motion. The wind carries the pungently clean odor of sage. Nowhere except at sea is there quite the same subtlety of color, quite the same feeling of vastness.

Still, it is a hard land. Weather is not merely capricious; it is implacable. Over every period of prosperity hangs the shadow of inevitable drought. Good years may dim a few bitter memories, and younger people who really disbelieve the inevitability of the cycle keep alive a tenacious optimism. But in truth few people seek out this land as such. Of those few, fewer still remain when the gauntlet is cast down.

There are, indeed, prosperous communities in the region. Basic to that prosperity today, however, is oil and the hope of oil. Billings, for instance, is Montana's fastest growing city. It has long been prosperous, pleasant, and clean. It has become the center of a great trade area, and its economy is becoming more diversified yearly. How, then, are such gems, such oases in the matrix of the formidable land, to be explained? The land and the weather are unchanged. But oil, an expanding national economy, and the fact that such communities have become vital ganglia in a regional transportation system actually set them apart from their immediate environment. Also, this is a new phenomenon in the eastern section, and we are dealing here primarily with the past.

As for the mountainous west, the general picture here will exhibit as many exceptions as are found in the east. In his great book, *The Great Plains,* Walter Prescott Webb remarked: "So far as civilization is concerned the mountains are negligible. Unless they contain minerals they are of relatively little importance in the development of human society." This may be true in the context of Webb's broad thesis, but it is questionable when reduced to particulars and local developments of significance. The mountains may not permanently have diverted the great course of the westward movement or produced, as the plains did, a new cultural complex. But man had to adapt to them, and they did produce unique institutions.

The mountains in the western section of Montana east of the Continental Divide are generally more barren than those west of the divide. Slabs of granite toss up in gigantic confusion. In the summertime these mountains shimmer in the sky. They seem to reflect everything and absorb nothing. The atmosphere the year around is startlingly clear—almost brittle. To view these ranges is to get a sudden sense of depth and perspective. The lines between sky, crag, and foothill are abrupt and clearly etched. In the spring the wild flowers cover the foothills with an almost bewildering variety of colors. When the ephemeral flora has withered in the sun, there are the red berries of kinnikinnick, the greens, browns, and reds of the tough scrub bushes, the serviceberry, huckleberry, and, always, the tawny grass. These ranges are less apt to be heavily forested than the ranges west of the divide.

On the western side of the watershed there is a touch of coastal verdancy to the mountains. There are giant larch and fir and pine. At lower altitudes and alongside the streams, there are cottonwood and quaking asp. The canyons are filled with white, rushing water. The area is dotted with clear lakes. The rivers, which flow generally northward and westward, are blue-green and swift. Between the ranges lie the high valleys. While these valleys vary widely as regards temperature, soil, snowfall, and water, all except a few are given a measure of protection from the wind by the ramparts that hedge them in. From the great peaks of Glacier Park in the north to towering twelve-thousand-foot Granite Peak in the far south, the innumerable, jumbled crags and folds, lakes and swift streams, interspersed with valleys, form a rugged, beautiful region.

But in the entire area the winters are long and the cold severe. Mountains are not good for growing things, and in the valleys, even though the soil is frequently rich and the water plentiful, the growing season is very short. Blizzards are little less severe than in the eastern section. To the man from eastern Montana the mountains are often oppressive. He feels hemmed in. But to the man used to them, mountainless country can be unbearable.

In any event, to fly over Montana—east or west—is to recognize how little man has really changed the country. The occasional ribbon of a highway or railway, lost as it is upon the plain or buried in the folds of the mountains, is poor testimony to man's conquest of nature. The occasional town or city, laid out with incongruous geometry, does little to take the edge off the impression of impenetrable wilderness. It is somehow startling to realize that man lived in this land thousands of years ago.

There are various theories concerning man's arrival in what is now Montana. That he existed here at least ten thousand years ago we know from physical evidence. It is probable that he came from Asia via Alaska and filtered southward when an intercontinental land bridge existed there.

The earliest-known Montanan was Folsom man. Because only a few small Folsom sites have been found in Montana, what we know of these people and their life in Montana must largely be deduced from broad evidence unearthed in the plains area outside of the state. We do know, however, from material found in the region of the Lower Yellowstone River, from the Medicine Lake area in northeastern Montana, and from a recent excavation near Helena, that the Folsom culture was rather widespread in Montana. All the evidence to indicate that they did not pass over the crest into the Columbia River country is, of course, negative, and it would seem that they were principally a plains' people whose probings into the mountain regions were probably tentative. In this very early period, indeed, we have no evidence at all of Folsom life in Montana west of the Continental Divide.

Following the Folsom culture, and probably for a time contemporaneous with it, came the Yuma culture. These people lived in Montana about 6,800 years ago. Anthropologists differentiate Folsom and Yuma by a myriad of small technicalities involving differences in stone projectile points, but these need not concern us here.

This unclear early period was followed by what anthropologists call the Redevelopment Period or the period of the Late Hunters. Beginning about three thousand years ago, clear changes in Indian culture are discernible in physical evidence. That evidence, in the form of projectile points, hearth fires, cave drawings, and tools is available for the region west of the divide as well as for the plains area.

By the time the first whites penetrated the region, the Montana Indians, ranging from west to east, could be identified as the Kutenais, Kalispels, Flatheads, Shoshonis, Crows, Blackfeet, Chippewas and Crees, Cheyennes, Gros Ventres or Atsinas, and the Assiniboins. These were the tribes whom the whites were to encounter. Some of them were peaceful;

some were not. But in either event, coexistence between Indian and white was to prove impossible. Relentlessly driven by ambition, the acquisitive scouts of empire meant to appropriate what they could as fast as they could. There was no room in the scheme of things for the Indian who sought to maintain his own way of life.

The white man did not merely wander aimlessly into the country. He was, indeed, propelled into it by the intense economic pressures in the old and the new world. At first the probers of the West were not motivated so much by the desire to exploit the region, because they regarded it as a barrier astride the new route revealed by Columbus from the West to the Far East. The first whites whose activities concern Montana were looking for a "Northwest Passage," a way through.

Three centuries passed between the voyage of Columbus and the discovery of the Columbia River by Robert Gray, and during those centuries the search for the Northwest Passage was recurrent. Even the Spanish sought it in the mythical "Strait of Anían," and even as trade with the new land grew and empires were being carved from it, the idea of a water passage through it persisted.

Impetus was lent the search by the report of a French explorer, Baron la Hontan. Between September, 1688, and May, 1689, La Hontan, who started from Michilimackinac at the head of the Great Lakes, presumably explored what he called the "Long River." His report included a map which we now know was so grossly inaccurate as to demonstrate that La Hontan wrote his account and drew his map from hearsay at best. Probably the Indian reports he received concerning the Missouri had something to do with it, but La Hontan obviously did not explore the Missouri region. What he had to say, however, lent support to the general belief that a water passage to the West Coast did indeed exist.

A French fur trader, Pierre Gaultier de Varennes, who came later to be known as Sieur de la Verendrye, was an agent for the French at the remote post of Lake Nipigon in the year 1728. To this outpost came Indians with a story of a great body of salt water somewhere to the south and west. Motivated both by a desire to find new fur country and the Northwest Passage, Verendrye succeeded in obtaining the support of the French government for an extensive exploration. An expedition in 1731 met with early disaster, and Verendrye returned to Montreal having lost much of his support. In 1738, with the backing of Canada's Governor, Charles de Beauharnois, he tried again. This time he visited the Mandans, who presumably knew the way to the Pacific; but the information he got there, while exciting, was insufficient, and leaving two men among the Indians to learn the language, he returned to Fort La Reine, just west of Winnipeg. The following fall the two men returned with the news that the Mandans had made contact with a western tribe who knew of a great body of salt water and of the presence there of white men.

A major Verendrye expedition was readied for the year 1742. But Verendrye's health was bad, and in his place he sent his two sons, François and Louis Joseph. Accompanied by two *voyageurs*, they set out in April, 1742. Because their astrolabe was broken early in the journey and hence no accurate celestial bearings were taken and also because the journal which François kept was skimpy and most general as regards direction and miles traveled, controversy has always attended any firm description of their route. One early theory brought them as far west as present Helena, Montana. This theory has since been largely exploded.

On January 1, 1743, they did sight a high range of mountains to the west. If, as may have been the case, they had been traveling across southeastern Montana, it was probably the Big Horn Range that they saw.

A lead plate buried by the Verendryes on a hill across the Missouri River from present Pierre, South Dakota, was unearthed by a schoolgirl in 1913, but save for proving that the Verendryes had been at that spot, it contributed little to settling the debate concerning their actual route. It is conceivable that the "mountains" they saw were the Black Hills and not the Big Horns. The preponderance of evidence at the present time, however, favors the latter. In any event, the expedition had epic qualities, and even if Montana was not probed as early as 1743, the quest for furs and the Northwest Passage was leading the whites closer and closer.

In 1792, for instance, we know that one Jacques d'Église, a Spaniard, was trading with the Mandans on the Upper Missouri. We know also that a rather mysterious figure named Menard, probably a French-Canadian, had, according to a report by David Thompson in 1795, been living among the Mandans for more than a decade and had also likely been trading with the Crows and Gros Ventres. Jonathan Carver had traveled into the interior, and in an account of his journey published in 1796, he made a surprisingly educated guess that "the four most capital rivers on the continent" all had their origins in a very small interior area.

It was in the context of this quest for a Northwest Passage and the increasingly competitive contest among the British, French, and Spanish that the newly conceived United

The uncommon land: mountain view from Bigfork, Montana.

The eastern Bad Lands, originally carpeted with "short grass" which sustained millions of buffalo, was quickly used up by the cattlemen in less than a decade.

States emerged on the Continent itself. By 1763, the British had defeated the French and effectively driven them from North America for the time being. Twenty years later the Americans emerged as an independent community and with startling vigor entered the contest for western empire themselves. The Spanish, meanwhile, disconcerted by the upset balance of power, were playing the British, Americans, and French against each other while they held grimly to Louisiana.

Louisiana, vague geographically, but in general the western half of the drainage basin of the Mississippi River (except for the region south of the Arkansas River, west of the 100th meridian, and east of the Continental Divide, all of which had been Spanish prior to 1762) had been ceded by France to Spain in 1762. Its western limit was a then hypothetical continental divide. Its northern limit was presumably the 49th parallel, although this, too, was vague and subject to dispute.

Spain was particularly fearful of the exceedingly aggressive Americans. She had held Louisiana during the American Revolution and subsequently had witnessed the relentless westward movement of the Americans in the face of which her political intrigues and machinations were ineffective. But it was the French, not the Americans, who wrested Louisiana from her. In the secret Treaty of San Ildefonso, which Napoleon forced Spain to sign in the fall of 1800, Louisiana was "retroceded" from Spain to France. The power politics behind all this need not concern us. What does, and must, is the effect the announcement of the retrocession had on Thomas Jefferson when he discovered it in May, 1801.

Jefferson was a man of extraordinary vision. He foresaw that the retrocession constituted a very grave danger to the United States because it substituted the world's greatest military power (France) for the weak and vacillating government of Spain on our western boundary. Moreover, Jefferson was one of the few Americans with an understanding of the force and inevitability of the American westward movement. While he was an outstanding Anglophobe, the retrocession of Louisiana wrung from him the famous statement: "From that moment we must marry ourselves to the British Fleet and Nation." From "that moment" also, Jefferson's efforts to secure the vital "free navigation" of the Mississippi for Westerners were unceasing.

Before turning the area over to France, the local Spanish intendant withdrew the American's "right of deposit" at the port of New Orleans, thus effectively choking off all American down-river trade and enraging Westerners to whom the waterway was an economic necessity. This particularly concerned Jefferson because he knew, as few of his compatriots did, how tenuous the West's allegiance to the East was. The Union was only twelve years old, yet already the peculiar independence of the Westerners, the frontiersmen, had asserted itself. Their suspicion of the federal government was already abiding. During the Spanish tenure at New Orleans, Jefferson could rely at least in part on Spanish timidity to keep the river open. Now, in a kind of last defiance, the Spanish had closed the river, leaving Jefferson to deal with Napoleon.

All this may seem to have little bearing on the history of Montana. In truth it has a great deal of bearing. It is not necessary to recount in detail the actions Jefferson took to forestall a crisis in the West. America's minister to France, Robert R. Livingston, was directed at once to proceed with negotiations for the purchase of New Orleans or, at the very least, to wring the right of deposit from the French. Fundamentally to convince the wrathful Westerners of the government's vital concern in the affair, James Monroe was appointed minister extraordinary and plenipotentiary to assist Livingston in dealing with Napoleon.

Napoleon was in no way concerned about the Americans. But since the retrocession other things had occurred which concerned him very much. His dream of a New World French colony with its heart at San Domingo and with Louisiana as a kind of breadbasket had been blasted by the failure of the French army in San Domingo. Initially he had thought also to renew his war with England via an attack in the Western Hemisphere. The loss at San Domingo convinced him that he should attack England in Europe. He knew that when he did so the mistress of the seas could easily wrest Louisiana from him. He would far rather that the Americans had Louisiana than that the English have it. Indeed, he was convinced that the Americans were the natural enemies of England, and at the time he was quite correct.

So to Livingston's and Monroe's surprise he proposed quickly that the United States buy all of Louisiana, not just New Orleans. As every student knows, the vast area of Louisiana which included most of Montana, was sold to the United States in 1803. As every student also knows, the Lewis and Clark expedition was promptly sent out by Jefferson to explore the great acquisition. But Jefferson's role in all this is less well known than it ought to be, as is the long background that attaches to the events. Since we owe to Jefferson the statesmanship which resulted in this tremendously significant accretion of property and wealth, as well as the creation of the political and organic systems (Ordinances of 1785 and 1787) which brought this vast contiguous area into the Union on an equal footing with the older states, and since, too, we owe to his curiosity and vision the exploration of the area by Lewis and Clark, it is proper to survey his concepts at least cursorily.

In the first place, Jefferson was not unaware of the problems of Napoleon. He had been secretary of state. He was and had been in touch with European chancelleries. Both as secretary of state and as President, Jefferson set the course of the United States with a realistic knowledge that in European wars there was American opportunity. He quite obviously had had an eye on the territory west of the Mississippi long before the retrocession. Indeed, he had approached the Spanish in 1802 for permission to send an expedition into their area. Both prior to and after becoming President, Jefferson had publicly and openly stated that in the event of European war the United States would seize the area west of the Mississippi. By 1803, a substantial number of Americans had already crossed the river and settled on foreign territory, and the inevitability that others would follow and build up strength there was well known to Jefferson.

An American expedition into then foreign territory had long been on Jefferson's mind. He had planned one such expedition to be led by André Michaux as early as 1793. He had offered the leadership of the expedition to Meriwether Lewis as early as February, 1801, one month before his inauguration. On January 18, 1803, in a secret message to Congress just five days after Monroe's commission had been approved, Jefferson asked the Congress to appropriate for and approve the expedition which was to be led by Lewis and Clark. This, be it noted, while Louisiana was still foreign soil.

It is unfortunate that this background of the Lewis and Clark expedition is not more widely treated in histories that touch on the subject because the meaning of the expedition itself is thus partially lost. That the United States acquired Louisiana was not by any means a mere European accident. That Jefferson's Lewis and Clark expedition succeeded so magnificently was not simple good luck. Both events bear the mark of Jefferson's long planning, his astute diplomacy, and the hard fact of his understanding that America would move west. Had this one man not understood that one fact and had he not made his cognizance of it a mainstay in his foreign policy, the history of Montana would likely have been very different.

What was the aim of the expedition? First of all, and after, lo, these many years it was still, in essence, a quest for the Northwest Passage. An American captain, Robert Gray, had discovered the Columbia River. Now more than ever Jefferson sought a water route up the Missouri and down the Columbia which would interconnect the Mississippi and the Pacific and would provide transport across the land to connect with the by then flourishing American maritime trade on the Northwest Coast. The expedition was also to mark off the potentialities of the fur trade and to prepare the Indians for the coming of American traders. In that sense it was an advertising expedition intended to wean the aborigines away from the British, French, and Spanish and to point out to them that they were now under American authority. As for the region west of the Continental Divide, there is little doubt but that Lewis and Clark were to pay it as much heed as that territory included in the purchase. Jefferson quite obviously had a covetous eye on Oregon country. And so in a larger sense, both in the secret message to Congress and in his explicit directions to Lewis, as well as what is implicit in the journals of Lewis and Clark reflecting what Jefferson must have told Lewis privately, the object of the expedition was to do everything possible to bind the land east and west of the divide to the United States. That in this process they were to find out everything they could about geography, flora, fauna, Indians, and weather is, of course, obvious.

Meriwether Lewis was twenty-nine years old in 1803. As a captain, First Infantry, U. S. Army, he had been serving as Jefferson's private secretary on detached duty. While he was a family friend, there were many people better qualified to serve as the President's private secretary. He was admirably equipped, however, to lead an expedition into the wilderness. Here, once more, we may suspect an ulterior motive in Jefferson's choice of secretaries. He doubtless briefed Lewis repeatedly on what he actually wanted of him. Lewis had fought in the militia during the Whiskey Rebellion and had then transferred to the regular army. While in the service he had met William Clark, a younger brother of the famous George Rogers Clark. Clark was thirty-three and, like Lewis, had served in the militia. Both had had command experience, and Clark had seen considerable combat.

Lewis picked Clark as his co-commander with Jefferson's sanction. Red tape prevented Clark's getting a captaincy, however, and throughout the expedition he was actually a second lieutenant. But he was called "captain," and in every sense he shared command with Lewis. Had the occasion ever arisen, Lewis was senior. But remarkable as it seems they shared command in effect without any single instance of acrimony.

Clark, who had had more Indian experience than Lewis, fell naturally into the role of negotiator and diplomat. Lewis, the more literary of the two, made celestial observations and took care of the scientific matters. Clark handled the boats.

Both were men of superior intelligence, and it is a tribute to that intelligence, and not to luck, that the expedition went so smoothly. The country the expedition traversed presented them with problems no frontiersman would have found in his experience; it was incredibly rugged, its streams were treacherous, its mountains tremendous, its weather capricious, and its dangers varied. Later expeditions by the Astorians, and many others, testified to the inherent dangers of the land. Less well-prepared, less experienced, and less vigilant subsequent expeditions, even when the routes and dangers were known, ended in tragedy. There was but one death in the Lewis and Clark party, Sergeant Floyd's. He probably died of a ruptured appendix which would doubtless have meant his end even had he been in St. Louis.

The party left St. Louis in mid-May, 1804. They reached the Mandan villages (north of present Bismarck) in October of that year and settled down there for the winter to prepare their gear and learn from the Indians what they could of the country to the west. They left the winter camp on April 7, 1805. There were twenty-three enlisted men and York, the Negro. This party was split into three groups, with one each under the commands of Sergeants John Ordway, Patrick Gass, and Nathaniel Pryor. Included in the group was a French-Canadian, Toussaint Charbonneau, who had traveled widely on the Upper Missouri, and his wife, Sacajawea. They traveled in two pirogues and six canoes. They made good time and on April 25 camped on the Yellowstone River. Lewis described the view from a near-by hill as "most pleasing." He could see the wide and fertile valleys formed by the Missouri and the Yellowstone which, occasionally unmasked by the woods on their borders, "disclose their meanderings for many miles in their passage through these delightfull [*sic*] tracts of country."¹ The whole "face of the country" was covered with herds of buffalo, elk, antelope, and deer, none of which bolted or ran as the party approached.

When the expedition reached the border of present Montana, it began to snow, causing Clark to comment on the interesting phenomenon of snow lying an inch deep over the flowers spread on the plains. Six days later they reached the Milk River, and on the nineteenth from the vantage point of a high hill, Clark saw the mouth of the Musselshell. It was cold—only a little above freezing—and the fog was so thick they were delayed two hours in breaking camp. Looking off in a westerly direction from the hill he had climbed, Clark got a glimpse of the Little Rockies. As usual, game was everywhere. That day Clark killed "a grey or white bear" (very likely a grizzly), which "not withstanding it was shot through the heart it ran at its usial [*sic*] pace near a quarter of a mile before it fell." That same day Clark killed three deer and a beaver; Lewis killed an elk, a deer, and a beaver; and others in the expedition killed three more deer and several beaver.

On June 2 the party reached the mouth of a large river which they called the Marias after Lewis' cousin, Miss Maria Wood, and because they were dubious about which might be the main channel, Lewis made a three-day journey up the Marias and returned fairly satisfied that they were still on the Missouri. Whatever doubt remained vanished when they reached the Great Falls of the Missouri on June 13.

Here, again, they encountered at close quarters the amazing grizzly. Lewis had shot a buffalo some distance from the camp of the main party. He suddenly became aware of a bear "within twenty steps" of him. He had not reloaded his

---

¹ All direct quotations are from *The Journals of Lewis and Clark*, edited by Bernard DeVoto.

rifle, and to his consternation the bear was "briskly advancing on me." There was no cover—not a bush within miles
nor a tree within three hundred yards. Lewis started a slow
retreat, but as he turned, the monstrous bear charged "open
mouthed and full speed." Although the bear gained on him
swiftly, Lewis reached the river and plunged in, thinking at
least that he would have a better chance in the water. At
this juncture, presenting the point of his *esponton* to the bear,
the latter suddenly wheeled and retreated. Lewis called this
merely a "curious adventure," but to anyone who has ever
seen a grizzly, Lewis' account of the affair is all the more
bloodcurdling for its understatement.

From the twenty-first of June to the fifteenth of July the
party was occupied by the arduous task of portaging around
the falls. It was killing work. The portage covered more than
eighteen miles. While they beached and concealed the remaining pirogue there, having in the meantime made dugout
canoes, they carried these heavy and cumbersome vessels up
the steep banks and then overland through cactus-peppered
ground. They had only moccasins now, and the entire party
had mangled feet. The weather was terrible, and mosquitoes
were thick. It hailed and rained and the ground turned into
gumbo. On the Fourth of July, exhausted and dispirited, they
drank the last of their "grog."

By July 13 they were on their way upstream again in
eight heavily laden boats. It was quickly apparent, as the
river became smaller and more swift, that they were somewhere near the approaches to its headwaters. But its con-
tinuing southerly direction concerned them. They could see
the mountains to the west, and they were understandably
anxious to reach them. They saw many Indian signs but no
Indians, and this, too, concerned them. On July 16 they passed

about forty small camps which they judged to have been abandoned only ten or twelve days before. On the eighteenth they saw and named the Dearborn River. Passing through the steep canyon, they observed mountain goats "walking about and abounding from rock to rock with apparent unconcern." The next day they reached the Gates of the Mountains, which Lewis named. He was impressed with the gigantic cliffs through which the river cut. He wrote in his journal: "Every object here wears a dark and gloomy aspect. The towering and projecting rocks in many places seem ready to tumble on us."

But once through the canyon they were cheered because Sacajawea recognized the country. (The Indian woman was a Shoshoni who had been kidnapped by the Minnetarees at the Three Forks some years before and had been sold to Charbonneau.) Whatever temptation existed to abandon the river and strike out westward vanished with Sacajawea's statement that they were no great distance from the Three Forks. But Clark noted with some apprehension that the mountains to the west were snow-covered. Lewis feared that Sacajawea's information was not accurate and that they would encounter falls or obstructions in the river. He could hardly believe that a river could pass through such jumbled and precipitous country without rapids or falls.

Clark and a small group went in advance of the main party and on July 25 reached the Three Forks. Despite the fact that they had walked some two hundred miles, Clark lost no time in exploring the west and south forks. When the main party arrived two days later, Clark felt relatively sure that they should follow the west fork. But so near in size were the three branches that the problem was perplexing. As Lewis wrote on July 27, "They appeared as if they had been cast in the same mold there being no difference in character of size, therefore to call either of these streams [middle fork or S. W. fork] the Missouri would be giving it a preference which its size does not warrant . . . ."

Clark was ill. He had a high fever with frequent chills, and he was exhausted. Lewis decided to spend several days at Three Forks. Clark's illness, their uncertainty about their course, and the fact that they had still encountered no Indians depressed Lewis. On the night of the twenty-seventh, he was low in spirit. With the mountains looming ever closer he knew that they had to have horses. Without them, he wrote in his journal, "I fear the successful issue of our voyage . . . ." He was worried, too, about food. "We are now several hundred miles within the bosom of this wild and mountanous country, where game may rationally be expected shortly to become scarce and subsistence precarious without any information with rispict to the country not knowing how far these mountains continue, or wher to direct our course to pass them to advantage or intersept a navigable branch of the Columbia, or even were we on such an one the probability is that we should not find any timber within these mountains large enough for canoes . . . ." The night of July 27 must have been a bad one for both the leaders.

They named the three streams the Jefferson, the Gallatin, and the Madison and on July 30 set forth up the Jefferson. It was rugged going. The river was swift, waist-deep, and not over ninety yards wide in many places. Hauling the canoes became an increasingly arduous task. Two of the men had "tumors," one had a bad stone bruise, one had dislocated an arm, another had strained his back, another an ankle. Their progress was painfully slow. Clark, himself, was developing a painful tumor on his ankle.

By August 5 it was clear that the Jefferson had become a mountain river, and they were encountering shoals over which the canoes had to be dragged. They encountered more forks in the river. A northerly one which Lewis called the Wisdom, is today known as the Big Hole; the other was the Ruby. Although Lewis continued to refer to the narrowing stream they followed as the Jefferson, it is today's Beaverhead, and the labor of following it was swiftly becoming prohibitive. On August 7 they abandoned one canoe. To make matters worse one of the party, Shannon, was lost, and Lewis had to dispatch Reuben Fields in search of him. The only high spot was the fact that on the next day Sacajawea recognized a promontory as what her people called the Beaver's Head, and she said that they were very near the range of her people.

By this time Clark was badly crippled by the tumor on his ankle. Accordingly, Lewis took three of the men with him and set out through a near-by pass (about twenty miles north of Dillon) in an effort to find the Shoshonis.

On August 11 they saw their first Indian. He was mounted and was coming toward them. Through his glass Lewis could see that he was of a strange tribe they had never encountered, and he was satisfied that he was a Shoshoni. He had a bow and quiver of arrows, and he rode without saddle and with only a thong fastened to the horse's lower jaw. Lewis was "overjoyed at the sight of this stranger" and immediately made signs of friendship by signaling with a blanket as was the custom among Indians with whom he was familiar. But the two men with Lewis—Drewyer (properly spelled Drouillard) and Shields, whom he had sent off previously to left and right—were now advancing precipitously, and to Lewis' bitter disappointment the Indian turned his horse and quickly vanished.

On August 13 they encountered two Indian women, a man, and some dogs. This time contact was made, and the three men were led to the Shoshoni camp. There they were received, as Lewis put it, "affectionately" by the chief. Lewis distributed presents, smoked a few pipes, and endeavored to inform the chief of the friendly object of their visit. Communication was not too difficult because Drewyer was accomplished in sign language. On August 15 the three whites, accompanied by most of the Indians, started back toward the main party. Two days later the two parties met.

For several days they remained with the Shoshonis, with Lewis pumping the Indians assiduously for information about the country to the west. The information he got was vague, although he was indeed warned that the river (Salmon) passed through a terrible canyon which was not navigable. But they traded trinkets for twenty-nine good horses and set out for the Salmon River anyhow. It was a mistake, and after probing the country, the party recrossed the mountains into Montana. They passed through this incredibly rugged country until on September 4 they dropped down into Ross's Hole where they encountered some four hundred friendly Flathead Indians. Here they traded for more horses, and the Flatheads were pleased to guide them for quite some distance. On September 9 they were in the Bitterroot Valley. Here they learned from their guide that they were but four days from the Gates of the Mountains and that had they left the Missouri there and turned westward they could have saved themselves the miserable fifty-two-day trip.

On the eleventh of September they started to ascend the main chain of the Bitterroots and found themselves in very high, rough country. They were on the Nez Percé "buffalo road" which followed the ridges instead of the valleys, and

there was much down-timber. On September 13 they crossed
Lolo Pass and camped on a stream of the Clearwater watershed. Thus they passed out of what is today Montana, dropped
down into the Columbia watershed through high and jumbled
mountains, and in early November arrived at the Pacific.
Here they spent the winter south of the Columbia and inland
from the coast in a stockade which they built and named Fort
Clatsop. Their sojourn on the West Coast is not a basic part
of this story; suffice it to say that life at Fort Clatsop was
characterized by singular monotony. The weather was almost
continuously bad. They ate elk meat almost exclusively and
grew very sick of it. But the two leaders were busy. Lewis
worked on his journal, systematizing his scientific observations. Clark was busy reviewing, organizing, and codifying
geographical data. This study of Clark's was particularly important as regards their return journey, for it became readily
apparent that the route they had taken west of the Great
Falls of the Missouri was neither the best nor the shortest one.
Clark realized that they should have left the river there and
headed due west to the Bitterroot. They determined that they
would avoid the Three Forks, Lemhi Pass, and Salmon River
area on their return, and they also determined that when
they reached the Bitterroot Valley they would split the party
to cover a greater area.

It must have been with genuine relief that the party left
the rainy coast in the spring of 1806. On June 29 they crossed
Lolo Pass, the last divide of the Bitterroot Mountains, and
dropped down onto Lolo Creek. They spent the next two days
resting and planning the division of the party. Lewis was to
take the direct overland route to the Great Falls of the Missouri. He planned to go up the Hell Gate and Blackfoot rivers,
cross the divide, and drop down on the Missouri via the Dear-

born or Sun River. He then planned to explore the Marias which they had been singularly curious about since they had first seen its waters. He selected nine men to go with him, three of whom were to remain at the Great Falls while the others explored the Marias. Clark was to meet these three at the Great Falls.

Clark, meanwhile, was to take the rest of the party to the forks of the Beaverhead. Here Clark was to split his party and send one detachment downstream with the boats and supplies (which had been cached at the forks of the Beaverhead) to join Lewis' three men and assist them in portaging around the falls. Clark was to take the remainder of the party overland to the Yellowstone. He was then to send Sergeant Pryor ahead with horses to the mouth of the Yellowstone. The entire party, in other words, was to meet at the confluence of the Missouri and Yellowstone rivers. This plan, devised at Fort Clatsop and worked out in detail in the Bitterroot Valley, is essentially the story of the return journey.

Clark made good time. He crossed by Gibbon's Pass into the Big Hole. There the party divided—one group going down-river, the other overland, to Three Forks. Without incident they arrived almost simultaneously. Here, again, the party divided—one group heading downstream with the boats, the other overland to the Yellowstone—and early in August both parties met at the mouth of the Yellowstone.

Lewis' excursion was no less rapid than Clark's, but it was attended by one blood-chilling incident. On July 7 Lewis had crossed the pass at the head of the Dearborn and dropped down to the Missouri. Here, according to plan, he left three men and pressed on to the Marias. With Lewis were the Fields brothers (Joseph and Reuben) and Drewyer. On July 26, 1806, the three men encountered a band of eight Blackfoot

Indians—as Lewis put it, "a very unpleasant sight." Although Lewis assumed that they were Gros Ventres, they were, in fact, Piegans, one of the three Blackfoot tribes. Lewis told his companions that "I apprehended that these were the Minnetares of Fort de Prarie and from their known character I expected that we were to have some trouble with them." But the initial contact was friendly enough. Since it was late in the afternoon, Lewis proposed to the Blackfeet that they camp together. After a general confab with the Indians that evening, Lewis turned the watch over to Reuben Fields, cautioning him to be alert, and fell into a sound sleep. This was a serious mistake. He was awakened at early dawn by a commotion. Joseph Fields had taken over the watch from Reuben and had carelessly laid his gun down behind him. One of the Indians slipped up and took the gun, while others took Lewis' and Drewyer's rifles. There was a scuffle, during the course of which Joseph Fields wrested his gun from one Indian and Reuben Fields stabbed another through the heart. All guns were quickly recovered, and the Indians then tried to run off the party's horses. Lewis promptly shot one through the belly. The Indians scattered, and the white party began a precipitous day and night retreat toward the Missouri.

Reading Lewis' account of the affair, full of his usual understatement, one is struck by the narrowness of the escape. It was sheer luck. One is also struck by Lewis' own carelessness because it was far from typical of him. He had been repeatedly warned by the Nez Percés and the Flatheads of the hostility of the Blackfeet and their allies, the Atsinas. His one lapse in the long journey came very close to ending in tragedy. But on August 12 at 1:00 P.M., Lewis' and Clark's parties joined forces on the Missouri. On Tuesday, September 23, 1806, Lewis and Clark arrived in the city of St. Louis.

Three Forks, where the Beaverhead, Madison, and Gallatin
rivers meet to form the Missouri.

Two early settlements on the frontier: *above*, Fort Union, the American Fur Company's post at the mouth of the Yellowstone on the Missouri; *below*, Fort Benton, as it appeared in 1862—the only fur post that survived the end of the trade.

The expedition had traveled farther into Montana and spent more time there than in any other area. Its most important discoveries and its greatest crises occurred in Montana. In a sense it opened up the country, although many decades were to elapse before actual settlement. A vast lot was learned about the Indians, and a land which had been shrouded in mystery for more than a century was mapped and described. Lewis and Clark left in their journals not only a story of hardship and courage but a story of wealth. It was all there, plain to see for anyone who cared to read it. Although they left only the ashes of their campfires behind, Montana would never be the same again.

III

TRAPPERS, POSTS, AND PRIESTS

With a whole new world to conquer, to cut up, and to exploit, Western Europe found itself rejuvenated and alive. The wealth from this new world found its way first into the pockets of kings and then, by percolation, into the hands of a new class of entrepreneurs. The destiny of the countries of Western Europe came more and more to be bound up with the ambitions of businessmen. Their flag followed them wherever they went.

When, as a new nation, the United States appeared upon the scene, the competition for the wealth of the great West was heightened. Spain, England, France, Russia, and the United States all made haste to claim the land and, above all, to mark off for themselves the regions where the beaver and other fur-bearing animals abounded.

The United States had purchased Louisiana; but purchase was one thing, and holding it inviolate was another. Fur trading was a mobile industry. Anyone with capital, courage, and luck could penetrate the wilderness and emerge with a fortune. And beyond the Rockies to the west, Oregon country and California were common ground for all nations.

Why did all this power and intrigue fasten on the lowly

beaver in his mountain stream? Because fur was of vital importance in Europe in terms of apparel. Wool was common. But there were no synthetic dyes, and wool was drab except for the brilliance lent it by indigo or cochineal. Even then it was uncomfortable and bulky. Thus, especially among the upper classes, furs were valued for their warmth, their luxuriousness, and the variety of texture and color. Indeed, the beaver hat was a symbol of af-fluence—the taller the hat, the richer the man. And there were fur coats, muffs, scarves, and trim. It is not too much to say that the first economic development of Montana was a consequence of fashion five thousand miles away.

W HEN LEWIS AND CLARK were en route back to St. Louis in 1806, they encountered, between August 3 and August 20, eleven separate parties of fur men bound up the Missouri River. In the year 1843 a former free trapper, James Bridger, built a post on a tributary of the Green River as a spa and trading establishment for the con-venience of emigrants. In the thirty-seven years between the beginning of the far western fur trade and the symbolic end of it marked by Bridger's post, the land which was to be known as Montana was crossed, recrossed, mapped, and probed. The mountain man, the free trapper, the fur trader, or whatever historians have chosen to call him, was an extra-ordinary breed. His direct imprint on history was faint. He usually left no records, kept no diary. We get at him only indirectly, through the records of the great fur companies who depended on his fearlessness and stamina, or through reminiscences of the few who survived the dangers of the towering country in which they plied their trade.

With the Louisiana Purchase the United States had acquired a vast and unknown region, the northern boundary of which was vague. But the great Hudson's Bay Company, chartered by the English Crown in 1670, had a grant to the north whose southern and western limits were tangent to the borders of present Montana. And, indeed, occupation was nine points of the law. No mere bill of sale could prevent the illusive traders of the Hudson's Bay Company from trapping and trading in the remote western area.

Then there was the North-West Company, formed by a group of acquisitive Scotsmen in 1783 in Montreal. From 1783 to 1821 this company, too, was probing into the region. As early as 1804 Charles McKenzie and François Antoine Larocque of the North-West Company journeyed far up the Missouri and satisfied themselves that beaver, in particular, abounded in the streams tributary to the "Big Muddy." A second North-West Company expedition in 1805 traveled over southeastern Montana and found great quantities of beaver both in the Yellowstone River and its tributaries. This, mark you, while Lewis and Clark were still en route.

But these discoveries of the North-West Company were not pursued. With the Hudson's Bay Company pushing vigorously southward, the Canadian Scotsmen could not spread themselves too thin. They retrenched and concentrated in the area around Lake Winnipeg.

At this juncture John Jacob Astor, an American, entered the picture. Astor, a German immigrant, saw the great potential in the fur trade. Through several American companies he built up the greatest American fortune of the nineteenth century. His activities particularly disturbed the North-West

Company, which then decided to expand westward with all possible dispatch.

By the end of the first decade of the nineteenth century, Montana was thus approached by traders from various directions. From the north both the Hudson's Bay and North-West Company were pushing southward. Hard on the heels of Lewis and Clark an American company, Manuel Lisa's Missouri Fur Company, was established. Lisa's partners were William Morrison and Pierre Menard, both from Kaskaskia, Illinois, and his chief lieutenant and interpreter was George Drouillard (sometimes called Drewyer), who had been with the Lewis and Clark expedition. It was also Lisa's good fortune to obtain the services of John Colter, who had not only been with the Lewis and Clark expedition but who, since 1806, had explored the Yellowstone region and probably the Absaroka Mountains region.

Manuel Lisa built the first fur post in Montana. It was known as Manuel's Fort or Lisa's Fort. It was completed in November, 1807, at the juncture of the Yellowstone and the Big Horn.

The winter of 1807–1808 was a severe one, and accordingly Lisa decided to get the Indians to come to the fort rather than to traverse the awesome country with his own men. John Colter was sent out to bring the Indians in.

Colter made no map of his incredible winter journey. But he told William Clark of his travels, and the latter, quite naturally interested in the man and the country, subsequently mapped Colter's route.

It would appear that Colter traveled up Pryor's Fork to Pryor's Gap—in the vicinity of the present Montana-Wyoming boundary. Traveling westward he came upon the Clarks Fork of the Yellowstone, which stream he ascended

43

probably to its juncture with Sunlight Creek. From there he traveled southwestward to the headwaters of the Wind River. Turning north he entered present Yellowstone Park, traveling west of Yellowstone Lake, then east to Clarks Fork from whence he retraced his steps to Lisa's Fort. It was this journey that gave Yellowstone Park its initial name Colter's Hell.

This incredible midwinter journey, which probably carried Colter as far south and west as Jackson Hole, has been the subject of considerable debate. In 1931, a peculiarly shaped stone with Colter's name and the date 1808 carved on it was found in the Jackson Hole region. The stone appears to be authentic. In view of Colter's subsequent activities and his Lewis and Clark experience, the trip of 1808 is less incredible. Colter, although little is really known of him, was one of those fabulous and reckless men with tremendous physical stamina and with a peculiar absence of fear. Like his compatriots in the fur trade, he was capable of extraordinary feats. Although he was widely accused of lying about his Yellowstone Park experiences, there is no doubt that Colter was the first recorded white man to visit the region.

Lisa's expedition returned to St. Louis in the spring, and his reports excited the city's businessmen considerably. A new firm was organized. Lisa, Menard, and Morrison were still active. They were joined by Pierre and Auguste Chouteau, Reuben Lewis (brother of Meriwether Lewis), Benjamin Wilkinson, William Clark, Sylvester Labadie, and Andrew Henry.

In the spring of 1809 a new expedition went forth. It was a large one, consisting of nearly three hundred men, and it was ill-fated. Near Three Forks eight of the party were killed by the increasingly hostile Blackfeet. Andrew Henry succeeded in crossing the mountains and establishing a short-lived post on the north fork of the Snake River. It was the first American post west of the Rockies, but by 1811 it had been abandoned, and Henry recrossed the mountains to the Yellowstone. The entire expedition was plagued with bad luck. The Blackfeet were hostile; a fire destroyed a big cache of furs. When Andrew Henry arrived at the post on the Big Horn, he found it abandoned.

The worsening relations between the United States and Great Britain, the various trade embargoes, and the strained American-Canadian relations had seriously damaged the fur trade. The price was down, and strict regulations had been set on Canadian and English trade. Lisa's partners deserted him, save for the shrewd Henry. The War of 1812 marked the end of the first era of the fur trade. It is too much to say that Montana had been explored, but enough of its streams had been sampled and enough of the word had gotten around so that it was only necessary for international conditions to change before the acquisitive traders were at it again. No one knew this better than Andrew Henry.

In the meantime, the British had not been idle. They had pushed resolutely westward in Canada. And they had probed southward. By 1804 one David Thompson was a partner in the North-West Company. In the spring of 1807 Thompson built a post which he called Kootenae House at the foot of Lake Windermere. This was in line with Thompson's and Alexander McKenzie's idea that the North-West Company must move swiftly and aggressively if they were to meet American competition.

From Kootenae House, Thompson dispatched Finan Mc-Donald down Kootenai River, where he set up a post in the neighborhood of present-day Libby, Montana.

McDonald himself was impressed with the country. His

reports to Thompson were encouraging. The latter visited the post in 1809 and then proceeded down-river to present Bonners Ferry. Turning south he arrived at Lake Pend d'Oreille, where he built still another post called Kullyspell House. A little later he built a third post near present Thompson Falls, calling it Saleesh House. By 1810, thus, the North-West Company had established three new posts athwart the American's route westward.

Finan McDonald remained at Saleesh House, made contact with the Indians, and during the winter of 1809–10 laid plans for an expedition to the east.

That summer the expedition crossed what was probably Marias Pass and pushed into the buffalo country east of the divide. The North-West Company was not content merely to remain in the country west of the divide, although their eastern ventures were abortive.

In the meantime, Thompson himself was exploring the country. In 1812 he was in the Missoula Valley. He had already explored the Columbia thoroughly from its mouth to its headwaters. And he had made a tour of his forts, spending most of the winter of 1812 at Saleesh House.

In 1813 his company purchased John Jacob Astor's Pacific Fur Company. The latter had little recourse, since the war was in progress and the Canadians were effectively in possession of the coastal area and were strong in the entire region west of the divide.

The War of 1812 ran its course. The American fur trade, while interrupted, emerged vigorously. The Canadian trade had continued unabated.

By 1818 the "brigade" method of trading had come into being. Instead of trying to prevail on the Indians to trap for the company and instead of sending out small expeditions, large and well-equipped brigades sallied forth to trap. In 1818 Donald McKenzie led such a brigade up the Snake River and into Yellowstone Park. Colter was redeemed, and the venture was highly profitable. But between 1818 and 1821 a series of brigades fell upon bad fortune. The furs were there, but trapping the animals, getting the furs to one of the posts, and shipping them eastward was no simple task. Overhead was high, and so were casualties.

Largely as a consequence of these several bad years, the Hudson's Bay Company and the North-West Company merged in 1821, and the entire enterprise was reorganized. Under the aegis of Alexander Ross, a former Astor man, an expansion took place. In 1823, a large party under Ross traveled to Saleesh House and thence into the Missoula Valley, up the Bitterroot, across Gibbon Pass, and over into the Big Hole. Here the expedition broke into small groups to explore the vast area of the headwaters of the Missouri. It is significant that one of these groups encountered an American trader, Jedediah Strong Smith, in the company of six other Americans. This was most upsetting to Ross, who probably realized for the first time just how much of a threat the aggressive Americans posed.

Ross's party re-formed and crossed over into the rugged Salmon River country and from there, turning north, reached the Bitterroot and then Saleesh House. The expedition had left Saleesh House in February, 1824. They returned at the end of November. Nine months had netted them some five thousand beaver, most of which they had taken in the Snake country. They had gained a vast amount of practical experience as well as a good knowledge of the vast and perilous land. While Ross had been startled and even alarmed at the presence of the Americans, the company was all the more determined to exploit the country Ross had traversed.

Thus in the years 1823–24 the company put its best men into the field. Working in concert and according to a careful plan, John McLoughlin was made chief factor of the Columbia district, which had its headquarters at Fort Vancouver. Fort Vancouver was the home base, and plans for the entire area were conceived there.

One district, under the supervision of Peter Skene Ogden, included the Clark Fork and Kootenai rivers. Ogden was given charge of the former Snake River brigade. In the winter of 1824 he set forth. Strangely enough, the Americans whom Ross had encountered came along. The ubiquitous Jedediah Strong Smith had shown up at Saleesh House a short time before, and he and the six men of his party now joined Ogden. Although they traveled only a short distance together, it was yet another harbinger of American predominance in the area.

Ogden's brigade turned eastward toward Three Forks. En route twenty-three of his men deserted to the Americans —lured by greater and quicker profits—and two were killed. With his remaining men Ogden crossed over Lemhi Pass and proceeded to Fort Walla Walla.

In the meantime, the company was also trapping and trading among the Selish and upper Pend d' Oreilles. Finan McDonald and John Work were busy in the Clark Fork and Kootenai rivers region. Spokane House was receiving great loads of furs. Nor was the company ignoring other areas. John Work, with a large brigade, was trading on both sides of the mountains by 1831. Sixty men, some women and children, and three hundred horses came into Montana via Lolo Pass in October, 1831. They came down the Bitterroot, turned east through Hell Gate, and explored the Big Blackfoot River without notable success. Plagued by hostile Blackfeet, they continued eastward to the Beaverhead country. That winter they crossed Lemhi Pass over into the Salmon River country. Still they had not done well. They turned back through Bannack Pass into the Big Hole country, where the Blackfeet appeared once more. Accordingly they recrossed the mountains and finally reached Vancouver in July, 1832. They had very few furs.

This big expedition spent more than nine months on the trek. They were in Montana's most rugged and formidable mountains in the dead of winter. In spite of hostile Indians they had traversed a country which should have been very productive of furs. The expedition had been costly and very dangerous. It was a failure. Thorough as the Hudson's Bay Company had been, something was wrong. Obviously, the number of men and horses and the quantity of equipment they carried had little bearing on success. The brigade system would no longer work. In the 1830's the Hudson's Bay Company was able to control only the Clark Fork and Kootenai River valleys. It remained for the Americans to devise a better way of getting the furs.

Before the War of 1812 it had been John Jacob Astor's plan to set up a series of trading posts stretching from the Great Lakes to the Pacific. The plan had failed because of the war. But American interest in the fur trade was tenacious.

Perhaps the most experienced trader of them all, Manuel Lisa, who was forty-six years old in 1819, had never deviated from his original purpose. The Missouri Fur Company was reorganized, and in 1812 and 1813 Lisa expeditions again traveled up the Missouri. Both expeditions were unprofitable, and Lisa's new backers grew discouraged. By 1819 Lisa alone was in control of the company, and because of insufficient capital he was confining his activity to the Lower Missouri while he perfected plans for yet another assault on the Rockies.

In the meantime, two events gave great impetus to American aspirations. The Convention of 1818 with England established the northern boundary of the United States east of the Rockies as the 49th parallel. Now if Canadian trappers entered the region, they did so in contravention of the law of their land.

The American government, more sanguine, perhaps, than practical, proposed to build a military post on the Yellowstone to enforce the law on foreigner and Indian alike. Major S. H. Long was assigned this task. The Major built no fort; indeed, he merely led an expedition up the Platte to its source. But inadvertently he did a vast lot for the fur trade. When he returned to civilization he wrote an official report regarding the "West"—encompassing the entire region from Mexico to Canada. This report became a kind of official bible. In it Long described the country as being uninhabitable, unfit for cultivation, and in the nature of a desert. One can readily understand Long's impression. It was, indeed, a formidable, semiarid, vast, and empty country. The appellation, "The Great American Desert," came to be applied to the whole area. Long's report, indeed, became the source book of those who wished, for political or other reasons, to check westward expansion. This gave a respite to the fur traders who, Long notwithstanding, knew that the streams teemed with fortunes in furs.

Manuel Lisa died in 1820 before he could launch another Rocky Mountain expedition. Joshua Pilcher took over the company and in 1821 sent an expedition into the Yellowstone country. He built Fort Vanderburgh above the mouth of the Knife River, and later, at the mouth of the Big Horn, near the original site of Lisa's post of 1807, he built Fort Benton (down river from the present Fort Benton).

The next year Pilcher had some three hundred men trading on the upper rivers. His chief lieutenants were W. H. Vanderburgh, Robert Jones, and Michael Immel. In the fall of 1822 these men sent some $25,000 worth of pelts down the river. It was a highly successful season. The Yellowstone trade seemed to be secure. Pilcher decided to expand, and in 1823 he dispatched Jones and Immel to Three Forks to open up the headwaters area. Their initial contacts with the perpetually hostile Blackfeet were strangely amicable. By early spring, lulled by the quiet of the Blackfeet, heavily laden with furs, they started downstream for the post on the Yellowstone. Just below the present city of Billings and presumably well within Crow country, the Blackfeet attacked. Jones and Immel were killed, and all their furs and equipment were lost. Once again the trade languished. Pilcher moved his operations to the Lower Missouri.

One man had gotten a taste for the country and its obvious wealth, however, and that was Andrew Henry, Lisa's old partner. Along with William H. Ashley, he now made a new assault on the fur country. Both Canadians and Americans had by this time discovered that the Indians could never be relied upon as trappers and traders. Both had discovered that brigades and large expeditions were no match for the vastness of the country and the hostility of the Indians. Forts and posts were expensive, and they had not been the answer. The great quiet land and its original inhabitants had all the advantages.

Therefore Ashley and Henry devised a new strategy. They would build no posts. They would use no Indians. They would send no brigades out into the field. They would, instead, send out individual white trappers or at the most, small groups.

They would not try to beat the country. They would elude rather than confront the Indians. They would send their men fanning out like shadows. There would be an annual "rendezvous" at a prearranged location. Supplies for the coming year, trade goods, traps, and equipment would be brought upriver to the point of rendezvous. The trappers would bring in their catch. In one quick operation the exchange would be made.

In 1822 Ashley and Henry put out a call for men. The Rocky Mountain Fur Company came into existence. Ashley and Henry gathered in a remarkable group. We have already encountered Jedediah Strong Smith. But there were others whose names were destined to be associated with the fur trade and with incredible tales of danger and hardship. There were Jim Bridger, Thomas Fitzpatrick, William and Milton Sublette, David E. Jackson, Etienne Provost, James Clyman, and Robert Campbell.

With Henry in command, this group ascended the Missouri in 1822. They broke up at the mouth of the Yellowstone and scattered out into the wilderness; Fitzpatrick, Smith, and Clyman moved southwestward. They found the Snake and Sweetwater country extremely rich in furs. They traveled through South Pass, marking it as by far the easiest route across the mountains. Others occupied themselves in the Snake River country, and they were equally successful. By 1824 Ashley and Henry had returned to the East—their fortunes made. Smith, Jackson, and Sublette took over the Rocky Mountain Fur Company and moved their principal operations southward into the Green River Valley and the Great Salt Lake area.

In the meantime, even though solemn agreement had been reached between England and the United States at the Convention of 1818, Canadian traders were still active in American territory. They were not agents of the Crown, nor was their activity concerted. Doubtless the consolidation of the North-West Company and Hudson's Bay Company in 1821 had left many of them at loose ends. These men were violating not only the Convention of 1818, however, but also an act passed by Congress in 1816 excluding "foreigners" from participating in the fur trade in the United States except in subordinate capacities under American traders. Laws and treaties were one thing; enforcing them was quite another. But John Jacob Astor saw advantage in an alliance with these enterprising "foreigners."

His American Fur Company had sustained great losses during the War of 1812. After the war he pulled together the loose ends of his business around the Great Lakes and began to plan western enterprises anew. A western department of the American Fur Company was set up in St. Louis in 1822. While there was opposition from the Rocky Mountain Fur Company, there was little they could do except compete. It was the intent of the western department to invade Ashley and Henry territory (or rather the territory now principally being worked by Smith, Jackson, and Sublette). It was left to the "foreigners," former nor'wester Kenneth McKenzie, in particular, to establish trade on the Upper Missouri. In September, 1828, McKenzie dispatched the keelboat *Otter* from the Mandans to the mouth of the Yellowstone. A post was built called Fort Floyd. Fort Union, with which Fort Floyd is often confused, was built the next year about two hundred miles above the mouth of the Yellowstone. But before the end of 1830 the name Floyd had been dropped, and the name Union had been fixed to the fort near the Yellowstone.

From his post on the Upper Missouri, McKenzie now decided to trap in the area hitherto made untenable by the Blackfeet. Where Lisa, Ashley, Henry, and all others had failed, McKenzie succeeded. An old trapper named Berger, who could speak the Blackfoot language, was dispatched from Fort Union. On the Marias River, Berger and a small group of terrified trappers encountered the dreaded Indians. Berger was able to persuade a party of about forty of them to accompany him to Fort Union. Here McKenzie had a conference with them which resulted in a treaty of trade and peace. The back of Blackfoot opposition was broken, and the western department had opened up the country between the Marias and the Missouri. James Kipp, who was assigned this area, shortly traded the Blackfeet for 2,400 beaver skins. Before the winter was over he had taken some 4,000 pelts from the area. The competition was on.

The winter of 1827 saw a "crowd" in the wilderness. McKenzie sent Samuel Tullock up the Yellowstone that fall with orders to work in the Snake River country. Tullock got snowed in and soon discovered that trappers from Smith, Jackson, and Sublette were in a similar predicament close by. Both groups then encountered Peter Skene Ogden of the Hudson's Bay Company. In the spring of 1828 trappers from the western department, as well as Smith, Jackson, and Sublette, were in the area. In 1830 these three traders sold out to Thomas Fitzpatrick, Henry Fraeb, Jim Bridger, and Baptiste Gervais. This latter combination formalized the name Rocky Mountain Fur Company.

In 1832 the largest rendezvous ever held in the mountains convened at Pierre's Hole. Both the American and Rocky Mountain men were there. It was at this rendezvous that the hard-pressed Rocky Mountain Company men sought a geographical division with the American Fur Company. The

Sidney Edgerton, the first governor of Montana Territory, was the only representative of organized government in 1863.

Indians also fought among themselves; here, the Assiniboins and Crees attack a small Piegan (Blackfoot) camp outside Fort McKenzie on August 28, 1833.

From a drawing by Karl Bodmer

latter company would not agree. The Hudson's Bay Company had already withdrawn from the Snake River country in the face of the American Fur Company's competition, and McKenzie was sure that he could eliminate the Rocky Mountain Company. He was quite correct. By 1834 the latter company had withdrawn from the area entirely. The American Fur Company's triumph was complete.

Astor, facing no competition, retired from the fur trade. The western department was sold to Pratte, Chouteau, Jr., and Company. McKenzie retired in 1839 and was succeeded by Alexander Culbertson.

The nature of the fur trade had changed. There was no sudden end to it, but the era of the silk hat had dawned. The textile industry was making tremendous strides. The mountain streams were depleted. The trappers who had survived, like Jim Bridger, became guides and scouts. The white hunters gradually found buffalo hides both easier to obtain and more profitable.

The fur trade in Montana, as elsewhere, was basically evanescent. But exploration and discovery, save for Lewis and Clark, was the consequence of the fur trade, not of formal or governmental expeditions. Before the emigrant's wagon ever rolled a mile, before the miner found his first color, before the government authorized a single road or trail, this inhospitable land had been traversed and mapped. Many things and places found by the free trapper were forgotten, only to be "rediscovered." But the emigrants who came across the land two decades later or who chose to stop short of the coast (as some did) owed far more than they knew to "this reckless breed of men."

The industry was exploitive, and here, too, a pattern was set. Montana was destined for a century of exploitation. The industry was extractive. It left little in return for what it took, and it took far more than furs.

The influence of the fur trade on the Indian was profound and destructive. The trappers brought smallpox, for which the Indian had no tolerance. The Blackfeet were decimated by it, their numbers reduced by half or more. The traders brought liquor which, diluted as it was, debauched the Indian thoroughly. Yet it must be added that the organizations behind the trappers were responsible for this destructive aspect of the trade. The trappers and mountain men themselves knew the Indians more intimately and understood them far better than the government agents who followed. There was extensive intermarriage. It was the trapper who took the pains to learn the language and customs of the Indian. Indeed, the influence of Indian ways on individual trappers was tremendous.

Save for a knowledge of the Indians and the country passed along from decade to decade, save for fortunes made and lost, what did the fur trade mean to Montana? It was indeed ephemeral. It left an aura of romance which exists to this day. But of all the forts and posts, none save Fort Benton had permanence. Between 1808 and 1821 the Missouri Fur Company established four posts. All were abandoned. Canadian fur companies between 1808 and 1846 constructed five posts in Montana. No settlements grew up around them. The Rocky Mountain Fur Company set up two posts, neither of which existed long. The great American Fur Company established Fort Benton in 1847 where Fort Benton is today. It alone of some eleven American Fur Company posts in present Montana survived the end of trade. Money had poured into the coffers of St. Louis merchants and New York financiers. The great Hudson's Bay Company had been enriched, and many an Englishman and Scotsman retired to a country estate to enjoy a leisure based on wealth from the white streams of Montana.

If the fur trade demoralized the Indian, it also brought him Christianity. But only a biased view of what happened as a consequence can establish the coming of Christianity to the Montana Indians as an unmixed blessing.

The Iroquois Indians had long been used by British and Canadian fur traders as trappers and canoemen. Some of these Indians, particularly those in the vicinity of Caughnawaga Mission near Montreal, had long been subject to Jesuit instruction. They were, in effect, Christians. When these Indians were brought out to instruct their western brethren in the techniques of trapping, they also passed along to them the rudiments, at least, of Catholicism.

The North-West Company's experiment in the use of Iroquois in the Rocky Mountain area was not universally successful. In the first place, they had a full measure of natural indolence. In the second place, they quickly gained unique stature among the western tribes, and it was often easier to retire and live among these people than to continue to work for the ambitious whites.

Thus it was that four Iroquois came to live among the Flatheads probably sometime in the early 1820's. One in particular, known as Big Ignace (or Ignace la Mousse), spoke at length about the Black Robes and the power of Catholicism. We know very little about Big Ignace save that in the estimation of Father Gregory Mengarini he was himself very virtuous and refused to teach the Flatheads any actual prayers lest he change the word of God. But one way or another, the rather gentle Flatheads (and the Nez Percés) developed a consuming curiosity about the Black Robes—a curiosity so great, indeed, that four separate Indian expeditions were dispatched from the mountain wilderness to St. Louis in 1831, 1835, 1837, and 1839.

There is a story about the expedition of 1831, doubtless apocryphal but of considerable importance because it had wide circulation in religious journals in the 1830's. A banquet was given in St. Louis for the two remaining travelers who were about to depart again for the mountains. William Clark was supposed to have been present at the banquet as were members of the clergy. There was much speechmaking. Finally one Indian is supposed to have arisen and said:

> My people sent me to get the "White Man's Book of Heaven." You took me to where you allow your women to dance as we do not ours, and the book was not there. You took me to where they worship the Great Spirit with candles, and the book was not there. You showed me images of the good spirits and the picture of the good land beyond, but the book was not among them to tell us the way. I am going back the long and sad trail to my people in the dark land. You make my feet heavy with gifts and my moccasins will grow old carrying them, yet the book is not among them. When I tell my poor blind people, after one more snow, in the big council, that I did not bring the book, no word will be spoken by our old men or by our young braves. One by one they will rise and go out in silence. My people will die in darkness and they will go a long path to other hunting grounds. No white men will go with them, and no white man's book to make the way plain. I have no more words.

However fanciful the story may be, its wide circulation had effect. This tale and the general interest in the Indians stirred the Methodist church to send Jason and Daniel Lee west in 1834 and the Presbyterians to send Marcus Whitman, Samuel Parker, Henry Harmon Spaulding, and W. H. Gray in 1835 and 1836. But the Flatheads were interested only in Black Robes, and, in addition, the Protestant missionaries saw wider and more fertile fields for missionary works farther west.

The Flatheads persisted. Again in 1835 they sent an expedition eastward, this time led by Old Ignace and his sons, Charles and François ("Saxa"). This party, like the first, failed in its endeavor; hence, in 1837 the Flatheads again sent a delegation. Big Ignace was again a delegate, but the entire group was killed by Sioux. The fourth delegation, consisting of Peter Gaucher and Young Ignace, reached St. Louis in 1839 and extracted a promise from Bishop Rosati to send them a Black Robe. We shall examine the nature of Flathead persistence in a moment, but it must be said that however it had come about, their interest in Catholicism, unclear as its nature may have been, was extraordinarily tenacious.

Bishop Rosati selected Father Pierre-Jean de Smet, a young Jesuit, to travel to the Flatheads. Less than a year after the Indians had seen the Bishop, Father de Smet was on his way westward with an American Fur Company caravan headed for the Green River. When he arrived, he was met by a delegation of Flatheads who escorted him to Pierre's Hole. Here the entire tribe had gathered, and many of the Nez Percés were present. A leisurely trip was made into Montana. In the late summer Father de Smet took leave of the Indians and returned to St. Louis to place his plans for the future before his superiors.

The St. Louis church itself had no funds for the establishment of a permanent mission among the Flatheads, but Father de Smet was given wide lattitude to raise funds on

59

his own. All that winter he traveled in the East and South, and by spring he had the necessary money to return with supplies and a staff to the Flatheads. He left St. Louis in April, 1841, accompanied by Fathers Gregory Mengarini and Nicholas Point and also by three lay brothers, Joseph Specht, Charles Huet, and William Claessens. They arrived in the Bitterroot Valley in September, 1841, and began the construction of St. Mary's Mission almost at once.

A chapel was built from cottonwood logs. It was twenty-five by thirty-three feet. Two small log houses were also constructed. Father de Smet was an inveterate traveler, and in late October he took off for Fort Colville on the Columbia. Forty-two days later, having traveled some six hundred miles, he returned to St. Mary's with seeds for potatoes, wheat, and oats. It was the intention of the fathers to introduce farming among the Flatheads with all possible dispatch. The religious instruction given the Indians was meanwhile intensive.

Before Father de Smet had arrived in 1840, the Flatheads were practicing some simple devotional exercises. They did pray, and they gave thanks for food. They did not move camp on Sundays. But there is evidence that what the fathers mistook for piety and adherence to certain Christian principles was something else entirely. Many of them, at least, did not see in the Cross a symbol of the Crucifixion with its attendant corollary meanings but rather conceived of it as a symbol of physical power. De Smet himself admitted that behind the Flatheads' intense desire for the Black Robes lay a conviction that through such offices they could defeat their enemies and preserve themselves. The Flatheads, after all, like their fellow mountain Indians, had a kind of heritage of fear. They did not live in the mountains by choice. They had been driven there by their fiercer eastern neighbors. They especially dreaded and hated the Blackfeet, a fact which was to have much significance in the story of their conversion.

From 1841 to 1846 things went smoothly at the mission. Then, suddenly, the relationship between the fathers and the Indians disintegrated. When, in the summer of 1846, the Flatheads left for their customary summer buffalo hunt on the plains, nothing was amiss. But when they returned, they revealed a startling change of attitude. Father Ravalli, who had come to the mission in 1845, was astonished at the Indians' behavior. They had as little as possible to do with the priests. They sold them a little meat, but it was the worst they had. They took up their old barbarous yells which had not been heard in the valley for five years. They reintroduced their old war dances, and they gave themselves up, as Father Ravalli put it, "to savage obscenity and shameless excesses of the flesh."

The change in the Indians was somehow connected, Ravalli knew, with Father de Smet's departure from their hunting camp. He was en route once more to St. Louis. Doubtless Ravalli was aware that the Indians were none too fond of the second in command, Father Mengarini, both because he was tactless and blunt and because he had once sheltered some hostile Blackfeet.

But what really lay behind the Flatheads' sudden reversion to savagery was probably a peculiar combination of circumstances coupled with a singular lack of perception on Father de Smet's part. For five years the Flatheads had prospered. They had had good hunting, and they had had almost uniformly good fortune in repelling the Blackfeet. During this good period the priests quite obviously overestimated the depth of the moral and abstract nature of the conversions they had made and underestimated the extent to which the

Flatheads thought of Catholicism as a practical protective cloak—in other words, simply as powerful medicine. Before his departure for St. Louis, Father de Smet had quite openly discussed the possibility of establishing real contact with the Blackfeet and Christianizing them. His willingness thus to deal with their dreaded enemies must have come to the Flatheads as a nasty shock. Since Father de Smet had spoken previously, and with pride, of the Flatheads' supreme confidence in "the god of battle" and had stated that the enemies of the Flatheads had to acknowledge that "the medicine [note the word] of the Black Robes . . . is strongest of all," it seems strange indeed that he would not realize how perfidious an act the baptism of a Blackfoot would appear to a Flathead. Perhaps, indeed, the Black Robes did not understand their charges nearly as well as they thought they did. Or perhaps it was merely that they thought conversion had gone much deeper than it actually had and that the Flatheads were more wily than they knew in disguising the pragmatic nature of their approach to the new religion.

The antagonism of the Indians was not enduring, but the bond had been seriously weakened. By 1848 it was clear that more than a *modus vivendi* had come about. Relationships were good again. During that winter, however, there was another peculiar reversion to the old ways. This, too, wore off. But by 1850 relations were again strained, and the Indians were remote. Most of them had given up prayer. They were hostile to the priests, and they were very suspicious. There is some evidence that Angus McDonald, a Hudson's Bay Company trader, was systematically planting seeds of doubt and suspicion in the minds of the Flatheads. Father Mengarini, then head of the mission, let himself become involved (albeit he probably had no choice) in tribal politics, and this garnered the enmity of Little Faro, an Indian of influence. So complete, in any event, was the break of 1850 that the priests felt that continued efforts were useless. The mission in that year was leased to Major John Owen, and the Jesuits departed, not to return until 1866.

Except for missionary activity and an insignificant fur and robe trade, Montana was somnolent for two decades—the forties and fifties. The white man had altered the face of the country not at all. He had merely started the Indian on the long and bitter trail toward his ultimate captivity on the reservations. There was a pause of twenty years, during which the wealth of the land lay hidden by the land's own formidable ramparts.

IV

GOLD

On a winter evening in the year 1848 James W. Marshall watching the millrace at Sutter's place in California, saw gold nuggets moving slowly along the sand, driven by the water's force. His cry of discovery was eventually heard around the world, and it brought to California and, in due course, to the whole West men from nearly every nation in the world.

From 1848 to 1858, gold mining was largely confined to the California fields. In the latter year prospectors began to fan out northward and westward. The old frontier, the agricultural frontier, was moving westward as it had since the seventeenth century. By 1870 the two frontiers were commingling in the intermountain region.

Swift fingers of the mining frontier probed out from California into the Southwest, into Colorado and Nevada, British Columbia, eastern Oregon and Washington, and, at last, into Idaho and western Montana.

Many of the miners who flooded into the mountain region had been in California or Oregon since the fifties. They had become western in every sense of the word. It was they who contributed most of the knowledge and most of the techniques. It was they who set the form for the laws and the courts.

But in the mountain region they were soon joined by veterans of the Civil War, especially from the disillusioned South, and the area became incredibly polyglot.

The rich placer deposits, fabulous as some of them were, were quickly gone. The camps and towns (or cities, as their residents called them) became ghost towns. Most of them had a brief and fitful existence. They were located, quite naturally, only with reference to gold. Accessibility was seldom other than a fortuitous circumstance.

But superficial as placer mining was, the miner, unlike the trapper, was more than a shadow. It was the miner that merchants came to sell to, that thieves came to steal from, and that farmers came to feed. And after every stream had been scoured of its dust and nuggets and the prospector had moved on, civilization kept a toe hold, however tenuous.

THE ARGUMENT concerning who first discovered gold in Montana (and where) is likely never to be settled. Father Pierre-Jean de Smet's biographer, E. Laveille, S. J., wrote in 1915 that Father de Smet had been aware of the presence of gold in Montana and Idaho for many years but that he so dreaded the consequence of its discovery that he kept the matter quiet. There is no document for Father Laveille's intimation that De Smet had discovered gold during the forties.

John Owen, who had bought St. Mary's Mission from the Jesuits in 1850 and who had established a trading post there known as Fort Owen, made a cryptic statement in his diary in 1852: "Gold hunting. Found some." This was on a Sunday in February, which would indicate that neither the search nor the "discovery" was of much consequence. Owen's diary contains no further reference to gold. The Bitterroot is mentioned again by Charles S. Warren, writing in 1876. He states that one Samuel M. Caldwell discovered gold on Mill Creek, which was close to Fort Owen, in 1852. There is no supporting testimony.

A more likely case can be made for John Silverthorne, a mountain man, who appeared at Fort Benton in 1856 with $1,525 worth of dust. But Silverthorne's gold could well have come from Canada, and, in truth, no one knows where he got it. It caused a momentary local stir but no rush.

We begin to deal more explicitly with discovery in the year 1850 and with a half-blood named François Finlay. Finlay was known as Benetsee, and he had been in California in 1849. Benetsee's story comes to us from Duncan McDonald. McDonald's mother was an Indian. His father, Angus, had built Fort Connah, a few miles south of Flathead Lake, while in the employ of the Hudson's Bay Company in 1847. In 1916 Paul C. Phillips and H. A. Trexler interviewed McDonald regarding Benetsee's discovery. McDonald testified that Angus, his father, had encountered Benetsee at Fort Connah in 1850. Benetsee had some gold with him, part of a teaspoonful. He told Angus that he had obtained it at Gold Creek (near present-day Garrison). Angus was immediately alert, but he said nothing. Again in 1851 or possibly 1852, Benetsee brought in about a teaspoonful of gold. On this occasion McDonald wrote a letter to the Board of Management of the Hudson's Bay Company at Victoria, B.C., informing them that there was gold in the Gold Creek (or the Benetsee Creek area).

According to Duncan McDonald, his father received a letter from the board instructing him to keep the entire matter secret because the company was interested in furs, not mining, and because they thought that a gold rush to the territory would ruin the fur business. Duncan McDonald also reported that his father told him that Major Owen in the Bitterroot "got wind of it," but that he kept quiet for the same reason. Duncan testified further that through some of Owen's employees the Stuart brothers (whom we shall encounter in a moment) were told of the event by some of Owen's men and that they "made a straight line to Gold Creek."

Legends and rumors dating back to the early fifties do associate Benetsee and gold. But Phillips and Trexler received only a third-hand report, and there are some dubious aspects to Duncan McDonald's testimony.

In the first place, Owen was a trader. He depended in large part on people passing through the country. He would have cared little whether their business was fur or gold. He would have been unlikely to keep such a discovery to himself for that reason. In the second place, there is no substantiation for the statement that the Stuarts were attracted to Gold Creek by rumors attributable to Benetsee's story. As we shall see, their trip there was due to other factors. Yet Benetsee was a Californian, and the possibility that he "discovered" gold in Montana, and that he talked about it, cannot be completely discounted.

In any event, "firsts" are relatively unimportant except to the antiquarian. What matters is effect. In this regard there is no doubt but that James and Granville Stuart should be credited with discovery. The Stuart brothers and one Reese Anderson were returning disgruntled from the California gold fields to Iowa. In 1857 they crossed Red Rock Divide into old Idaho territory. They spent the winter of 1857–58 in the Beaverhead Valley and in the spring moved toward the Deer Lodge Valley. On Gold Creek (then known as Benetsee Creek) they sank a shaft and found colors. Granville wrote later: "This prospect hole dug by us was the first prospecting done in what is now Montana and this is the account of the first real discovery of gold within the state."

But it was not until 1862 that the party got adequate tools to exploit their find. A community known as American Fork grew up at the mouth of the creek. It was more hope and expectation than profit that kept American Fork alive. There was no bonanza. Even though it has been commonly assumed that the operation of the Stuarts started the rush to the Northwest and in particular to Montana, such was not the case. Phillips and Trexler state rather boldly that American Fork was the magnet. The mining frontier's principal authority, William J. Trimble, disagrees. In the first place, there is simply no causal relationship between the Stuarts' discovery and the three real "rushes," namely, Bannack, Alder Gulch, and Last Chance Gulch. In the second place, the Gold Creek operation was not very successful. Moreover, the Salmon River mines in Idaho had been discovered in July, 1861, predating any real operations at Gold Creek. Perhaps a majority of those who came to American Fork in 1862 were actually headed for the Salmon River country. In spite of the fact that the Salmon River mines were very shallow and quickly exhausted, men from both east and west converged on the area. In any event, there were some sixty people in American Fork by the summer of 1862.

There is another weakness in crediting the Stuarts too exclusively. General regional conditions were most favorable for a Montana influx. By 1862 the bloom was off the rushes in Nevada, Colorado, and even Idaho. The vast majority who had flocked to those areas had not realized their dreams of quick wealth. They were, in any event, a restless type, anxious to press on. The Indian menace, although destined for a recrudescence at a later date, had diminished. The Stevens Treaty of 1855 had made possible the building of the Mullan Road from Fort Benton, Montana, to Walla Walla, Washington, so that it was now possible to reach the mountain areas (and carry equipment) with comparative ease. The entire road was completed in 1863.

Even more important, the first steamboat had reached Fort Benton on the high waters of the spring of 1860. Thus the mountain region of Montana was really accessible for the first time.

All this brought prospectors almost by the droves in the early 1860's. There is, of course, no way of knowing how many came or what remote gulches they sampled. But if gold was there, they had the determination to find it.

In July, 1862, Montana's first real strike took place on Grasshopper Creek, a tributary to the Beaverhead River. Bannack was born. By late fall there was no doubt of the richness of the mines. A train was dispatched to Salt Lake City for provisions, and a town was laid out. At first, as was usually the case, it was wickiups and tents. Then came log structures, and a little later still, when a sawmill became operative at Virginia City, some miles away, the clapboard building took over. By mid-winter, 1863, there were perhaps five hundred persons in Bannack. By spring there were nearly one thousand. Now, with typical pretentiousness, the community became "Bannack City." It was a crude, rough, and somewhat dangerous place in which to live. It attracted not only miners but an assortment of peculiarly evil men. While the road-agent plague of these years has been somewhat overdone by local historians, it was nonetheless severe. It is understandable that this element should have been attracted to the camp, because during the first year of operations it is estimated that nearly five million dollars' worth of gold was taken from the gulch.

After Grasshopper Creek, discovery followed on the heels of discovery. When the richest bars had been located at Bannack, the latecomers fanned out into surrounding gulches. Alder Gulch, or Virginia City, was next. This discovery in the Ruby Valley in May, 1863, caused at least a momentary exodus from Grasshopper Creek, and settlements sprouted like rampant weeds along the course of Alder Gulch. Virginia City, Nevada City, Circle City, and Central City housed some six thousand people by late 1863.

Here again, the rootless men were quickly poised and attuned to the rumors which were constantly boiling in the bars and hostels. That winter there were stories of a new strike on the Kootenai River, and spring saw the exodus from Virginia City. Four such men, John Cowan, D. J. Miller, Reginald Stanley, and John Crab (subsequently to be known as the Four Georgians), got as far west as Hell Gate on the Clark Fork of the Columbia when they met discouraged miners returning from the Kootenai country. Discouraged themselves, they turned back, prospected on the Little Blackfoot River, and then decided to try the Marias. En route they stopped and tried their luck on a stream which came to be known as Prickley Pear Creek. They found colors but moved on, probably as far as the Marias.

They had no luck in the Marias area, and "Last Chance

Hunted and hunter: *above*, Chief Joseph of the Nez Percés, master of strategic retreat; *below*, General Nelson A. Miles, who pursued him.

Two headstrong generals: *above*, Major General George Armstrong Custer, whose defeat at the Little Big Horn was one of the signal disasters of United States history; *below*, General Thomas Francis Meagher, who longed more for glory than for Indians.

Gulch" (as they now called it), in the Prickly Pear Valley, stuck in their minds. They decided to have one more try at it before they left the country. They retraced their route, and on July 14, 1864, they found enough colors to warrant a trip by Cowan to Alder Gulch to purchase supplies and equipment. The secret, if, indeed, there was any real attempt to keep one, was quickly out. On his return Cowan was accompanied, or at least was followed closely, by the usual horde of men. The rush to Last Chance Gulch was on, and Helena was born. Be it said for Stanley and Miller that they were ready for the contingency. They had drawn up a code of "laws" protecting their own locations, and they provided for an orderly system for locating new claims. Within the span of a few short weeks these "laws" or regulations had been ratified by the assembled miners. That fall a general meeting was held, and the new community was named Helena. Streets were laid out, the size of town lots was determined, and a government, based principally on mining rights but nonetheless the essence of order, was established.

Although government and law and order were difficult to maintain, the rapidity with which the framework, at least, was established is amazing not only with respect to Helena but in the case of all such communities. These governments were strictly improvised, but they were also strictly imitative, There was no theorizing and no experimentation. Laws were utilitarian. These men were hotly engaged in the business of mining. They wanted regulations sufficient to protect themselves, but they wanted nothing more. Politics arose initially from economic necessity. It finer developments awaited a later period.

In December, 1864, the pattern was repeated again across

the Prickly Pear Valley, and Confederate Gulch (note the Southern influence) and Diamond City came into existence. They varied little in character from the other camps.

On the eastern slope of the Rockies gold was found in Emigrant Gulch in the Yellowstone Valley. Yellowstone City was the hub of this area. Butte, which became a silver camp in 1875 and a copper camp in 1882, was initially a gold camp. There were, of course, a large number of abortive rushes and short-lived communities whose brief and sometimes bizarre existence was the stuff of hope and not of substance. But Elk Creek, Bear, Lincoln, and Highland gulches, in what became Deer Lodge County, took hold. It would serve little purpose to chronicle the discovery and early development of each camp. They were remarkably similar in every instance. They did not take on either physical or governmental (or even human) individuality until they began to diversify. Suffice it to say that by the early seventies there were some five hundred gold-bearing gulches in Montana.

The population in the mining camps was heterogeneous. It was representative of every part of the United States and almost every part of the globe. Southwesterners were very predominant after 1864. The Fisk expeditions of the early sixties contributed Minnesotans. Californians, as has been pointed out, were in evidence very early. There was a curious mixture of eastern "tenderfeet" and western "yon-siders."

Quite naturally, men predominated at first. Early in the winter of 1862–63, out of a total approximate population of 670 in the territory, 59 were "respectable" females. But after 1865 women came in appreciable numbers, and the dearth of women in the mining camps has been considerably exaggerated.

Unfortunately no study has been made of the Chinese in

Montana, but there were thought to be about eight hundred of them in the territory in 1869. There was considerable hostility toward them because of their willingness to work long, hard hours for a pittance. But they were important economically because they were willing to rework the "tailings" of the claims which white men had supposedly exhausted.

The white population lived less precariously than has often been indicated. Foods were rather monotonous—the staples being bread, bacon, beans, and coffee. But by paying a good price a man could usually buy green fruit, eggs, and butter. Fresh meat was always available because the cattle industry developed quickly. Trout abounded in the streams, and west of the divide there were salmon.

As for recreation, the miner was attracted to horse racing and boxing—both on an impromptu basis. Saloons were much in evidence, and heavy drinking, especially during the long winter months, was at most a venial transgression. Gambling was wide-open. Three-card monte, strap game, thimblerig game, patent safe game, black and red, any dice game, and two-card box at faro were all regarded as "legally unfair" in Montana, but a great variety of other games of chance existed.

What is often overlooked, however, is that the steady part of the population—those who were doing most of the real building—gathered neither in saloons nor gambling houses. They gathered at church functions or, more frequently, at "the store," such as George Chrisman's at Bannack or Pfouts' at Virginia City. Also, there were fraternal organizations; the Masonic Order was almost coeval with the founding of Virginia City. And there were social clubs, dances, and special events.

Virginia City was perhaps typical. Seen from the top of "Boot Hill," a primitive cemetery most of whose occupants were road agents, the community sprawled down Alder Gulch without design or plan. Paint was a rare commodity, and almost as soon as they were built the buildings had a look of decay. Within three months Alder Gulch probably had a boom population of nearly ten thousand people. They lived at first in everything from tents and wickiups to hewn log cabins. Unplaned lumber structures began to take over in 1864. The populace lived also among disfiguring heaps of gravel, sluice boxes, flumes, and washes. The streets became quagmires in the spring and fall, and they were inches deep in dust in the summer. The sidewalks of the main street were board. All told, the whole area of disfigurement and activity was perhaps twelve miles long, snaking down Alder Gulch with shoots probing off into near-by gulches. It was, undeniably, a tough community.

But after a year in the camp, J. H. Morley wrote in his diary: "I shouldn't have the patience to count the places of business, but can say that the market is so well stocked that all necessaries and many luxuries can be obtained in the stores." "Luxury," of course, is a relative word, but Morley was an educated and perceptive man.

Virginia City and Bannack (and thereby most of the early gold camps) have been painted most colorfully for us by Thomas Dimsdale and N. P. Langford, both of whom were there. Each wrote a book on the Vigilantes. The pictures that emerge are of almost unrestrained violence, murder, and drunkenness. Unfortunately the other side of life in these camps has been submerged by the short-lived Vigilante era. Before we examine the status of law and order, therefore, we should get at least a glimpse of the more basic tenor of society.

It is notable that in Morley's diary there is but one notation on a hanging. Yet Morley was there at the height of the road-agent scourge. What was he doing? He was mining and tending his own business. He was, it is true, preoccupied with his own affairs, but he was also observant. It is noteworthy that he would comment on the community's remarkable growth, the nature of its business houses, and the affairs of its miners but that the picture of violence and murder is almost totally absent from his writing.

Virginia City was also seen in those days by one J. K. Miller. Miller was a youth of some seventeen or eighteen years, who kept a detailed diary. It gives us a picture of Virginia City that is totally different from Morley's and also totally different from Dimsdale's or Langford's. Miller was adolescent and naïve, and his perspective is therefore all the more revealing. He was obviously homesick but intrigued with his surroundings. Although he was as often at church as he was playing billiards, his "peccadilloes" caused him considerable remorse. On Sunday, October 22, 1865, he wrote in his diary: "*Resolved:* That from this date I do not spend a cent for foolishness such as Billiards, Drinking, Eating, Driving, Riding, Smoking. That I limit my monthly expenses for Dancing and Gifts to $10.00."

Even though he repeatedly reaffirmed this resolution, he could not resist a little carousing. On one occasion he drank "an immense quantity of Tom and Jerry" and got violently ill. But on the other hand, he "took the initiatory steps to organize the Virginia City Social Club." In succeeding weeks one gets no glimpse of the riotous, bloody camp. Miller went on a sleigh ride sponsored by the "Literary Association." He attended the inauguration ball of the society. He did see a prize fight on January 10 and was constrained to remark that it was attended by "a very rough looking crowd consisting in great proportion of Irish, a sprinkling of Dutch and a smaller percentage of Gents"; but shortly thereafter he attended the theatre and saw Julia Dean Hayne Cooper in *Griseldis*.

Miller's free time was largely taken up with French lessons (from Mr. Hammel, who was "a shining light in the Catholic choir of this city") and various social activities. Nowhere, again, does the grim picture of Dimsdale and Langford emerge.

What is the true picture of life in these camps? It is a composite of all these views. Gunmen and violence were there, but beneath the primitive and raw surface churches were emerging, and social and economic institutions of substance were taking form.

Law came to the mining camps almost invariably with discovery. Discoverers and early arrivals sought first of all to protect their claims. Thus, regulations bearing on ownership had to be drawn up immediately. They varied only in detail from camp to camp, and all were based on previous codes developed elsewhere on the frontier. The regulations usually adopted at a miner's meeting provided for the size of claims, water rights, a miners' court, a president of the district, a recorder, and a sheriff. The ordinary term was six months.

The miners' court was a powerful institution. It tried both civil and criminal cases. Attorneys usually appeared on both sides, and while the rules of evidence were less stringent than they were in more settled communities, they did exist in the event that the judge had legal training, which was often the case. Civil matters were usually determined by a jury, but criminal matters were often left to the judgment of the entire body of miners. Sentences were clear-cut and simple. Since there were no prisons and, indeed, few effective jails, punishment seldom involved incarceration. The miscreant was either flogged (which was rare), banished (which was common), or hanged (which, for a time, was predominant).

But distance made appeal to regularly constituted authority an impossibility. The great wealth in negotiable material (gold dust and nuggets) which was everywhere attracted the West's most unsavory group of cutthroats. For a while, because the miners were preoccupied and because, indeed, the evil elements were better organized than the good, the road agents held bloody sway. Their unlikely leader was a graceful, softspoken, and charming man named Henry Plummer. We do not know a great deal about him save that he had a bad record in California, Nevada, and Idaho. He was undoubtedly psychopathic. His cold-bloodedness stood in contrast to his charm. His unpretentious good manners and his obvious appeal to men (and women) were such that he was elected sheriff of Bannack. In that capacity he gathered around him an unholy crew and preyed on the populace. This band came to be known as "The Innocents," and they congregated principally in Bannack. Between the winters of 1862 and 1864 they murdered a known 102 victims. But perhaps a score more may have been killed by them. There were many cases of missing persons. Some, at least, probably fell prey to The Innocents. Thomas Dimsdale describes them thus:

> The usual arms of a road agent were a pair of revolvers, a double-barrelled shotgun of large bore, with the barrels cut down short, and to this they invariably added a knife or dagger. Thus armed and mounted on fleet, well-trained horses, and being disguised with blankets and masks, the robbers awaited their prey in ambush.

Although the number in the band varied, there were

twenty-four principal members. All were hanged by the Vigilantes between December 21, 1863, and January 11, 1864. There is no evidence that these hangings were without justification. Subsequent Vigilante activity in Montana, especially with respect to the "strangler" activity in central Montana in the early eighties, cannot be so readily justified. But the record of Plummer's band was so bloody, and so plain for all to read that there can be little doubt of the rectitude of the stringent methods of the early vigilance committee. As Langford puts it:

> What else could they do? How else were their own lives and property, and the lives and property of the great body of peaceable miners in the places to be preserved? What other protection was there for a country entirely destitute of law?

But Langford also says:

> The reader will find among the later acts of some of the individuals claiming to have exercised the authority of the Vigilantes, some executions of which he cannot approve. For these persons I can offer no apology. Many of these were worse men than those they executed.

The Vigilantes organized on December 23, 1863. There was an executive committee consisting of Paris Pfouts, James Williams, and Wilbur F. Sanders. The remainder of the forty-five men who signed the original Vigilante Oath were organized into teams, each headed by a captain. During the bitterly cold midwinter of 1863 these groups ranged the mountain country from Virginia City to Fort Owen, searching out the road agents who were now alerted and scattering. Fortunately one of the early captives, Erastus "Red" Yeager, confessed not only his own crimes but gave the Vigilantes the names of most of The Innocents. Further, under the expert questioning of James Williams, "executive officer" of the vigilance committee, most of Plummer's band confessed specific crimes.

By the spring of 1864 they had hanged all of Plummer's principal band and an additional eight miscreants. Their activities were shrouded in a secrecy which has lasted to this day. Their mysterious sign, 3–7–77, which they often left pinned to the corpses of the road agents, is still not subject to accurate interpretation. Many of them went on to become leaders in territorial and state affairs.

In the meantime, crime had in no way discouraged the boom. Montana's mines (almost exclusively gold and largely placer produced about $90,800,000 between 1862 and 1876. This, in the strict sense, was "new wealth," but it is only very partially representative of the tremendous economic stimulus which the gold rush produced in Montana.

Economic growth in the western part of the territory (and it must be borne in mind that eastern Montana enjoyed none of this boom) was rapid. The embarkation point for the men and supplies bound for the gold fields was principally St. Louis. The several Fisk routes from Minnesota overland and the route up from Corinne in the South contributed some of the flow, but Fort Benton, headwaters of navigation on the Missouri, received the vast bulk of its business from the up-river trade. Indicative of the magnitude of the change wrought in the western country by the gold rush are the figures with respect to Benton itself.

Starting with the *Chippewa* in 1859 (which didn't quite reach the Fort), from two to eight steamboats arrived during every spring season from 1860 to 1865. From 1866 to 1868 so great was the demand for supplies in the mining country that thirty-one steamboats arrived in 1866, thirty-nine in 1867, thirty-five in 1868, and twenty-four in 1869. Fort Benton was a veritable cauldron. Its levee was towering with boxed goods, barrels, tools, bales, and equipment. In 1867, 8,061 tons of freight and about 10,000 passengers spilled out at Fort Benton. Since each passenger paid a fare of $150, some $1,500,000 was spent in that year in passenger fares alone. Captain La Barge of the *Octavia* is reported to have cleared $40,000 from one trip in 1867, and profits from other vessels in the preceding year ranged from $16,000 to $65,000 net. The warehouses which had sprung up along the levee were jammed to the rafters. Freighters could not keep up with the business. It is significant to note that one steamer bound downstream in 1867 carried $1,250,000 in raw gold to St. Louis.

Prices for all provisions in the mining areas were high. And this economic inducement led to agricultural settlement in the remote valleys which, had it not been for the mines, would have waited long for settlement. Had the farmer been looking only for good soil, proper moisture, and a long growing season, he would have forsaken the mountain valleys and moved on westward. But at prevailing prices and with apparently unlimited demand, he could afford the hardships and risks. Agriculture was so firmly rooted in the Gallatin and Bitterroot valleys that the farmer survived the trying times of the decline of placer mining with little adjustment.

To consider only the camps and towns themselves and to deal only with the figures involving gold production per se is to set the lens too narrowly. These settlements in many cases vanished completely; in others they languished and hung on for several decades. But the point is that they were the wedge of settlement, and thus their contribution was lasting. This fact is far too often overlooked when the "ghost town" is pointed out as evidence of the passing nature of the precious-metal industry.

Nor, indeed, did all the camps vanish. Helena is a good example of a mining camp that became a city. There were two factors involved which enabled Helena to survive. In the first place, although placer gold was quickly depleted, rich quartz lodes were discovered. Quartz mining required capital, technicians, and longer range programs.

In the second place, Helena had become a trade center. By late 1866 the mining flush was gone. But it continued in surrounding valleys, and the supplies needed there came from Helena stocks. The summer of 1867 witnessed the erection of a substantial number of stone buildings in Helena. By the fall of that year a United States Land Office had been opened. Dahler's Bank, a brick building, had been erected, and a $26,000 courthouse was started. The assessment of property in the county for 1866 amounted to $1,320,386.

By 1876, Helena had a settled population of about four thousand, and Lewis and Clark County had about six thousand. This indicates the nature of the country's growth. The population figures themselves are not impressive when it appears that Helena grew from nothing to only four thousand people in twelve long years. But a different standard applies in the context of an immense and inhospitable country. These western settlements, of which Helena was typical, were in no sense "villages" or "towns" in the eastern or particularly the New England sense. It is not a matter of mere pretension that the word "village" had no place in the western lexicon. There was an intensity and vitality about these communities that was all out of proportion to the actual number of people participating. Such population centers served a tremendous area with all their needs. And they themselves were peculiarly cosmopolitan and independent. It is only with this relativity in mind that the student can avoid the distortion of comparative figures.

West of the Continental Divide the mining rush had produced similar, though not identical, results. According to the census of 1870, Missoula County had a population of only 2,554 persons. Even that figure is deceptive because a portion of these people were essentially transients drawn to the area by the Cedar Creek mines. The significance of the Missoula example, however, lies in the fact that ordinarily one does not think of today's community of over 40,000 people as having had its origin in mining. Yet directly and indirectly gold was again a cornerstone of permanent settlement.

In October, 1864, rich but shallow placer discoveries were made on Silver Bow Creek (Butte), and during the winter of 1864–65 there were probably 150 men in the vicinity. But by 1867 the claims were almost entirely worked out, and Butte seemed destined for the parched end of most of such camps. By 1869 it was on the far edge of extinction. Its satellites, Rocker and Silver Bow, were already crumbling, and Butte itself had less than 60 tenacious residents. Notable among these was William L. Farlin, whose steady belief that there was promise in quartz gold and silver was fundamentally responsible for Butte's rebirth. By 1875, Farlin was actively and profitably engaged in silver mining, and within three months Butte had become a bustling camp once more.

Butte and Helena are typical examples of a basic development in the mining industry—not only in Montana but in the entire western mining area during the decades of the sixties and seventies. Placer mining featured the individual miner or, at most, a loose partnership. The economy, thus, was extremely simple and undiversified. But quartz mining, which in most instances replaced placer mining, demanded corporate organization and capital. It was therefore a tremendous stimulus for banking, for the legal profession, and for promotion. Moreover, because quartz mining required mine timbers, it ushered in the allied lumber industry. Because it required stamp mills and reduction plants of various kinds, there developed a demand for overland transportation and hence for roads. Further, the industry required technicians, mill hands, and bookkeepers. Thus in the seventies the base of the economy was greatly expanded.

A chronic problem was development capital. Hardly a week passed that the Butte *Miner,* for instance, did not proclaim the opportunities for investment. Editorial after editorial set forth the promise of fabulous return. Stern lectures were read the populace on the necessity of making the most of feelers extended by outside investors. Men like Z. L. White, staff correspondent for the New York *Tribune* who visited Butte in 1879, were treated like uncommon royalty. Other camps in Montana, making the same transition and plagued by the same shortage of capital, were no less solicitous of visiting bankers and engineers. When such eastern publications as the *Engineering and Mining Journal* began to take note of Montana mining developments, the endeavor to get capital sometimes became almost frenzied.

Local miners, however, were not relying on any such chamber-of-commerce activity. Men such as William Andrews Clark, Samuel T. Hauser, Marcus Daly, and others now engaged in enterprises of significance made regular pilgrimages to the East or Far West to get development capital. Their mines were financed in some part by banks or individuals in St. Louis, Chicago, New York, or San Francisco. This trend is noticeable in the late seventies, it is pronounced by the early eighties. Slowly, in a comparative sense, but perceptibly, the top of the profit was siphoned off, and more and more frequently policy decisions were made by investors who had never seen the country or the enterprises which were producing for them.

Nevertheless, a spirit of optimism reigned in Montana's mining camps in the eighties—and not without justification. Prices were high, but wages were good. There were clear indications that the wealth still beneath the earth was fabulous. Many a miner had been in the territory since the sixties. Such men could look back to the beginnings and see the signs of progress all around them. Twenty years had produced profound changes. There was little to indicate that it was not all for the better. Now, with the railroads approaching both from the East and South, the dark hills fretted with tracks and crowned with headframes, the sound of stamp mills echoing in the canyons, the wagons lumbering over improving roads, and the shafts penetrating ever deeper into the hills, it was a dim vision that did not see a great future for the territory.

While Montana was still terribly remote, trails, roads, and the fast approaching railroads gave the citizens a sense of proximity to "the States" which had not existed a few years before.

The principal highway to Montana for many years had been the great Missouri, curving into its heartland. This had been the route of Lewis and Clark. It had borne the keelboats of the trappers and the steamboats from St. Louis.

But when gold turned the eyes of Middle Westerners

toward the mountains, other routes were opened. The news of the Montana discoveries caused much excitement in the Northern Great Lakes region. But even prior to this, James L. Fisk, a private in the Third Minnesota Regiment, had proposed a northern route to obviate the long trip down to St. Louis. Since the government saw some military value in such a route, $5,000 was set aside for Fisk to open the northern route. With the new rank of captain, Fisk was ready in the summer of 1862. It was in July of that summer that the first real Montana gold strike occurred.

Gathering at Fort Abercrombie, near present Fargo, a party of 130, led by Fisk, set forth. They crossed the plains to Fort Union, ascended the Missouri and the Milk to about the location of present Havre, and then, turning southwestward, reached Fort Benton on September 5. The trip, which took a little less than two months, was uneventful, and it established the feasibility of the northern route.

Four separate Fisk expeditions left Fargo (or Abercrombie) between 1862 and 1866, the last of which consisted of 160 wagons and 500 people. While there were variations in the northern route, the fact remained that for Minnesotans the Northern Overland Route was both easier and faster than the trip up the Missouri.

The country was being probed by still another road from another direction, this time a military wagon road. The idea for such a road had its inception in the mind of twenty-three-year-old John Mullan (lieutenant, U. S. Army), who had accompanied General Stevens into the Montana area on the Railroad Survey of 1853. The Stevens survey party left Fort Benton for the Bitterroot in September, 1853. The party was divided into three groups, each of which was to investigate a separate route. Mullan had charge of the group which in-

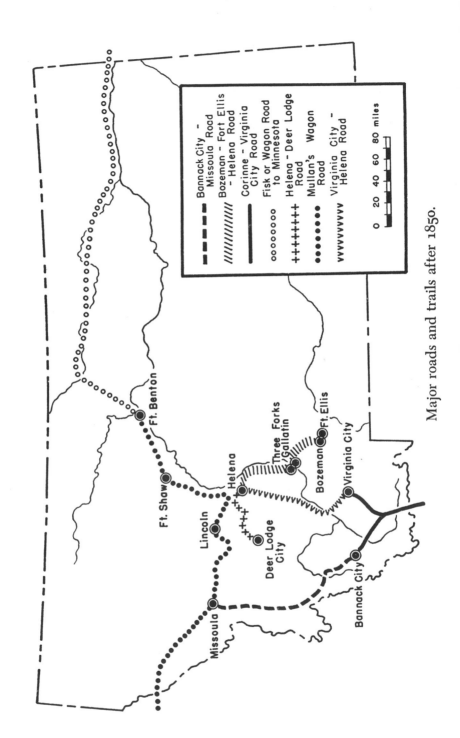

Major roads and trails after 1850.

Legend:

Bannack City – Missoula Road
Bozeman – Fort Ellis – Helena Road
Corinne – Virginia City Road
Fisk or Wagon Road to Minnesota
Helena – Deer Lodge Road
Mullan's Wagon Road
Virginia City – Helena Road

0   20   40   60   80 miles

Ft. Benton
Ft. Shaw
Helena
Three Forks
Gallatin
Bozeman
Ft. Ellis
Virginia City
Lincoln
Deer Lodge City
Missoula
Bannack City

Civilization came all at once; homesteaders arrive in the Flat-head Valley.

Hoping to make their fortune were these homesteaders in Custer County.

vestigated the Bitterroot, and, moreover, he remained in the valley all winter to study winter conditions.

The route which Stevens ultimately recommended was from Fort Union up the Missouri and Milk rivers, then down to Benton, over the main range via either Cadottes or Lewis and Clark Pass, through the Hell Gate, then westward over the present Mullan Pass and into the Coeur d' Alene country and on to Spokane.

Mullan was by now thoroughly familiar with the country, and he understood that the need for both prior and auxiliary transportation was great. Mullan proposed an overland military road from Fort Benton to Walla Walla. The time (1855), however, was not propitious. Congress favored the central railroad route and not the northern route.

But the need for military roads was impressed on the government when the Yakima Indians caused trouble in 1855 and again when the Mormon trouble broke out in 1857. In 1858 the secretary of war authorized the building of the road proposed by Mullan, and he was placed in charge of the project.

Not until 1859 was Mullan ready to go to work. By this time another event had occurred which was of singular importance to Mullan's project and to the next phase of Montana's development. The steamboat *Chippewa* was the first vessel to navigate the Missouri above Fort Union and reach Fort Benton. This meant that there would be, when Mullan's Road was completed, continuous and easy transportation from St. Louis to the Pacific Northwest. There would be a tremendous saving in time and money over the route around Cape Horn.

Starting his expedition at The Dalles on May 15, 1859, Mullan and his men were caught in heavy snow a few miles above the mouth of the St. Regis River. The heaviness of the snow in that area convinced Mullan that the Clark Fork route was the better one. During that winter he changed his plans, also, and brought some three hundred troops up the Missouri to Fort Benton, the road's eastern terminus. He used the equipment and wagons which were at Fort Benton to transport the troops back over the road to the Northwest. The road was completed to Fort Benton in the late summer of 1860, and four days later the troops (which had been transported up the river by Pierre Chouteau at a contract price of thirty dollars a head) set out for Walla Walla. They made the six-hundred-mile journey in fifty-seven days.

The Mullan Road was no highway, but it was a tremendously important project in view of the soon-to-occur gold rushes. Had there been no such road making it possible to transport heavy equipment into the gold fields, the settlement of Montana would have been greatly retarded. As it was, the road was completed just as the rush began. Lest the presence of the great highways which cut swaths across our land today lead us to underestimate Mullan's accomplishment, it should be borne in mind that with only the equipment wielded by hand or dragged by horse Mullan cut his road through 624 miles of wilderness, 120 miles of it through dense forest where the road was 30 feet wide. There were 30 miles of earth excavation and rock. While the road was not finally finished until 1863, it was usable in 1860.

In the meantime, the Oregon Trail to the south had been worn deep by the wheels of immigrant wagons since the forties. With the discovery of gold in Idaho and Montana, a northern offshoot of the trail became desirable. John Bozeman had come to the Deer Lodge Valley in 1862. Following the stampede to Bannack, he met John M. Jacobs, and together they planned to open a route from Fort Laramie to Bannack.

In the early spring of 1863, Bozeman and Jacobs began to plot the route. Accompanied by Jacobs' eight-year-old half-blood daughter, they set out for Fort Laramie. The trip was ill-fated. They were captured by Indians and narrowly escaped death, but in due course, half-starved, they reached Fort Laramie. There, nothing daunted, they began collecting a train for a trip back along their route.

Actually their cutoff left the Oregon Trail some one hundred miles northwest of Laramie. On July 6, with forty-six wagons and eighty-nine people, they set off over the trail. Plagued by Sioux and Cheyenne, the train had to turn back, but Bozeman and eight others followed the proposed route which ran east of the Big Horn Mountains to about present Buffalo, Wyoming, then slanted northwestward into Montana, crossing the Big Horn River southeast of present Hardin, and then up into the Yellowstone Valley. The trouble was that this offshoot east of the Big Horns passed through the very heart of Indian country. Bozeman advocated it primarily because of the excellent grass and water and because he felt that large and heavily armed trains would be secure from Indian attacks.

The old scout Jim Bridger disagreed, and he set about guiding trains westward from Casper, through the Wind River Canyon, and down into the Big Horn Valley. Bozeman's route, however, proved the more popular, and beginning in 1864 it was heavily traveled.

Another route into Montana, from Corinne, Utah, to Virginia City, became perhaps the principal road for hauling heavy equipment in and hauling ore out. Part of the Corinne–Virginia City road had been in use since the fifties. Stretching from western Montana through the Big Hole Basin, over Monida Pass, to Fort Hall on the Oregon Trail, the road had been used by early traders and trappers. When the Union Pacific–Central Pacific joined to form a transcontinental railroad in 1869, the southern terminus of the Montana road became Corinne, some thirty miles west of Ogden. Here the heavy freight destined for the Montana mining camps was taken off the railroad and reloaded on massive wagons for the rugged trip north. Here, too, Montana ore—silver and even copper—arrived for shipment to the east. The trip to Corinne by fast stage could be accomplished with relative ease in four or five days. But a round trip for the freight wagons took about two months.

The Corinne–Virginia City road, of course, branched out once it reached Montana. The first cutoff, as a matter of fact, occurred just south of the present boundary. Part of the road forked northwestward, entering Beaverhead County through the Sheep Creek Basin; the other fork entered near present Monida. From Bannack one road led into the Bitterroot, and another led northward into the Deer Lodge Valley. And from Virginia City there was a heavily traveled road northward to Helena, where a juncture was made with the Mullan Road.

From the myriad accounts of both stage travelers and freighters we get some concept of the ruggedness of the country. The stage traveler could expect a "station" every twenty to fifty miles. Such stations had very primitive accommodations. Their principal function was to provide fresh horses. Stages usually ran day and night, and six to eight days and nights of jouncing, dust, heat, cold, rain, snow, and mud were hardly calculated to bring the passenger to his destination refreshed. Nor was such travel cheap. It cost about $65.00 to get from Corinne to Helena.

Freight outfits usually used mules or oxen. There were ordinarily three loaded wagons per unit with an eight-mule or -oxen hitch. The lead wagon, and the largest, could carry about 6,500 pounds; the second wagon, 5,500; and the third, 4,500. It was a rough, sweaty, and grueling job to drive such outfits, and it is not surprising that mule skinners and bull-whackers developed profanity to the fine point of art.

All this changed, as did the entire economy of the region, with the coming of the railroads. The Utah Northern, a branch of the Union Pacific, was the first road to reach the state.

Promoted by John W. Young (Brigham's son) and financed largely in New York, the Utah Northern had reached the border of Montana Territory by 1879. There now arose conflict between the westward building Northern Pacific and the Utah Northern, with the latter attempting to get special legislation locally for a tax-exempt status for fifteen years. A special session of the Territorial Legislature in 1879 defeated such a measure. There was a growing realization on the part of Montanans, a realization voiced most succinctly by Martin Maginnis, that local subsidies were not necessary to encourage railroad building in Montana and that local communities should not mortgage their futures.

The Northern Pacific had reached Montana's eastern boundary in 1881. By 1883 the Utah Northern and Northern Pacific made junction at Garrison, west of Butte. The Utah Northern was narrow gauge, and this led to considerable difficulty as the Northern Pacific pushed westward. All goods had to be unloaded and then reloaded. But the road was converted to standard gauge in 1888 and was leased by the Northern Pacific. In 1897, it was incorporated into the Oregon Short Line Railroad Company.

The financing of the Northern Pacific had been characterized by one crisis after another. It was originally financed by Jay Cooke, but then a controlling interest had been purchased in the Oregon Steam Navigation Company in order to assure an adequate right of way west of the mountains. It was via this company that Henry Villard replaced Frederick Billings as president of the parent company. Villard sometimes ran dangerously close to financial catastrophe and at one time was facing a deficit of some $14,000,000. But by showmanship and shrewd manipulations he kept the company on its feet and pushed construction rapidly. By 1882 the road had passed up the Yellowstone Valley and into the mountains. By the fall of 1883 it had reached Garrison.

The land subsidy given the Northern Pacific was substantial. Where construction was relatively simple (in Minnesota and Oregon) the railroad received ten alternate sections on either side of the right of way. But in mountainous country, including all of Montana, it received twenty alternate sections on each side. All in all the company got about fifty million acres, some fourteen million of which were in Montana. The Northern Pacific thus became a landholder of consequence in Montana, and this, in turn, led to its sustained promotional campaign designed to bring in settlers.

In the meantime, James J. Hill had conceived the plan of a northern railroad to the coast. Hill was a Canadian who had had considerable railroad experience with a route between St. Paul and Winnipeg and who had been interested in a Canadian road to the Pacific. He came to St. Paul in 1876 and transferred his interest from a Canadian to an American road. Initially he called his road the St. Paul, Minneapolis, and Manitoba. By 1886, both by new construction and by the absorption of already existing lines, his road had reached Minot, North Dakota. Here, by virtue of his friendship with

Paris Gibson, he became interested in the Great Falls area. Through Gibson and C. A. Broadwater he established the Montana Central Railroad Company, the object of which was to pre-empt the Helena and Butte area by a line connecting them with Great Falls. This would compete with the Northern Pacific.

But Hill had a problem which the Northern Pacific had not encountered. Northern Montana was practically all Indian reservation area. The government, and President Cleveland in particular, had qualms about any additional violation of Indian rights. It was perfectly clear that a railroad would quickly lead to the further alienation of Indian lands. Once again, however, the pressure on the government was relentless and strong, and in 1887 the Great Northern Railroad was granted a seventy-five-foot right of way through reservation lands with the further stipulation that the railroad could use the adjacent timber and stone for construction purposes. Hill, however, had to pay approximately fifty cents an acre for land.

Construction west of Minot started in the spring of 1887, and in a tremendous burst of activity the road reached Great Falls in the early fall. More than five hundred miles of road had been constructed, constituting an average of more than three miles a day. That same fall, the Montana Central completed its line to Helena. While the branch to Butte was delayed for several years, the Great Northern had effectively made its bid against the Northern Pacific for its slice of the Continental Divide region's business.

In 1889, in dead winter, the Great Northern's engineer, John F. Stevens, found the long elusive and often sought for Marias Pass. The pass had, of course, been used for years both by trappers and Indians. But, even though it provided one of the lowest and easiest passages through the mountains, neither the Stevens party of 1853 nor subsequent railroad explorations had revealed it. Now the Great Northern could proceed westward without having to drop southward toward the already existent Northern Pacific or push northward toward the area which was serviced by Canadian roads. The Great Northern reached Everett, Washington, in the summer of 1893.

In 1894 the Chicago, Burlington, and Quincy reached Billings. This was a branch that began at York, Nebraska, then ran to Edgemont, South Dakota, and thence to Newcastle, Wyoming, and Billings. Later the Burlington extended its line for a direct connection with Denver.

The Milwaukee, which had confined itself to the Middle West, extended into Iowa and the Dakotas in the early 1870's and then in 1905 determined to build on to the coast. The road reached Gold Creek, Montana (near Garrison), in 1909 and in 1914 was electrified between Harlowton, Montana, and Avery, Idaho.

The railroads put an end to navigation on the Missouri, Fort Benton became a sleepy village, stage companies and freight outfits went out of business, and the bullwhacker became a legend.

But Montana was ready to enter the industrial age—in its own peculiar and plunging way.

V

POLITICS

In the bitterness of civil war the Democratic party became the party of rebellion. The taint of treason bore down heavily on it. Even the northern Democrats, to whom the preservation of the Union was as dear as to the Republicans, shared through the party name, if in no other way, the odium of their errant southern brothers' rebellion. From 1860 until 1884 no Democrat was elected to the Presidency, and the Congress was overwhelmingly controlled by the Republican party. Until 1872, the most militant Republicans, the Radicals, controlled the Congress. Bent on vengeance and punishment, Lincoln's benign policy of reconstruction for the South was converted into a policy of malice by the Radicals.

But neither defeat, coercion, nor punishment could kill the spirit of the Southerner, nor was the Democratic party permanently eclipsed. Both the Southerner and his party found latitude and a relief from pressure and disillusionment in the West. Southerners came to Montana in great numbers.

Prior to the spring of 1864 Montana had undergone a bewildering process of political organization, division, and subdivision. On May 26, 1864, it became a territory unto itself. In 1863 the only representative of organized government was Sidney Edgerton, who had been named by President Lincoln as chief justice of Idaho Territory. The federal government, having only the vaguest notion of western geography, assigned Edgerton to Bannack instead of Lewiston. Once Edgerton became aware of the immensity of the country he was supposed to administer, he realized that the area east of the Bitterroot Mountains could never be effectively governed from Lewiston and that it should not be a part of Idaho Territory. He joined with W. F. Sanders and others in petitioning Congress for a separate territory. Edgerton himself made the trip to Washington and was successful. Lincoln then named Edgerton governor of the new territory of Montana.

The political story which now unfolds has its ludicrous elements. Government, when it functioned at all, did so only in the midst of near chaos. Frequently there simply wasn't any government. Civil War hatreds were very prominent in the territory, where southern sympathizers were predominant. The Democratic party was the party of strength, but a strongly Republican national administration appointed only Republican territorial officials. Such officials were supported locally by an aggressive minority from the northern states. Also, there were a good many northern Democrats who, even though they were supporters of the Union cause, simply could not bring themselves to join either the Republicans or the southern Democrats. The latter, many of them former Confederate soldiers, were all thoroughly Democratic.

This admixture was reason enough for political acrimony, but there was an even more fundamental cause of trouble. Almost all Montanans resented the far-removed national government. In this respect they were no different from other frontiersmen of that and other times. Part of the trouble was inherent in distance, poor communications, and a primitive resentment of "outside" interference. The rest was the consequence of genuine blundering and ignorance in Washington. The administration could not be much concerned about the remote and sparsely settled frontier. Congress itself was preoccupied, first with the war and then with the vast problems of reconstruction. When it turned its attention to the West, it did so only momentarily and incompletely. While particular territorial resentment was aroused by the federal military and Indian policies, there were many other things that frustrated and galled Montana residents.

So strong was southern sentiment in the spring of 1864 that Edgerton's daughter wrote: "Threats had been made that anyone would be shot who dared to raise the star spangled banner. . . . The threats proved to be mere bravado; but drunken horsemen galloping by at night often fired random shots at the red, white and blue target while hurrahing lustily for Jeff Davis."

Yet Montana Republicans waved "the bloody shirt" with a vengeance. They lost no opportunity to equate the Democratic party with treason and rebellion. Even though it was edited by the mild and almost timid Thomas Dimsdale, Montana's first newspaper, the *Montana Post*, attacked the Democrats as "the meanest and most heterogeneous compound ever foisted on the political world of the 19th Century."

97

Edgerton, Sanders, and other Republicans rode this horse of treason constantly. But the territory remained strongly Democratic.

A kind of legend has grown up in Montana that the "left wing of Price's army" and a host of secessionists stood in fair train to separate the territory from the Union and attach it to the Confederacy. This is strictly a hand-over from early Republican propaganda. There is no doubt that Edgerton and Sanders in particular assiduously sought to create this impression. They were certainly no more violent than Republican politicians in the nation as a whole, but there was no substance to their charges. Indeed, the First Territorial Legislature was divided politically. The Council was Republican by one vote, and the House was Democratic by the same margin. It is a commentary on Edgerton's strong feelings (and perhaps on his political ineptitude) that in his address to the first legislature he called Southerners "uncultivated savages" and referred to the "imbecile administration of James Buchanan." The address was full of violent expletives and unrestrained condemnation of Democrats. It was not a very auspicious way to launch a new government. Yet that divided legislature adopted a resolution proclaiming itself loyal to the Union, a rather clear indication that there was no substantial secessionist sentiment.

Majority opinion manifested itself in the first election for a territorial delegate to Congress. The popular and widely known Wilbur F. Sanders was defeated by Samuel McLean, a Democrat. The Democratic position was that the war had become a war of attrition, that there could be no victor, and that a negotiated peace was the proper solution. Sanders was as violent as Edgerton in his condemnation of such moderation. He cried that the left wing of Price's army was "skulking

in the gulches of Montana, inciting treason." He called Southerners "rebels, copperheads and traitors to their country." But
there was an obvious lack of enthusiasm in Sanders' audiences
—so much so that the Governor was called upon to come from
Bannack to Virginia City to help out Sanders' campaign.
Edgerton was venomous, but Sanders lost the election.

Upon the death of Lincoln and the fiasco of Johnson's impeachment, radical Republicanism became the order of the
day. Congress created the punitive "Iron Clad Oath," designed to eliminate from public office all those who had borne
arms against the Union. In Montana one John H. Rogers had
been elected to the first legislature, and he had been in the
Confederate Army. He believed that the oath as constituted
could only be signed by a perjurer, and he proposed an alternative oath in which he would swear his support of the government of the United States and the Organic Act relating to
Montana Territory. But Edgerton would have none of this,
and he declared that if Rogers took his seat in the legislature,
he (Edgerton) would declare all the acts of that legislature
null and void. Rogers did not press the issue at that time, and
Edgerton's victory was Pyrrhic because of Rogers' popularity.
The Governor found it increasingly difficult to deal with the
legislature, and in eight months' time he had given up and
returned to the East. Rogers was re-elected in 1866, and he
was seated without challenge.

Edgerton seems to have been somewhat less than astute
in his handling of the legislature. Aside from that, he was well
aware of the problems of the Territory. With respect to roads,
in particular, taxation of mineral lands, Indian affairs, mail
facilities, and education, his message to the first legislature
revealed a clear understanding of the country's necessities.

It was Edgerton who first encountered the absurd situation which was to plague several of his successors. There was money in the federal treasury with which to administer the territories, but the expenditure of such money required the signature of a territorial secretary. The trouble was that no secretary had been appointed. Nobody wanted the job. Accordingly, Edgerton had paid most of the expenses of government out of his own pocket. This was an understandable part of his general discouragement. After Edgerton had left, Thomas Francis Meagher was appointed secretary, only to become acting governor upon his arrival. He, himself, then, was without a secretary. Not until the fall of 1866 was a permanent governor appointed, and in the interim Meagher "acted"—which is to say, he engaged in many activities, few of which contributed to any kind of territorial stability.

There is an equestrian statue of Thomas Francis Meagher standing on the front lawn of the Capitol in Helena—charging, sword drawn, forever into the future. He is a legend in Montana, especially among the Irish. But he is not an easy man for the historian to treat. He is described by his principal biographer as "truculent, noisy, brash, verbose and belligerent. He was restless, high-strung and eager for adventure and change. In his judgment he was hasty, and he thought of force before he considered reason." He was also a man whose time was running out. Driven relentlessly by a consuming ambition for fame, he had been a brigadier general during the Civil War, but subsequently his star had waned. His activities in Montana can probably best be explained in the context of this last chance to recoup.

He was born in Waterford, Ireland, in 1823. He was educated and trained in law. By the time he was twenty-two he had become deeply involved in Irish agitation against the English, and the French Revolution of 1848 fed the fires in him. He was arrested and convicted of sedition, and he was sentenced to be hanged. This sentence, however, was changed to banishment in 1849, and he was shipped to Tasmania for life. But in 1852 he escaped from Tasmania and, via Brazil, landed in New York. Here he found himself in his element. He became editor of the *Irish News*, took out citizenship papers, wrote widely, and lectured throughout the East.

The Civil War gave the mercurial Meagher a further opportunity to engage in action. He organized an Irish brigade and became a general. His unit acquitted itself well. But then the war ended, and the excitement was over. Where now? It is not surprising that at the age of forty-two Meagher sought further adventure in the West.

He arrived on a scene which was already confused. Montana Republicans accepted him at once because, even though he had been a northern Democrat, he had fought for the Union. To people for whom the issue was clear-cut, i. e., loyalty versus treason, this was a reasonable approach. But Montana's northern Democrats expected Meagher to serve them. Initially, Meagher was captured by the Republican side; after all, he was a Republican appointee. But in a few months he discerned that the Democrats constituted a majority. Whether he switched sides because of opportunism or confusion, switch he did. Let it be said in his favor that any man might have been confused. There simply was no government in Montana. There was no secretary, and, worse, there was no legislature. This had come about because Edgerton had vetoed an apportionment bill which would have provided for the election of the succeeding legislative body. He felt that it violated the Organic Act. But the original Organic Act had now expired; there was no legal basis for government.

In the late fall of 1865, Meagher was petitioned by a group

of citizens to order a new election for members of the legislature and at the same time to provide for the calling of a
constitutional convention. On this Meagher had mingled
feelings. He wanted the constitutional convention because,
should Montana become a state, he would "become master
of the situation," as he put it. He had in mind to run for the
Senate. But convening a legislature was another thing. He
did not think he had the authority to do it. He also had other
qualms. In December, 1865, he wrote to Secretary of State
Seward: "Were Montana admitted as a state tomorrow the
Union Cause would have to encounter in Congress equivocal
friends, if not flagrant mischiefmakers, from here whilst the
government of the State of Montana and the branches of the
government would, I sincerely fear, be monopolized by men
who in their hearts regard with aversion and vindictiveness
the great triumph of the nation . . . ."

This was good Republican sentiment. The party had no
desire for statehood, knowing that all offices would go to
Democrats. As a man of action, however, Meagher was in a
quandary. He could not abide a stalemate. Here he was, a
governor without a government. Two months after his initial
letter to Seward, he had changed his mind about the situation
in Montana. "I frankly confess," he now wrote, "that I was
greatly in error . . . these very Southerners and Southern sympathizers are now as heartily to be relied upon by the Administration and its friends as any other men in the Territory."

It is perhaps true that Meagher had to act, but these were
the very men he had called "flagrant mischiefmakers" two
months earlier. The extent of Meagher's switch from the
Republican to the Democratic side is apparent in the new
Montana Democrat, which suddenly became an ardent

Plowing up the prairie; the land would never again be like this.

Conservation practices recently adopted by Montana farmers: *above*, contour strip cropping; *below*, a partially completed pattern of windbreaks.

Meagher supporter. Men like Sanders and George M. Pinney had completely parted company with "the acting one."

His political troubles did not occupy Meagher completely, however. He was convinced that the Indian threat to the territory was grave and that he needed an army. While most Westerners usually saw a greater Indian threat than actually existed, Meagher was persistent in his badgering of Washington. He either called plaintively and frequently for troops, or he sought permission to organize a militia. Troops were spread very thinly throughout the entire frontier area, and the last thing that army officials wanted was unnecessary Indian trouble. General William Tecumseh Sherman was commander of the Division of the Missouri, which included Montana. The harassed Sherman wrote General Pope in 1866: "I fear civilians in the style of T. Francis Meagher may involve the frontier in needless war . . . ."

When direct appeal for troops failed, Meagher then sought permission to raise one thousand volunteers "at the expense of the gov't." This, too, was refused, but Meagher persisted. As we shall see, the results were ludicrous.

In the meantime, Meagher had done an about-face on the matter of providing for a legislative election and a constitutional convention. He called the first legislative assembly (1864) back into session. The session was supposed to transact all necessary business and to validate the calling of a constitutional convention. Two distinct sessions of this assembly were held (the second and third). The Republicans regarded the entire procedure as illegal, and two of the three Republican Supreme Court justices declared the sessions null and void. A righteously indignant W. F. Sanders carried the matter to Congress, and in a very unusual move

Congress declared the acts of the second and third legislative assemblies of 1886 null and void.

There is a case for Meagher's actions. It can be summed up by the question, what else could he do? Properly he should have referred the matter to Congress himself. But he doubtless felt that he could not leave the Territory; he had no secretary to replace him, and he was deeply involved in what he thought were military affairs. He also knew full well that his actions had been popular with the Democratic majority. In truth, Sanders ruined himself politically. The move to prevent a petition for statehood, which was the way the Democrats interpreted it, was galling to most Montanans. Even as late as 1876, when Sanders ran again for territorial delegate to Congress, he was defeated largely on the basis of what he did in 1866. One leading Democrat, Martin Maginnis, termed Congress' action "the most unjust act ever perpetrated by the Congress of the United States on a territory." The legislature of 1867 demanded the resignation of the Supreme Court justices who had handed down the decision. It would not seem that Meagher had hurt himself politically.

But any perceptive person, politics notwithstanding, could have seen that a move for statehood was very premature. And anyone politically astute could have seen that, all other things being equal, a radically Republican Congress would hardly admit a new Democratic state. Indeed, the principal business of that very Congress was its attempt utterly to destroy the "party of rebellion."

So the constitutional convention that, strangely enough, met in Helena instead of the new capitol at Virginia City met in an atmosphere of unreality. Its deliberations were never taken seriously, and its chief result was merely to confuse an already mightily confused situation.

In the summer of 1866, President Johnson at last got around to appointing a permanent governor, Green Clay Smith. Meagher became secretary. Like Meagher, Smith was a brigadier. He had served in both the Mexican and Civil Wars. He had twice been elected congressman from Kentucky. He had been a delegate to the Baltimore Republican Convention of 1864 and missed becoming Lincoln's vice-president by one-half vote. It is on such small margins that great events are often determined. Montanans, stretching a point, are proud to point out that they had a man who missed the Presidency by the narrowest margin in American history.

In October, Smith arrived in Virginia City. Everyone was weary of political statemate and strife, and there was a lull, that fall, in acrimony. Smith did a great deal to pacify both sides, and even though, like Meagher, he had been a Union Democrat, he was now a Republican. Both sides were willing to accept him. His long personal friendship with Lincoln and his intimacy with Johnson gave him a particular stature, and Montanans did not feel that a lesser man had been foisted upon them.

The new legislature decided that Smith should return to Washington to present Montana's particular problems in person. Soon after the session adjourned Smith left, and Meagher took over once more.

During the winter of 1866–67 there had been more Indian talk than usual. There was a widespread belief that Red Cloud and his Sioux were awaiting only the spring to ravage the Gallatin Valley. There was no evidence to buttress this belief; but the residents of the valley were nervous, and they put increasing pressure on Meagher. He was not reluctant to press their case. Meagher received a report from John Bozeman that entire families were getting ready to evacuate the valley, which prompted him to wire General Grant as follows:

> . . . the most populous and prosperous portion of our Territory . . . is threatened by the Sioux. The greatest alarm reasonably prevails . . . . Danger is imminent . . . we earnestly entreat permission from the War Department to raise a force of one thousand volunteers for menaced quarters to be paid by General Government.

Even this request would doubtless have been denied, but shortly after Meagher's wire the well-known John Bozeman was killed by the Sioux. Now came a deluge of entreaties from Meagher. Without authorization Meagher impetuously issued a call for six hundred volunteers. But merchants in the Territory had to have more to go on. They refused to issue rations. Meagher kept bombarding Washington with urgent messages predicting terrible bloodshed.

The government in Washington, the military particularly, was not now totally ignorant of the Montana situation. General Sherman had sent Major William H. Lewis to Montana to get a reliable firsthand account of affairs. Secretary of War Stanton found himself in agreement with Sherman, who wrote that "Meagher, in Montana, is a stampeder, and can always with a fair share of truth raise a clamor." At this juncture Sherman sent Major Lewis a wire which Meagher either inadvertently or by design interpreted as a green light for the militia. The call went out for volunteers, and the merchants were officially informed that all expense would be borne by the general government.

Meagher gathered around himself a motley crew, consisting mostly of commissioned officers, and placed himself at the head of his "troops" in the field. At last he was again in his element. The threatened Sioux invasion did not materialize in the spring, but this did not prevent the militia from running up bills which ultimately totaled $1,100,000. There was much charging hither and thither, and planning was done on a scale which would have been suitable for nothing less than full-scale catastrophe. While the government ultimately settled the many claims against it for $513,000, this was an immense amount of money when considered in light of the fact that not one redskin bit the dust.

On July 1, 1867, Meagher was in Fort Benton awaiting a shipment of arms. He had been ill for several days. He retired that evening in a berth aboard the steamer *G. A. Thompson*. During the night a sentry aboard the vessel saw a white figure moving about the stern and shortly thereafter heard a loud splash. He immediately awoke the crew with the cry of "man overboard," and a search of the ship and water was made. Meagher was missing. There was little point in searching the swollen Missouri at night, and subsequent daylight patrols of the riverbanks failed to turn up the body. It was never found.

Meagher's militia was kept in the field until October, but they encountered no Indians. It then disbanded. The whole venture was ill-starred, as were so many of Meagher's activities in Montana, and he left the Territory in worse shape than he had found it.

When Green Clay Smith returned from Washington after Meagher's death, he found the government in its usual state of chaos. Now that Meagher was dead, there was again no secretary to sign vouchers. The laws of the two preceding legislative sessions had been declared null and void, and there had been no effective legislative action in three full years. Governor Smith called a new legislative session, which convened in December, 1867.

The first thing that Smith urged that session to adopt was a good militia law which would prevent the haphazard raising of volunteers for dubious purposes. This legislation took form while debate was raging concerning Montana's $1,100,000 claim against the government.

Smith also initiated the first effective tax measure. "If," he said, "ninety-nine and three fourths percent of the assessed taxes can be collected under the Internal Revenue law without resorting to penal provisions, save in a dozen cases, a tax law under which the county collectors collect but thirty percent and still do their duty must me manifestly defective." This was quite true, but it did overlook the fact that Montana's first collector of internal revenue was Nathaniel P. Langford, a man of implacable determination and great personal courage. Langford's collection techniques were a little like those of gun-carrying law officers, and he himself was often in danger. Unlike county officials, he did not have to remain in the locality where his collection activity had stirred up a hornets' nest. Still, Smith was quite right in believing that the laws for collecting local taxes badly needed revision.

Smith also saw that outside capital was swiftly growing necessity if the Territory were to prosper, and he fully realized that gold, as the only medium of exchange, created a situation too close to primitive barter to encourage Eastern capital to come west. The "greenback" had been inflated greatly by the war, and there was lack of faith in it in the West. But Smith urged the legislature "to recognize greenback currency as the only currency of this Territory."

Unfortunately Smith left the Territory after the session and never returned. Washington had still failed to appoint a secretary, and doubtless Smith was as discouraged as Edgerton. A belatedly appointed secretary, James Tufts, served as acting governor from 1867 until the spring of 1869 when, at last, President Grant appointed James M. Ashley as governor. The appointment was unfortunate.

The Territory had by this time become overwhelmingly Democratic. From a nearly evenly divided legislature in 1864, the preponderance had swung almost completely to the Democrats in 1869. There were only three Republicans in the twenty-four-member House, and there were none in the Council.

Yet Ashley was an uncompromising and intolerant radical Republican. He was outspoken, opinionated, and vain. Smith had poured oil on the troubled waters of territorial politics; Ashley roiled those waters again with a grim intransigence.

The Democrats felt that they were entitled to patronage. Aware that the government in Washington was almost hysterically Republican and aware, too, that Ashley had been one of the leading lights in the impeachment of Johnson, they asked Ashley for half of the appointments, a not unreasonable request in view of their numerical superiority. The Governor totally ignored them and presented them with a straight Republican list. However, he was not dealing with a beaten Southern community but with a highly individualistic and independent Western territory. The legislature flatly refused to confirm his appointments and moreover immediately repealed an act which had given the governor and secretary an additional one-thousand-dollar pay raise. A stalemate had been reached, and neither party to the argument would move an inch toward compromise. Ashley was determined to "make Montana a republican state"; the legislature was just as determined to keep it Democratic. For reasons still obscure, Grant suddenly recalled Ashley and left Montana with its old schisms and governmental confusion.

Thus between 1864 and 1870 political developments in Montana reflected national problems to an extraordinary degree. Politics did not develop in response to indigenous economic factors but was a superficial reflection of the stresses of war and reconstruction. Local issues in campaign speeches, for instance, were negligible. The war and its aftermath dominated the scene. Of the several governors only Meagher actually sought to become part of the local scene, and he, unfortunately, was too erratic and perhaps in too much of a hurry to assure himself of fame to take a contemplative view of the Territory's actual problems. All this took place in the setting of federal neglect.

A belated kind of political maturity arrived with the appointment of Benjamin F. Potts in 1870. He, too, had been a brigadier and before the war ended had become a brevet major general. One can imagine at least some Montanans groaning at the thought of still another "civilian general" guiding the political destinies of the Territory. Fortuitously, however, Potts was not only an able administrator, but he had no inclination to make Montana a stronghold of Republicanism. Neither did he propose to use the Territory for glory, fame, or a sight-seeing trip. During the twelve years of his tenure he put territorial finances on a businesslike basis, encouraged outside capital, and, above all, balanced with consummate skill on the shaky wire between local demands and the abiding suspicion which the national administration had for "western radicals." He satisfied both parties, even when the depression of 1873 gave rise to a hot demand in Montana for inflation in the form of the free coinage of silver.

President Arthur removed Potts in 1883, but he had become so much a part of the territorial scene by that time that he bought a ranch near Helena and lived there until he died in 1887.

In the six years between the removal of Potts and the advent of statehood, little that is noteworthy transpired on the administrative political scene. A good deal was happening in the background, because the economy of the area was getting complex and politics was beginning to assume its classic form, i. e., political events were arising essentially from economic interests. Men were coming on the scene whose concern with political matters stemmed from their desire to protect or augment their mining, banking, or other business enterprises.

Montana convened two abortive constitutional conventions prior to 1889—one in 1866 and another in 1884. It will be recalled that Meagher succumbed to Democratic pressure in 1866 and that a constitutional convention met in Helena. There was no grass-roots movement for statehood at the time, and Republicans vehemently opposed the convention because the Territory was so strongly Democratic. The procedure of the convention of 1866 was farcical. Mid-January was no time to travel in Montana, and for a while there was doubt that a sufficient number of delegates would show up to do business. The resultant draft was presented neither to the people nor to Congress but, after being sent to St. Louis for printing, was lost. The Republican *Post* referred to the convention as being "sired by the Acting-one, and damned by the people."

But in the next decade, as the Territory grew and as federal neglect continued to work its hardship on Montanans, a genuine sentiment for statehood was engendered. By 1884 it seemed to be a possibility at least. The iron grip of radical Republicans on the Congress was ended. Indeed, the most powerful political figure on the national scene, Grover Cleveland, was a Democrat. Montanans were sick and tired of arbitrary gubernatorial and other territorial appointments. As early as 1867 the Helena *Herald* came up with figures demonstrating that of the appointed officials serving in Montana there were five from Pennsylvania, three from New York, three from Kentucky, two from Virginia, and one each from New Hampshire, Massachusetts, Vermont, Ohio, North Carolina, and Missouri. One hailed from Scotland, and one from Ireland. What irked the *Herald* was that there were no appointments from Montana. Said the Rocky Mountain *Gazette* for March 22, 1870: "We are onlookers in Venice." A particularly strong editorial in the *Herald* for March 27, 1879, put it this way:

> Our Territorial governments are false in theory, and are rendered worse by the vicious practice of making the places under those governments a sort of lying-in hospital for political tramps. With every appropriation the government nominally makes for our benefit, a dozen hungry wolves are sent with it to devour all and still more of our substance.

By the early eighties practically every Montana newspaper was railing at the government. There was clear indication of swiftly growing discontent. In the age-old process of self-government, another stage had been reached; another constitutional convention was called. Its forty-five members assembled in Helena in January, 1884. Nineteen of the delegates were Northern by birth, twelve were Southern, and the remainder were foreign-born. There were twenty-five Democrats, twelve Republicans, and one Independent. The majority had been in the Territory a long time. The deliberations were earnest and, with a few exceptions, harmonious. The discourse of North versus South had dwindled to a whisper, and there was no widespread Republican opposition to statehood. The following November the constitution was put to a vote of the people, and they responded 15,506 for and 4,266 against —nearly four to one in favor of the constitution.

Seldom in the admission of any state to the Union has the case for acceptance rested solely on its statistical merits. But 1884 was not a propitious year for Montana's petition. In the first place, the great power of the Republicans had been weakened. A precarious national political balance had resulted. The national Senate was Republican, but the House was Democratic. Both the election of 1884 and, it was thought, the election of 1888 would be very close. Neither party therefore wished to rock the boat.

Moreover, Montana's case was bound up with other western territories. Hence, after the presentation of Montana's proposed constitution to the Congress, there were numberless committee hearings and delays.

But the Fiftieth Congress, which convened in 1888, could no longer resist the western clamor. This was a "lameduck" second session, since it was already known that a Republican, Benjamin Harrison, had been elected President. While the Democratic Fiftieth Congress would have opposed admission ordinarily, they were now in a position to claim credit for what was, in effect, a *fait accompli*.

On January 15, 1889, Territorial Delegate Joseph K. Toole formally presented Montana's case to the Congress. Among other things he pointed out that the Territory had a surplus of $130,192.70 in the treasury, that four-fifths of her population were American born, and that $13,318,000 had been taken from the mines in the year 1888.

In mid-February a conference committee provided for the admission of Montana, North Dakota, South Dakota, and Washington. But it was necessary for each of these territories to call new constitutional conventions. This was done with dispatch in Montana, and in the late summer of 1889 the job was done. Montana became the forty-first state in the Union.

The politics of the territorial period, which seem so chaotic and at times absurd when viewed at close hand, should be viewed in the remarkable setting of the whole territorial system. Whatever else is said, it worked. The concept of Thomas Jefferson as set forth in the Ordinances of 1785 and 1787 brought the great contiguous territories of the West into the Union in orderly fashion. This was done in spite of the wrenching dislocations of a great civil conflict, in spite of intense partisanship, and in spite of suspicions of Easterners concerning Westerners and vice versa. The political scene in Montana between 1864 and 1889 has the superficial appearance of disorder, chaos, and even comedy. The fact is that there was deep consensus concerning the maintenance of the Union, there was a basic agreement about what the Territory needed, and Republican and Democrat alike shared a conviction that Montana was destined for great things. Indeed, their optimism seems strange in retrospect. What they sought in common, however, far outweighed what they sought otherwise.

VI

THE INDIAN AND THE MILITARY

THE WHITE MAN has almost always seen the Indian through his own eyes. There is nothing remarkable about this, save for the proportion of the tragedy it has wrought. The American of today would Americanize the Arab if he could, along with the Gold Coast native and the Chinese. We have always been somewhat Messianic about our "way of life." But the Indian was a resident of our own continent, and therein lay the core of the tragedy. Our "policy" toward the Indian has been no policy at all. It has run an extraordinary gamut from extermination to impractical Christian humanitarianism, but it has always been a "policy" which ignored the Indian himself and his peculiar heritage.

The Plains Indians were the most formidable of opponents. Not only were they nomads in the true sense, but in an age when there was still a kind of stiff propriety to warfare, they were true guerrillas—superbly mounted, ruthless, and courageous. They fought each other as incessantly as they fought the whites. The white concept of property and boun-

daries was anathema to the very basis of Indian existence—
the right to follow the buffalo wherever they went, the right
to roam for their livelihood. Neither the men of God nor of
war who sought to deal with them really understood this. In
Jackson's Removal policy and in the concept of the reservation we see some portrayal of the dilemma. It is as if we had
said, "We cannot deal with them. Let us seal them off, somehow, and forget about them." But, in truth, we could neither
remove them (because we were too greedy to occupy the
desert lands which we assigned them), nor could we seal
them off. We steadily encroached on their reservations.

Nothing on earth could have stopped the juggernaut of
manifest destiny. To the extent that the Indian tried, he was
doomed. But inevitable as the white occupation of western
America was, there is little in our attitudes or policies toward
the Indian that we can justify in retrospect.

The historical tribes of Montana—ranging from west to
east—were the Kutenai, Kalispel, Flathead, Shoshoni, Crow,
Blackfoot, Chippewa and Cree, Cheyenne, Gros Ventre (or
Atsina), and the Assiniboin. We will not consider here the
many groups who made periodic incursions into the area but
only those who, within the period of recorded history, depended for a living on the resources within the present boundaries of the state.

The Kutenais, also spelled Kootenays or Kootenais, originally were centered in three areas. The Plains Kutenais extended southward into Montana from a center in Alberta near
present McLeod. The Upper Kutenais lived west of the divide
in the region near present Eureka, Montana. The Lower
Kutenais extended from the area near Bonners Ferry in Idaho
eastward to about present-day Troy in Montana.

Unrelated linguistically to any other tribes, the Kutenais

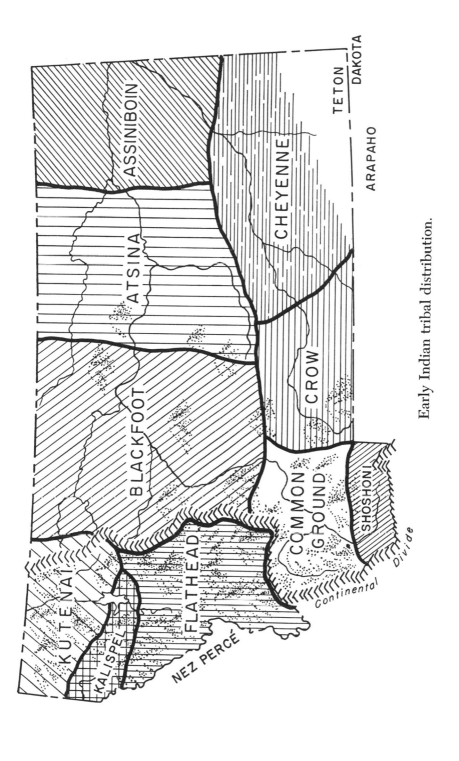

Early Indian tribal distribution.

had an amicable relationship with their neighbors, the Kalis-pels, although there is some evidence of early conflict between the two. The Plains Kutenais were probably forced westward by the Blackfeet. They were, in any event, one of Montana's most isolated tribes, whose contacts with the whites were few and late.

Gradually the Upper Kutenais developed their own pe-culiar speech dialect, but a certain unity continued to exist between the main divisions of the tribe. This unity had as its core the strong feeling all the Kutenais held in regard to the Kootenai River. It was not only a physical link between the various villages, but they all had a feeling of possession about it. It was their river, and all the land it drained was their domain.

The Kalispel Indians, frequently called the Pend d' Oreilles, were closely related to the Flatheads on the south and the Spokans on the west. Although the center of their domain was in northern Idaho, they were to be found as far upriver as Flathead Lake. Some of them settled in the Mission Valley in the early 1800's, and it was among the Kalispels that the Jesuits began operations at St. Ignatius Mission in 1854. Even though today's reservation bears the name Flathead, the Kalispels are actually more numerous and have more political power than the Flatheads.

The Flatheads once occupied the lush Bitterroot Valley. Their territory also once extended for some distance on either side of the divide. But they were driven progressively farther into the mountains by the eastward-pushing Plains Indians and came ultimately to occupy principally the Bitterroot Valley. It was there that Lewis and Clark found them and there, likewise, that Father de Smet set up St. Mary's Mis-sion in 1841.

All these tribes in northwestern Montana had a common background. They had been driven from the plains into the mountains by the bowling-pin effect of the white advance. They kept some of their old traditions but adapted themselves admirably to the new and rugged environment. They gave the whites very little trouble. Lewis and Clark, the fur traders, Father de Smet, and subsequent whites found them clean, intelligent, and honest—none of which qualities availed them much in their ultimate relations with the whites.

While Montanans do not usually think of the Shoshonis as being native to the state, they were very important in its early history. In 1742, when the first whites penetrated eastern Montana, it was the Shoshonis or "Snakes" who struck terror to the hearts of their Indian guides. But while the Shoshonis had horses, they did not have guns. They had relied heavily on the Spaniards in the south for trade goods, and the Spaniards did not trade guns. Accordingly, the Shoshonis were driven westward. Horses from the Spaniards and guns from the English and French met in Montana. Blackfoot and Hidatsa Indians began to take a fearful toll of the Shoshonis. Hence, although Lewis and Clark expected to find Sacajawea's people (Shoshonis) in the region of the Great Falls of the Missouri, they did not encounter them until they had moved over the divide into the Salmon River country. While these Indians continued to make sorties into Montana, they never regained their former territory.

Behind the Shoshonis were the Crows, who, by the time of the arrival of the whites, had pushed as far westward as present-day Billings. Originally the Crows were probably Minnesota and Iowa Indians, and they were a more sedentary people than they subsequently became. They raised corn and made pottery. But as they were driven westward they became true nomads, and the basis of their economy became bison.

The Blackfoot Indians seem once to have lived far to the east. They are of Algonquian extraction linguistically. In the eighteenth century they moved westward. By 1780 the three divisions of the tribe (Blood, Northern Blackfoot, and Piegan) held a large body of land. In Canada and Montana they were as far west as the Rockies. The general boundary of their domain may then be determined by drawing a line eastward from the Rockies through Edmonton to Battleford, then due south to the Missouri in Montana, then westward to Great Falls, and back to the Rockies south of Glacier Park. Here the Blackfeet had their backs to the impregnable mountains. On the east, however, they were open to the attacks of the Crees and Assiniboins. Probably because they were thus almost literally backed against a wall, the Blackfeet developed an aggressive attitude which gave them a reputation for great fierceness. The Piegans held the southern and southeastern front, also subject to periodic attack, and the Crees and Assiniboins were pressing on the northeastern front. Once the Blackfeet had horses and guns, however, they were more than a match for their enemies. Indeed, they soon took the offensive.

The Blackfeet were at the height of their power about 1830. There were perhaps ten thousand of them, and they held their domain against Indian and white alike. In 1836 the scourge of smallpox swept the tribes, and about half the population died. Subsequent incursions of the disease in 1845 and 1857 reduced the Blackfeet to a shadow of their former power. The disease weakened their defenses and opened the way for white conquest.

The Cheyennes were another Algonquian-speaking people. Pushed westward by the Dakota Indians in the latter part of the eighteenth century, the main body of the Cheyennes moved to the Black Hills. From this center point the tribe broke up, and one segment had reached Montana by the 1830's. Here they adapted themselves to a strictly nomadic, bison-based life, and here the pattern repeated itself. At war with their aboriginal neighbors, at war with the whites, their ranks were decimated. The mass slaughter of the buffalo by white traders cut the base from their livelihood.

Like the Cheyennes, the Arapahos and the Atsinas (or Montana Gros Ventres) were once probably sedentary Minnesota Indians who were pushed westward. They probably moved westward before the Cheyennes. A little after 1700 they had gone beyond the mouth of the Little Missouri. Again the story was repeated. Between the Blackfeet and the Assiniboins, the Montana Gros Ventres allied themselves with the Blackfeet. By the early 1800's they were settled in north central Montana—settled, that is, to the extent that any of these nomadic people could properly be called settled. It was the Montana Gros Ventres who were ultimately placed on the Fort Belknap Reservation with the Assiniboins.

The latter tribe was a member of the Dakota branch of Siouan stock. In the middle of the seventeenth century they probably lived in the region of the Lake of the Woods and Lake Nipigon. From there they moved northwestward toward Lake Winnipeg and ultimately got as far west as the Assiniboine and Saskatchewan rivers. At the time of the Lewis and Clark expedition, the Assiniboins were in close contact with the village tribes of the Missouri. They were also frequently at war with the Dakotas, Crows, and Blackfeet. Prior to 1836 there were probably between eight and ten thousand members of the tribe, but smallpox decimated their ranks in 1836.

At no time, of course, did these various tribes of Indians present a united front to the whites. To the old warfare with each other, the whites added the corrosive concomitants of whisky, the devastation of smallpox, and the destruction of the bison. There were a few occasions, such as Custer's fight on the Little Big Horn, when the Indians seemed to effect a plan and a union. But even momentary cohesion was more apparent than real.

The Indians made periodic attacks on the fur traders, and between Lewis' experience on the Marias in 1806 and the period of the late fifties, no one who ventured into Montana could afford to be other than alert. But except for the missionaries and a few isolated traders, Montana in the forties and fifties was largely by-passed by the westward movement. Gold changed all that, and in the first few years of the sixties contact and friction between Indian and white increased enormously. When the Civil War was over, the situation became critical.

The military problem in the entire American West subsequent to the Civil War was a severe one. True to American tradition, demobilization after the war was quick and complete. At the same time hordes of settlers were moving westward, and there was an unprecedented series of economic assaults by miners, cattlemen, merchants, and traders on an area which until the sixties had been the almost exclusive domain of the Indian. There was no stemming this tide; there was no effective way to regulate or channel it. The fur trader had not expected the flag to follow him. The miner, the cattleman, and the merchant did. They not only expected it; they demanded it.

The Indians repeatedly struck at the invader. They rarely did so in concert with each other, and in the main their internecine warfare continued. Indian attacks were sporadic, but they produced, if not retreat, howls of anguish and indignation. Where were the troops? The hard-pressed army, its ranks decimated by precipitous demobilization, with a vast area to cover in which transportation facilities were abominable, did its best. But its best was far from good enough for the Westerners.

Worse, Indian affairs were now the business of two departments of government—the Army, or War Department, and the newly created Department of the Interior. These two departments constantly bickered with each other. The Interior Department pursued a policy of "pacification by feeding." But when the Indians departed from the reservations and sallied forth to attack the whites, the army pursued them, in some instances killed them, and drove them back to the reservations. The army, quite naturally, felt that unless it had complete control it could not be responsible for the safety of the frontier. While the frontiersmen demanded Indian extermination, the Interior Department demanded pacification, and Eastern humanitarians (now turning from abolitionism to the Indian) demanded assimilation. The army was caught in the middle.

In 1866 a military district for Montana was created with Fort Shaw as regimental headquarters. General Sherman became General of the Army, and General P. H. Sheridan became commander of the Division of the Missouri, which included Montana.

It was obvious to Sherman that the army's principal problem lay on the high plains. Here the Indian was mobile, well armed, and well fed by buffalo. It was clear that the army would somehow have to adapt to the country. It could not mass its forces. So Sherman devised a plan that, he hoped, would protect both the settlers and the Indians. The plains were like the seas—vast, undulating, and of limitless sweep. Far out and widely interspersed on the grassy sea were the islands of settlement and a few military outposts. Sherman determined that mobile army forces would keep the lines of communication open between these outposts. To do so, troops had to be used sparingly, and they had to stay close to the main lines of communication. They could not dissipate themselves by pursuing the Indians across trackless wastes. The posture of the troops was to be essentially defensive.

Sherman wanted travel beyond the area of actual cultivation and settlement to be channeled, therefore, into the fewest possible principal routes. Immigrants were to follow these routes after having organized themselves on a semimilitary basis. There were to be at least thirty armed men, a captain was to be elected along with other officers, and violators were to be arrested by the army. It was hoped that this plan would reduce contact between Indians and whites to a minimum and that, should contact occur, the well-armed whites could take care of themselves.

The trouble was that the immigrants simply would not be channeled. In Montana, for instance, the gold rushes were leading to all kinds of formal and informal new routes toward and into the mountains. An overland route, the Fisk route, took four rather distinct paths from Minnesota. The Bozeman Trail branched north from Fort Laramie, passed around the Big Horns, and went into Montana through Sioux country. Contributing to the tinder-like situation was the fact that the buffalo were rapidly disappearing; this drew the Indians in toward the settlements and travel routes. It was clear to Sherman that conflict was in the offing.

Between 1866 and 1892 the army established a dozen forts

in Montana—from Fort C. F. Smith in 1866 to Fort William Henry Harrison in 1892. They pursued as best they could a policy of containment. But they could not prevent Indian and white clashes, the casualties from which stirred up both races.

The Sioux and Cheyennes were now crowded into eastern and southern Montana. As they pushed into the Montana area, they, in turn, pressed the Montana Indians westward toward the mountains and the white settlements. We have already seen that fear of this movement in the Gallatin Valley, exacerbated by the killing of a prominent citizen, John Bozeman, had led to Meagher's Militia and a measure of white hysteria.

By 1868 the Montana frontier was undergoing real Indian trouble. Army patrols had to be established because of Blood, Piegan, and Blackfoot attacks on the Montana-Minnesota overland route. The now busy route from Fort Benton to Helena was also subject to repeated attacks by the same Indians. The winter and spring of 1868 saw raids at Dearborn Creek on the Upper Yellowstone, near Fort Ellis, Camp Cook, Camp Reeve, and Fort Buford. During the summer of 1869 several white men were killed in an attack near Fort Benton, and two friendly Indians were shot in the streets by the tense citizens of the Fort. In retaliation the Piegans, Bloods, and Blackfeet launched a series of raids, stole some eight hundred horses, and killed a number of whites. A Helena newspaper, the *Herald*, estimated that a total of over one thousand horses were stolen in these raids and that fifty-six whites were killed.

In August, 1869, one Malcolm Clarke, who was considered a close friend of the Indians and who had married a Piegan woman, was killed by the Piegans near Helena. This launched the so-called Piegan War of 1870. In response to increasing pressure, General Sheridan sent a personal representative,

Inspector General James A. Hardie, to investigate the situation. Hardie reported that he thought the Indians should be punished for Clarke's death and that only punishment would restore peace. Sheridan acquiesced, and Major Eugene M. Baker from Fort Ellis was assigned the task. He left Fort Ellis for Fort Shaw in January, 1870, with four companies of the Second Cavalry. Striking out from Fort Shaw in the bitter cold of January 19, Baker's command encountered a band of Piegans on January 23. One hundred and seventy-three Indians were killed, fifty-three of whom were women and children, and it subsequently developed that the Indians were not of the band which had killed Malcolm Clark. "The Baker Massacre," as it was called, caused a furor in the East. Baker's actions were considered bloodthirsty, unnecessary, and cruel. But both the army and Montanans supported Baker in the investigation which followed.

There were further encounters with the Indians in 1872 and 1873. But the situation reached critical proportions again in 1874 when General George Armstrong Custer led an expedition into the Black Hills. Rumors of the existence of gold in the area were increased by the expedition, and there was a rush to the Black Hills. While some eleven thousand of the Indians in the surrounding country were now on reservations, about three thousand were not. The rush to the Black Hills seriously disturbed these Indians. Sitting Bull, a Sioux, was particularly resentful and intransigent.

The Commissioner of Indian Affairs was sufficiently concerned to send a representative to the area. The report given him led him to believe that while momentarily acute, the problem was rapidly solving itself. He did not believe that the Indians could ever again muster more than five hundred warriors or that there was any danger of a general Indian war.

But as the roving Indians kept causing trouble, the Secretary of the Interior concluded that only concerted military action would bring substantial peace to the frontier. As of February, 1876, with the agreement of the Secretary of the Interior the matter became one principally involving the War Department.

The culmination of this move was, of course, the "Custer Massacre" in the Battle of the Little Big Horn. While the battle is a dramatic incident in Montana history, it has been exhaustively treated elsewhere and will not be considered in detail here. It did not, in any event, involve Montana Indians or troops to the extent often assumed.

Pursuant to the aggressive policy now agreed upon by the two branches of government concerned, General George Crook turned northward from Wyoming to join forces with General A. H. Terry, who was marching westward from Fort Abraham Lincoln near present Bismarck, North Dakota. In the meantime, the available forces in Montana from Fort Shaw, Camp Baker, and Fort Ellis were to join Terry and Crook, thus putting the Sioux in a three-headed vise. The overall command was Terry's, although he did not want it and had suggested that it be given to Custer. Crook's column of about one thousand men was constantly and dangerously harassed by the warriors of Crazy Horse as he moved slowly northward. He had one encounter with Crazy Horse, but it was indecisive, and he retired for reinforcements. Then he moved to join Terry.

Terry left Fort Abraham Lincoln, reinforced by Custer's Cavalry, in May, 1876. In late May he was joined by Colonel Gibbon with the Montana forces. On the Yellowstone at the mouth of the Powder this force encountered an Indian trail up the Rosebud, and Custer was dispatched to follow the trail with orders to stay well in the rear of the Indians so that an attack could be made by the entire force. Custer's Seventh Cavalry departed on its fateful trip.

Custer, at thirty-seven years of age, disappointed that he had not been given Terry's command, driven by the fear that his star was waning, and convinced that his Seventh Cavalry could defeat all the Indians on the plains, encountered the Sioux on June 25, 1876. He gave hot pursuit. In a short time he and about 260 of his men—the entire unit—were wiped out.

In the fall of 1876, Colonel Nelson A. Miles with the Fifth Infantry was building a cantonment at the mouth of the Tongue River when a pack train of supplies bound for the cantonment was attacked by a sizable force of warriors, and its mules were driven off. Miles pursued them and in eleven days caught up with them. He turned the main body back to the area south of the Yellowstone, but Sitting Bull with part of the force broke away and headed for Canada. Miles then prepared for an aggressive winter campaign.

In one engagement in November, three more in January, and a fifth in the early spring, Miles kept relentless pressure on the Indians. During that winter Crazy Horse surrendered with over eight hundred people and two thousand horses. In March over two thousand Indians surrendered at Camps Sheridan and Robinson. By spring only Sitting Bull was still at large, but, wily as he was, he had little support, and he shortly took his people across the border into Canada again.

In spite of the success of Miles' campaign, there was no general feeling in Montana that the trouble was over. There was great fear of Sitting Bull, even in Canada, and it was believed that the Sioux on the northern plains were still capable of war. Because the Indians could cross the border into Canada with almost complete impunity, both Canadian and American officials were highly nervous. Attempts by a joint

Canadian-American delegation to come to terms with the chief were to no avail, and he remained a threat until his his surrender in 1881.

The year 1877 saw the now famous retreat of Chief Joseph. The events which led to this remarkable retreat followed the monotonous pattern. Driven out of their original Oregon home into the Clearwater country in Idaho, the Nez Percés found themselves beleaguered by white miners on all sides. Their annuity payments were not sufficient to sustain life. There had been increasing conflict between their young "hotheads" and the whites. The Nez Percés' chief was a peaceful man, but he was also intelligent. He saw the handwriting on the wall. Accordingly he determined to move into Canada, peacefully if possible but using force if he had to.

The army was then building Fort Missoula, and Captain C. C. Rawn moved into Lolo Canyon from Fort Missoula to intercept the Nez Percés. In spite of the fact that barricades were constructed at a point in the canyon where passage around them seemed impossible, Joseph easily gave Rawn's forces the slip and proceeded slowly, and without committing depredations, up the rather heavily populated Bitterroot Valley. Meanwhile, with concern rapidly spreading throughout western Montana, Colonel Gibbon left Fort Shaw on a forced march westward. He caught Joseph's forces in the Big Hole. In spite of the advantage of surprise, Gibbon was defeated, and his casualties amounted to about 40 per cent of his men. Meanwhile, Joseph had been pursued from the beginning by General O. O. Howard, who was commander of the Department of the Columbia.

With all his women, children, and gear Joseph traversed the rugged country of Yellowstone Park. The forces of Colonel S. D. Sturgis were grimly waiting for them to emerge from the canyon of the Stinkingwater River. To the Colonel's chagrin, they emerged instead from the Clarks Fork and passed on out to the plains. Sturgis followed, and the Indians defeated him just north of the Yellowstone and, before he could regroup, eluded him altogether.

Now Colonel Miles joined the chase. He marched swiftly to the Tongue River, and at the foot of the Bear Paw Mountains, only a few miles from Canada, he finally caught the exhausted Nez Percés and defeated them. Joseph surrendered.

General Howard had marched over eighteen hundred miles in pursuit of Joseph. Encumbered with about three hundred women and children, about seven hundred horses, and only one hundred warriors, Joseph had outmarched, outthought, and outfought the U. S. Army.

The Nez Percés War, as it came to be called, was the last event of substance in the Indians' effort to resist the whites. Thereafter they could not mount any kind of offensive. But the events of 1876 and 1877 were far too fresh in the minds of Montanans (and of the military) for them to relax. They continued to bombard the army with demands for more protection, and the army, with Custer and Joseph in mind, was less inclined to deprecate the fears of the whites than it had been in 1875. After all, Sitting Bull was still in Canada, there were still roving bands of Indians on the loose, and conditions of great hardship on the reservations made for much tension. One more event in 1878 caused the army at last to set up additional permanent forts in Montana.

The Bannock Indians of Idaho had been prevented from hunting in Montana in 1877 because of the army's fear that they would join the Nez Percés. As was the case with the latter, conditions on their Idaho reservation were bad. They could not hunt, and their allotments were insufficient to sus-

The movements of the "Yellowstone Command" of General
Nelson A. Miles, in 1876–77.

tain them. In 1878, therefore, large bands of Bannocks, began moving into Montana. Like Joseph, they avoided troops sent to intercept them, moved through Yellowstone Park, and down the Clarks Fork onto the plains. Unlike Joseph, they had the misfortune there to meet the ubiquitous Colonel Miles, who promptly defeated them. However, the affair pointed up the army's plight. Prior to 1876 and the Little Big Horn, there had been only about six hundred soldiers in Montana to police approximately thirteen thousand Indians. At the time of Joseph's defeat there were a little over three thousand troops in the field, but the alarm was greater even if the danger was actually less. Thus, between 1877 and 1892, eight additional forts were built in Montana. They were Forts Logan, Missoula, Keogh, Custer, Assiniboine, Maginnis, and Harrison, and Camp Baker. During this period there were seldom less than two thousand troops in the area.

Between 1880 and 1887 circumstances conspired to make the Indians' lot on the reservation a hard and demoralizing one. In the late seventies they had managed to get along well on the thriving buffalo-robe trade. The trade was more important by far in reservation economy than was agriculture. As a consequence of this lucrative business, the government cut down its allotments, and the agents did not push agricultural development. But in 1880–81 the buffalo were simply gone. In view of the terrific slaughter of the animals in the seventies, the inevitability of their near extinction in the future was obvious. But neither the Indians nor reservation whites were prepared for it. Crop failure in 1882–83 added to the problem. So severe was the situation on the Blackfoot reservation that actual starvation occurred. In 1884, the government was sustaining the Indians at an actual cost of about seven dollars an Indian per year. At the same time it was costing the government about one thousand dollars a man per year to maintain soldiers in Indian country. Agriculture developed slowly from 1886 onward, but the years from 1881 to 1884 had deeply demoralized the reservation Indians. Just three years later the land allotment act was passed, and the process of removing from the Indian the best of even his reservation lands began.

In the twenty years between 1860 and 1880, in other words, a proud, nomadic people were subdued, deprived of their hunting grounds, herded onto ever shrinking reservations, and utterly broken in spirit. It is true that the terrible incursion of smallpox in the thirties, the introduction of whisky, and, in general, the trauma of the meeting of savagery and civilization predated the sixties. But it was really in the decade of the seventies that the last resources of the Indians gave way, the last ramparts were stormed, and the white juggernaut rolled implacably over the red men.

It is too easy to look back on this tragedy, extract it from context, and oversimplify its elements. Since the seventeenth century the white man on the westward moving fringes of his own civilization had been in conflict with the Indian. Always the Easterner and the Westerner had disagreed on how the problem should be handled; always the government had been subjected to explosive pressures it could never contain and rarely control. But the rush across the plains and into the mountains accelerated the problems and the clash between all those involved. What was done to mitigate conflict was always too little and too late, and usually it was shortsighted and cruel.

The government sought to deal with the Indians on the basis of a legal fiction, namely, that these people composed independent nations, each with partial sovereignty. The government assumed that they owned the land they occupied and that hence they could be dealt with only by treaty. Negotiated by the executive branch but confirmable only by the United States Senate, this "treaty" approach to the Indians was obviously a bad one. It presumed an independence which the Indians did not in fact have; it presumed a state of tribal organization and consensus which did not exist. In many instances the Senate modified treaty terms which in turn necessitated an effort, usually completely futile, to have the modifications signed by the original participants. The paradox was that the government dealt with the Indians as if they had sovereignty and as if they inhabited foreign territory, when in fact they lived within the territorial limits of the United States. They were not recognized by foreign powers and could not be dealt with effectively on the basis of this legal fiction.

Further, government policy in a democracy is very directly formulated by public attitudes. Government officials are not free agents. The government might devise what rules it chose concerning the Indians and western lands, but the Westerner pursued his own course, and to him killing Indians was like killing snakes. The almost explosive movement of the frontier was something the government could not control— either with respect to the Indians or in many other respects.

In his second annual message to Congress in 1870, President Grant stated his Indian policy. He announced that the nomination of agents would be essentially a matter to be handled by the representatives of religious groups and that it should be the fundamental function of such agents to Christianize and civilize the Indians. He went on to state that he hoped that within a few years all the Indians would be on

The beginning of the end of the grassy plains: a beef herd
in the Bad Lands in 1896.

"Waiting for a Chinook": a painting by Charles M. Russell depicting the last of a starving herd.

WAITING FOR A CHINOOK

reservations, living in houses, going to schools and churches, and that they would be self-sustaining.

It would seem that this system was more desirable than its predecessor under which agency appointments were purely political. But unhappily the Methodist church, which was soon assigned all the tribes in Montana except the Flatheads, did not do an adequate job. There is abundant evidence of this on the contemporary scene. Before Grant's "Peace Policy" was abandoned in 1885, it had further compounded the confusion in the Indian mind.

In 1887 the Dawes Act was passed. It was perhaps an inevitable consequence of the white insistence of long standing that the Indian have the same concept of the individual ownership of land which was so deeply ingrained in the white. The Dawes Act provided for the allotment of lands in severalty to Indians on various reservations, that these allotments be selected by the Indians, that any Indian entitled to an allotment must make his choice within four years or the agent would make it for him, that the land would be held in trust for twenty-five years, that after allotment the secretary of the interior could negotiate with the tribe for purchase or release of the unallotted lands, and that all such released lands were to be held by the government for the sole purpose of securing homes for settlers.

In the Congress only Senator Teller of Colorado, who was to demonstrate again and again that he understood Western problems, protested the legislation. He warned his fellow congressmen that they did not understand Indian character and that he foresaw that within a generation the Indians would have parted with their title and would then have nothing. But the act passed without difficulty.

Teller's statement was prophetic. In 1902 the Dawes Act was modified to permit the heirs of deceased allottees to sell the land they had inherited. By 1907 any Indian could sell his land.

In 1887 about 130,000,000 acres of land were held in trust for the Indians by the government. By 1933 this had dwindled to 49,000,000 acres of marginal land. In 1934 the Dawes Act was repealed, and the Indian Reorganization Act took its place.

Looking backward from the vantage point of 1933, John Collier, commissioner of Indian affairs, saw clearly the havoc wrought among the Indians by the allotment law of 1887. Above all Collier saw that the Indian functioned best in his age-old context, as a member of an integrated group or tribe. He saw, too, that this was as much a spiritual as an economic necessity. It was principally Collier's philosophy that lay behind the Reorganization Act of 1934. Now, under the aegis of the New Deal, the government reversed itself completely. After years of insisting that the Indian forget his tribal heritage and his basic concepts of community property, the government now began to emphasize the tribe and tribal property.

The Reorganization Act provided for incorporation on a tribal basis. It provided that each member of the tribe should also be a member of the corporation which, in turn, had the power to manage its own property. A credit fund was set up, and the corporation could borrow from this fund, could execute contracts, sue and be sued, and distribute its profits. No land, power sites, water rights, or oil, gas, or mineral rights could be sold or mortgaged. Timber could not be leased for more than ten years.

Special elections were held on all Indian reservations in 1934 and 1935. A total of 172 tribes accepted the provisions of the act; 72 rejected it. In Montana, residents of five of the seven reservations adopted constitutions and bylaws and began to function under the act. The Crows have never accepted the act, and the Fort Peck Indians did not really begin to function until 1956.

The Flatheads, or the Confederated Selish and Kutenai tribes, as they officially became, were the first Montana tribes to incorporate and begin functioning. In 1910 these Indians had owned 1,250,000 acres. By 1930, 750,00 acres of their best land had been lost, their stock industry had been to all intents and purposes ruined, and 1,400,000,000 feet of their timber had been dissipated. Under the Reorganization Act, 192,425 acres have been redeemed, tribal income from its enterprises has been good, and tribal management has been competent. Not all tribes have shown equal acumen, but in the main the Indians' situation showed marked improvement after 1934.

While the Indian became a citizen in 1924, he is a ward of the government in the sense that control is still exerted over the sale or leasing of his land. Collier's philosophy, even though watered down by his career associates and weakened because he was branded a dreamer and a sentimentalist, still has a profound influence on Indian policy. The reservations, although called "open air ghettoes" by a recent critic of Montana's reservations,[1] still provide the Indian with a sense of belonging and security he cannot find elsewhere. The majority do not like to leave them for long.

There has been a very recent trend in government circles aimed at "assimilating" the Indian again—making him "an individual American" who can "stand on his own feet." Even though couched in terms of progress and inevitability, this

[1] Leslie Fiedler, "The Montana Face," *Partisan Review*, December, 1948.

is, in fact, a reversion to a policy that failed tragically. There is, on the basis of past performance, little reason to suspect that future Indian policy will be either consistent or wise. But the opportunity to deal with a proud and independent people has long since been lost. All that can be done now is to deal both understandingly and practicably with a people whose final heritage consists of a built-in and ineradicable tragedy.

VII

THE ECONOMY EVOLVES

AFTER THE CIVIL WAR, except for the South, the United States enjoyed a tremendous economic growth. A nation whose energies had been consumed with the moral problem of slavery and the military problem of whether it was to be one nation or two now turned its attention to building.

In the half-century following 1850 the country's population tripled. Swollen by natural increase and by tides of immigration, it reached 75,000,000 in 1900. The post–Civil War period witnessed the rise of big business and the formation of ever larger corporate structures. While the growth in the West was great, it did not keep pace with the Northeast. The center of the new financial and industrial system lay along the axis from Boston, New York, and Philadelphia to Chicago and St. Louis.

The prevailing economic philosophy was laissez faire. It did not occur to government either to regulate or control the excesses of business. While the depressions of 1873, 1884, and 1893 were sharp and painful, they only checked the business trend momentarily. More and more, consolidations and mergers became the order of the day, and tremendous "paper" profits were made from stock transfers and "watering."

It was from the West and the South that the first stirrings of reaction and the first demands for control by government came. The Western origin of the protest is not surprising, because in spite of an industrial trend the West was still overwhelmingly agrarian. Moreover, it was at the mercy of the railroads and other eastern enterprises which seemed to Westerners to have too much control over their destiny.

THE MOUNTAIN MEN did not like beef. They were accustomed to the dry, wild taste of buffalo, and they found beef almost sickeningly sweet. But you could not domesticate buffalo and, except for horses, the only kind of wealth a man could amass in the mountains was beef, because wealth had to be mobile in the wilderness.

Accordingly, cattle were driven to the Green River rendezvous in 1830, and Charles Larpenteur drove four cows and two bulls from this herd up into Montana in 1833. Fort McKenzie boasted a Durham bull in 1843; the American Fur Company had a number of cattle on the Upper Missouri by 1846; Father de Smet had forty-six head at St. Mary's Mission by 1846; and by the middle fifties Richard ("Johnnie") Grant, who had built up a herd at Fort Hall in southern Idaho from stock obtained from immigrants on the Oregon Trail, drove some six hundred head northward into Montana.

Even though it is commonly assumed that the mining rushes accounted for the swift rise of the cattle industry, the industry was already existent. Indeed, that is why the initial demands of the miners could be so readily met, and that is why the cattle on Montana's western ranges so quickly spilled over onto the plains region.

With the advent of Nelson Story's Texas Trail drive in 1866, eastern Montana enters the economic picture for the first time. Story's 600 head of longhorns were the first. But within a decade they were joined by other trail herds and by herds from the West.

There was no provision in this vast plains area for the selling or leasing of land. Cattlemen simply commandeered it. This led not only to ultimate conflict with the government but to conflict with each other. Recognition of sorts was given "prior occupation" by the federal government in 1877, but it was still true that the owners of 20,000 or 30,000 head of cattle might actually own but a few hundred acres. Cattlemen could neither buy nor lease sufficient acreage to conduct their business. So they simply took it. They took it from the Indians, who retaliated with raids. They took it from the public domain and fought among each other for it. Rustling was a chronic problem which neither the government nor the newly arisen cattlemen's associations could effectively stop. The result was vigilance activity in the mid-eighties which was often a bloody business, unco-ordinated and undisciplined.

Thus, eastern and central Montana began to participate in the boom which had struck the western part of the area twenty years before. But if in the west the boom had a transient aspect, based on the purely extractive industry of taking minerals from the earth, it was even more so in the east. There was at least some diversification in the west—lumbering, merchandising, farming, and allied developments. There was no such diversification in the east. Everything depended on grass, weather, and luck. A normal loss in one year on account of the vagaries of nature would amount to about 10 per cent. Thus, a rancher had to increase his herd a good 20 per cent to make a profit. With literally hundreds of ranchers on the open range, it is not surprising that overstocking resulted quickly. Not only were herds pouring over the divide from the Beaverhead, the Gallatin, and the Missoula valleys in the early eighties, but there was now a steady stream of long-horns pouring onto the northern ranges from Texas. By 1880, a count, which was doubtless very conservative, placed 48,287 horses, 1,632 mules, 249,888 sheep, and 274,321 cattle in Montana Territory. In the fall of 1880 there were enough cattle within a six-day drive of the Northern Pacific's rail-head to fill 250 boxcars. One J. L. Driskin, formerly of Austin, Texas, had driven 6,000 head into Montana and was shipping 2,260 East in the fall of 1880.

The number of stock on the Montana open range had tripled by 1883. The U. S. Department of Agriculture estimated that there were nearly 600,000 cattle and 500,000 sheep in the Territory, the great bulk of which were east of the mountains. In 1880 the majority of cattle had been on the western ranges and in central Montana, in Meagher and Chouteau counties. By 1883 the center had moved eastward to Custer County. While the Texas drives were primarily responsible for this shift, it is also true that the central Montana ranges were already crowded and there was a movement toward the east.

This expanding business, like the mining business, required capital. And once again we see the influx of outside money. The N Bar was backed by the Niobrara Cattle Company of Nebraska; there were the Atlantic Livestock Company of Boston; the Concord Cattle Company of Concord, New Hampshire; the Green Mountain Stock Ranching Company of Minneapolis (formerly of Vermont); and many companies from St. Louis and points east. In the early eighties, too, the Scotch and English began to invest heavily in Montana's booming cattle industry. A vast percentage of the fortunes made between 1879 and 1887 enriched stockholders and owners who had never seen Montana and knew of it only through glowing company reports of quick profit. The nature of the business was summed up by Julian Ralph, who wrote in 1893:

> The cattle owners, or cowmen, are in Wall Street, the south of France, or in Florida in the winter, but their cattle are on the wintry fields where now and then, say once in four years, half of them, or 80% of them, or one in three (as it happens) starve to death because of their inability to get at the grass under the snow . . . . But the cowmen do business on the principle that the gains in good years far more than offset the losses in bad years . . . .

There were, it is true, Montana-owned enterprises; the DHS was a Montana ranch started by Granville Stuart and Reese Anderson. The capital came from A. J. Davis of Butte, Erwin Davis, his brother, of New York, and S. T. Hauser of Helena. The DHS became one of the truly big outfits. Even by 1883 it had some 12,000 head of cattle. A union of the DHS people and Conrad Kohrs in 1885 led to incorporation for $1,000,000 and to the founding of the Pioneer Cattle Company.

But on the other hand, the immense Continental Land and Cattle Company, which owned such brands as the Hashknife, Bridle Bit, HS, and Mill Iron, was a $3,000,000 enterprise incorporated in St. Louis. The Continental Company may have had as many as 80,000 head of cattle in Montana at the height of its activity. Small and medium-sized outfits simply could not compete, and they did not stay in business very long. As with mining, it took great capital to get in the business and to tide a company over a bad year. Although some Montana outfits made it, most did not. Thus, of the eleven major British cattle companies about half had heavy investments in Montana, and other Montana enterprises were mainly owned by absentees.

But all this ended in 1886–87. To the Montanans who had first driven cattle onto the plains in the late seventies and early eighties it was inconceivable that this vast and limitless land could ever be "overcrowded." Had it not sustained buffalo by the millions? Surely the eye alone could testify that it could support almost limitless numbers of cattle for a century. Indeed, it was not really good for anything else. That is what it was made for.

Yet in the shockingly short span of six years the whole empire came crashing down. It took only a brief malevolence of nature and a few years of man's abuse.

During the spring and summer of 1885 there had been plenty of rainfall. The grass was good. The fall was dry, however, and there were a good many range fires. But the winter of 1885–86 was a mild one, with neither severe winds nor heavy snow. The cattle business in the summer of 1886 should have been at a new height. Three things were wrong. The summer was hot, with baking winds. The price of cattle had dropped a little in 1885 and more sharply in the early part of 1886. Believing this to be only temporary, most Montana cattlemen held off on Eastern shipment awaiting a price rise. Thirdly, a bad winter to the south in 1885 had forced some 200,000 head northward to better ranges. The ranges were crammed with cattle.

As the fall of 1886 approached, there were a goodly number of perceptive ranchers who foresaw trouble. The Glendive *Times* remarked on August 1 that the situation facing the stockmen was anything but comfortable and stated further that while the price situation did not encourage shipment, neither did the range situation warrant holding.

"Much," said the Helena *Independent* on September 11, "depends on the coming winter." The fall rains did not come. The grass was thin; the earth baked. And in November the winter howled down out of the North with a vengeance. These storms were violent, and, one on the heels of another, they lasted until the end of November. There then occurred a combination of circumstances that presaged disaster. There was heavy snow in November, then a thaw in mid-December, followed by several months of uniformly low temperatures and bitter winds. The thaw produced a nearly impenetrable ice sheet which was then covered by more snow. The cattle lacerated their noses and legs trying to penetrate the ice. But even when they got through, the grass was skimpy and lacked nutrition. January was bitterly cold. The hope was that February would see a thaw. No one really knew what shape the cattle were in, but it was assumed that the great majority would survive, even though they would be weak, if February proved mild. It did not.

In late January another storm howled down from the North. Temperatures at Glendive from February 1 to February 12 averaged –27.5 degrees Fahrenheit. At Bismarck it was –43 degrees on February 1, –34 degrees on February 3, and –43 degrees on February 12.

In March the "chinook" came. The hot winds cut the snow and ice away in a few days, and the cowmen set off over the ranges to assess the damage. The losses were appalling—

so much so that the old cattleman Granville Stuart was sickened and vowed never to ranch again. In every gully, every arroyo, along the stream beds, and dotting the level plains were the rotting carcasses of thousands upon thousands of cattle. Estimates of losses came in slowly. But the cattle which had lived were drifting, and an accurate count was impossible. Not until the spring and fall roundups would the full extent of the disaster be known. Contemporary newspapers were full of statistics, and estimations of loss ran from 13 per cent to 70 per cent. Even by the next fall estimates were at variance with each other. But some idea of the magnitude of the loss can be garnered from individual cattle company estimates. The Hashknife placed its loss, according to one estimate, at about 75 per cent; the Crosby Cattle Company at 80 per cent; J. L. Driskin estimated that he last two-thirds of his herd; many other estimates ranged between 70 per cent and 90 per cent. When the winter began the E6 and Turkey Track ranches had 27,000 head. By spring they had 250 head.

The Montana range-cattle industry was in ruins. Bankruptcy followed bankruptcy. In Custer County, for instance, where there had been 200 operators in 1886, there were but 120 in 1888. There was a rush to sell the poorly conditioned surviving cattle and a kind of exodus from the range. Those few shrewd cattlemen who bought instead of sold, men like Pierre Wibaux and Conrad Kohrs, built fortunes on the remnants because only the very fit had survived, and new herds bred from these survivors were unusually sturdy. But few, indeed, were buying.

A new and different kind of cattle industry rose from these ruins. The days of the "open range" were gone. They had, in truth, been doomed from the beginning. The boom of 1880–

86 had been speculative. The aim of the majority involved in it had been to make quick and high profit over the short term in a business in which the basic element was risk. There had been no attempt to prevent overstocking. There had been no attempt to prepare for the inevitable inclemency of the weather. Bulls had been turned loose to produce calves in the late fall—calves that had no chance in severe weather without shelter or feed.

The new cattle industry, with men of vision and adaptability involved in it, was quite another matter. The nineties witnessed a remarkable recovery—so remarkable that by 1890 there were about 175,000 head back on those ranges that had been reduced to perhaps 82,000 in 1887.

The rancher was no longer a nomad. He could not overgraze and then move on. The railroads had put an end to the "long drive." Barbed wire forced him not only to become more self-contained, to husband his resources, it made him into something of a conservationist. He was forced, also, to improve his blood lines. Profit now, lay not so much in quantity as in quality. He had, increasingly, to compete with sheepmen, and all this forced him to plan thoughtfully and manage carefully. The railroad was at once a curse and blessing—a curse because both by the fact of its existence and the persistence of promotional campaigns it brought the "sod buster," a blessing because it lent stability to his business.

Subsequent to the "Hard Winter" the cattle business reverted to the hands of Montanans for quite a long period. Not until boom conditions followed the country's emergence from the depression and until the income tax made the quest for investments in lands almost a necessity after World War II, did Eastern capital again venture into the business. The story of Montana's early cattle industry was, once more, a story of too much too soon. It was a story of absentee ownership and the devastating exploitation of a natural resource.

In the meantime, the sheep industry had also enjoyed a phenomenal growth. No romance ever associated itself with the sheepherder. Indeed, sheepherders and sheepmen have come to be reviled in the Western myth. And because myth and fact are so interwoven in Montana's history, mention is seldom made of sheep in the books which presume to tell us about our past. Yet at one time Montana raised more sheep and produced more wool than any other state in the country.

Sheep in quantity did not come to Montana as early as cattle. But there were sheep at St. Ignatius in 1857, at Fort Owen in 1862, and Conrad Kohrs drove a band of 400 head up the Montana trail in 1863. Like cattle, sheep were driven in from Oregon in the late sixties, and the first big drive (1,500 head) was from The Dalles to Dillon in 1869.

If the sudden increase in cattle in Montana between 1880 and 1885 was impressive, the swift growth of the sheep industry was overwhelming. In 1870 there were about 3,000 sheep in the Territory. Within five years there were 60,000, and within another five nearly 400,000. As early as 1878 a wool clip estimated at $1,000,000 was taken from Montana.

Montana newspapers in the seventies made frequent references to sheep and wool. *The Rocky Mountain Husbandman* in Meagher County noted in December, 1875, that there were some 20,000 sheep in the county, that the wool would bring in about $20,000, and that if the increase continued sheep and wool would mean more to the county than mining. The wool, analyzed by Edwards Bros. in Boston, was announced to be of excellent quality.

In its analysis of the past year's business on January 1,

1881, the *Husbandman* noted with some amazement that the wool yield in Montana for 1880 had amounted to a $250,000. Wool exports had reached 1,300,000 pounds, and approximately 100,000 sheep had been driven into the Territory from Oregon, Washington, and California.

The "Hard Winter" wreaked considerably less havoc among sheep than among cattle, with the consequence that some investors, at least, cast an interested eye on the sheep business. But whereas men who were experienced in the cattle business were legion, experienced sheepmen were few. This led to some strange partnerships between the providers of capital and the providers of experience. For instance, one W. D. Ellis of New York City contracted with Lee Simonsen of the Castle Mountain country in Montana as follows:

> This agreement between Lee Simonsen and W. D. Ellis— We are leasing Lee Simonsen 2,000 ewes for five years— Ellis takes half the wool and Simonsen takes half. Ellis furnishes half the bucks and half the twine and wool sacks. He also furnishes half the money at 6% if needed. Ellis takes away the wether lambs every fall. At the end of five years Simonsen pays Ellis back 2,000 ewes, including what is left of the original bunch.

This contract was profitable for both men. At the end of five years, 1,354 of the original flock remained, and they had been constantly on the range, being fed no hay. Simonsen did not have to borrow on the contract because half the wool took care of the expenses. He had set himself up in the sheep business.

By 1885 there were a million and a half sheep in Montana. Like the cattlemen, who had felt the need for a stockgrowers' association and had formed one in 1885, the sheepmen also organized. They met in Fort Benton in January, 1883, and formed the Montana Woolgrowers Association. By this time sheepmen were erecting sheds and fences, and there was beginning to be trouble over grazing land between cattlemen and sheepmen. This conflict never reached the stage of violence, however. Cattlemen were in no position to engage in warfare. As Joseph Kinsey Howard put it in *Montana: High, Wide and Handsome:*

> A Montana cattleman, riding his range one day, found a sheepherder camped upon it, with his flock. He ordered the herder to get off. Returning the next day, he found the lamblicker still there. Again he demanded that the interloper quit his range.
>
> The herder looked up calmly at the mounted stockman. "You own it, pardner?" he asked.
>
> The cattleman admitted that he didn't. "But it's my range," he retorted, "and I want you off!"
>
> The herder got up slowly, drawing a Winchester rifle from the ground as he did so.
>
> "Listen, friend," he said quietly. "I just got out of prison after shooting one sonofabitch like you, and I'd just as soon go back for shooting another."
>
> The cattleman rode home. "Looking into the barrel of that gun," he told this writer many years later, "you know, I realized for the first time that I didn't own that range . . . . And, by God, I didn't even have a gun on me!"

Thus, in contest, the illusion of "customary range" vanished. Sheepmen could go where they pleased and did so. By 1885, according to the territorial auditor, there were 593,-896 sheep in Montana as compared with 509,768 cattle. This was real competition.

The "Hard Winter" accelerated the process of shed- and

In the war of the sheep and the cattle, grass was the victor's prize. Here, a sheepherder watches his flock.

Riches in wool: *above*, the sheep were sheared by hand;
below, the wool had to be hauled long miles before it could
be freighted to the East for sale.

shelter-building, and whereas the cattle industry was teetering on the brink of ruin, the sheep industry was glowing with health. In 1886 there were 968,298 sheep in the Territory. By 1890 there were more than 1,500,000. Many ruined cattlemen had turned to sheep. In 1890 it took about $20 a head to get a start in the cattle business. It would thus take about $2,000 to put 1,000 head on the range. But the value of sheep in 1890 was approximately $2.35 a head. The cost of starting business with 1,000 head of sheep was only $2,350. Returns on sheep per head, of course, were much lower, but they were much quicker. Breeders ordinarily calculated on a net profit of from 25 to 30 per cent. While lambs became producers the first year, calves were unproductive for several years. And as time went on, sheepmen began to concentrate on mutton breeds as well as wool breeds.

From 1870 to 1875 the average price of wool per pound in the Eastern market had been $0.516 for fine wool, $0.506 for medium, and $0.457 for coarse. After 1875 there was a drastic decline in wool prices. By 1887 the three grades were respectively worth $0.261, $0.294, and $0.248, with medium wool bringing a better price than fine but with all prices low. This brought about a concerted effort on the part of Montana sheepmen to improve the bloodline of their sheep and thus make up in lamb and mutton what they had lost in wool. In this they were largely successful. By 1890, there were 1,555,-116 sheep in Montana, and there was a total wool production of 7,783,007 pounds. Billings was now the center of the sheep area and was the shipping center not only for all of eastern Montana but for many Wyoming operators. The nineties were the golden days for the sheepmen. Big operators considered 50,000 head a "Fair-sized bunch." Such men as J. B. Long, who ran his sheep in the vicinity of the Fort Peck In-

151

dian Reservation, would shear approximately 160,000 head each year. In the northern part of the state, N. J. Bielenberg and Joseph Toomey ran about 130,000 head, and in Custer County, formerly the center of the cattle kingdom, Bob Selway had one hundred bands which ran 2,000 or 3,000 sheep to the band. Almost all these enterprises ran on a share basis, and a man who was ambitious and who could take the loneliness and hardship of herding could get himself in the sheep business often with no capital at all.

It occurred with increasing frequency to sheepmen and lawmakers alike that the real cream of the industry, however, was being bled off. Just as meat-packing facilities for the cattlemen had been in far-off Chicago or Kansas City, Montana's wool was shipped raw to Boston. Why not, reasoned the legislature, establish mills in Montana and keep that money at home? Accordingly, in 1887, the Territorial Legislature passed a law exempting the first woolen factory from all taxation for a six-year period. The incentive did not prove sufficient. But again and again the newspapers of the nineties bemoaned the "bleeding of the state" and pointed to the millions of dollars that could be saved and made were Montana to become a wool-manufacturing center. But a woolen mill at Big Timber in 1891 failed to make the grade. The simple and unhappy fact was that woolens produced in Montana still had to be shipped east for sale, and high labor costs plus freight charges meant that Montana products could not compete on the Eastern market. Here, again, was the old problem and the old pattern. By 1900, Montana had more sheep than any other state in the Union—more than 6,000,000—but it could not sustain woolen mills, and the business was dependent upon the market price of wool determined by the East. It was, again, an extractive industry; it was also an industry that depended on "range." After the turn of the century, when unrealistic federal land laws encouraged the "sodbuster" and "honyocker" to pour into eastern Montana with a plow, a horse, and the hope of quick profit, the sheep industry, like the cattle industry before it, fell on evil days. "I begin to see my finish," one of the big sheepmen, P. B. Moss, said in 1902. He continued:

> As the cattlemen found their nemesis in the hard winter of 1886–'87, I predict that the large owners of sheep have found their's in the small owner of sheep . . . . I have seen my position on the range gradually eliminated and forced to retreat under the crowding in of the small holders of sheep, and like the poor Indians, I have gradually fallen back to new ranges . . . and I feel that I am now about at the jumping off place.

Moss was right. The size of Montana bands was reduced drastically from 1910 onward. The great boom was over. The new "farmer" ran sheep and cattle but on a much reduced scale.

Both the cattle and sheep industries in Montana, in other words, enjoyed a period, brief but spectacular, of extraordinary boom-and-bust proportions. Yet in each case there had been insufficient foundation. The idea both of a range meat-packing industry and of a range woolen-manufacturing industry came early and were persistent. But in neither case were such enterprises successful because of the basic economic facts involved. The boom industries themselves were foredoomed. The attempt to extend them by fabricating as well as growing sounded reasonable but ignored time, distance, labor costs, freight rates, and other abiding factors, all of which together constitute a colonial economy. The industries survived but only by giving way to and becoming mingled with a generally diversified agricultural economy.

Other aspects of Montana's economy had also been changing rapidly and significantly. Until the Utah and Northern Railroad crossed into Montana in early 1880, reaching Butte in late 1881, and the Northern Pacific reached the Montana border in late 1880, Fort Benton remained the hub of the empire.

The town itself was hardly prepossessing. Behind the mile-long levee it stretched along one main street. During the sixties it was dirty, "a squaw town, a scalp market, the home of cutthroats and horse thieves . . . ." Like many such communities its most prominent structures were saloons and *bistros.* In the spring its main street was a sea of mud with wagon ruts feet deep. In the summer the street was inches thick with a whitish dust. It was treeless, its water was brackish, and it smelled strongly of hides, mules, oxen, and whisky. The people who lived in or near Benton and the people who passed through were incredibly polyglot. There were French, Indians, Negroes, Minnesotans, Southerners, Canadians, miners from the coast, wolfers, bullwhackers, whisky runners, and a few solid citizens. Accommodations in Benton were understandably poor, and most travelers in this early period left the town as soon as they could. Benton itself lived on transportation and storage. A tremendous freight and warehouse business was well under way by the late sixties. Freighters initially charged what the traffic would bear—as much as ten cents per pound in gold for the 140-mile trip to Helena. But competition quickly developed. Such firms as the Diamond R Transportation Company, one of the big ones, found itself undercut by a dozen or more small competitors like Garrison and Wyatt, E. G. Maclay and Company, or Carroll and Steel. Some idea of the tremendous growth of the freight business can be garnered from the fact that by 1866 there were perhaps 2,500 men, 3,000 teams, and 20,000 oxen and mules involved in the business of hauling goods over the trails that radiated out from Benton. The town changed dramatically from a fur outpost and a haven for wolfers to a commercial center of tremendous importance to the Northwest. It became, instead of a place of *bistros,* a place of stores and warehouses, manifest lists and account books. Everything boomed. Wages were half again as high as in the East. Artisans, wheelwrights, carpenters, and mechanics were in such short supply that businessmen in Benton would do almost anything to get them. But the shortage was acute and chronic. Even up into the eighties this shortage of skilled men was a plague.

Here there arose, too, Montana's first businessmen. While little has been written of them, they were of the same mold and were produced by the same drives as the Vanderbilts, Rockefellers, Fisks, and Carnegies. In this, the age of laissez faire and rugged individualism, these men became second-echelon tycoons. But there was nothing second echelon about them for Montana. Enterprising, tough-minded, and sometimes ruthless, they created their own dynasties and in the process created wealth in the Territory. But it is vital to note that Benton's boom was of a colonial nature nonetheless. Once again the familiar pattern emerged. Profits went disproportionately to stockholders in New Jersey and to bankers in New York, Montreal, and London. Benton businessmen were, in a real sense, the outpost agents of that vast entrepreneurial system which placed the products of the furnaces at Pittsburgh, the looms at Manchester, the distilleries of Kentucky, and the manufacturers of the entire East at the portals of the hungry mining frontier.

I. G. Baker and Company, T. C. Power and Bro., Klein-
schmidt and Bro., and many other such organizations fed
the hungry maw. The Bakers and the Powers soon outdis-
tanced all rivals. Theirs was not a local but rather a regional
business.

The Northwest Mounted Police had moved into the region
to the north. The whisky trade among the Indians and the
illicit hide and fur trade had greatly disturbed the Hudson's
Bay Company. But the Mounted Police assigned to keep order
and restore law on this frontier were operating far from their
own centers of supply. And so they turned to Benton. I. G.
Baker, for instance, was paid $122, 771 and $122,057, respec-
tively, in 1875 and 1876 for supplying the Mounted Police.
One can imagine the importance of this Canadian trade to
Benton and to Baker.

T. C. Power, in the meantime, financed by Joseph Field
of Chicago, launched the Benton Packet Line for the river
trade and also extended his activity into southwestern Canada
in the form of company posts at Forts Walsh and McLeod.
Canadian trade was vital to both these firms because, although the population in Montana was rapidly increasing
and the demand for goods was constant, the Union Pacific
Railroad had reached Corinne, Utah, and was supplying much
of the Montana area.

In 1873–74 Baker sold his interest in the firm to the Conrad brothers, William and Charles. There was no change in
the nature of the company's business. There was no change
in the uniformly good relations with T. C. Power. Both firms
expanded; both had varied interests as a hedge against the
failure of any one aspect. They were involved in the fur
trade, up- and down-river shipping, warehousing, banking,
milling, and mining. They carried on a flourishing trade with

the Gros Ventre, Blood, and Blackfoot Indians. Both were involved in the illicit whisky trade, and there is evidence that both sold illegal arms and ammunition to the Indians. And they had peripheral interests.

I. G. Baker, for instance, received the contract in 1877 to provide beef for the Blackfeet on the reservation. This involved about $500,000 worth of beef. T. C. Power imported coal from Canada at $25.00 a ton for fuel in Benton. If the cost was high, so was the cost of inferior wood at $8.00 a cord.

In the meantime, Samuel T. Hauser had become a power to the West, in Helena and Butte and environs. He had set up a kind of integrated financial empire. It was important to the merchants of Benton because it was through Hauser that they received much of their financing. Hauser, in turn, got his backing in St. Louis, New York, and Montreal. In 1880 the First National Bank of Fort Benton came into existence, backed by Hauser, the Conrads, and Powers. But there was still a shortage of investment capital, and wealthy as these men quickly became there was never a time, significantly, that they did not have to have recourse to eastern centers to expand in Montana.

In 1879, forty-seven steamboats disgorged their loads on the Fort Benton levee. This amounted to about 10,000 tons of goods, of which the Benton Packet Line carried 2,529, and the Baker Line 2,015. The year 1879 was the high point for Benton. Thereafter, commerce dropped off sharply. In 1872 the Northern Pacific Railway reached Bismarck, and upriver trade was cut off from Sioux City. In 1880 the Utah Northern crossed into Montana and further cut Benton's trade. In 1883 the Northern Pacific pushed into the upper Missouri Valley. Now the river trade diminished still further, and when, in 1887, the Great Northern Railroad reached Helena, Benton's excuse for existence was essentially gone. The Conrads and Powers sold their stores and supplies in the north to the patient and abiding Hudson's Bay Company, to which, in the long course of its history, their sharp competition had been hurtful but momentary. The Conrads sold out to a Great Falls firm in 1891, and I. G. Baker ran the last steamer in 1882. By 1885, Benton lay quiet and somnolent on the banks of the Missouri, in the backwaters of the wave that had swept over it.

In the meantime, the boom moved west to Helena, Butte, and the Continental Divide region. Here the economy was emerging from the placer period into the quartz period; in some regions silver was replacing gold, and there were even early attempts to smelt copper ores. With railroads pressing close to the territory, heavy equipment, mills, crushers, and steam plants were replacing the sluice and rocker. But there was the chronic shortage of capital.

It was in 1880 that Marcus Daly, an Irish immigrant who had mined in Calaveras County, California, and had served out an apprenticeship in the hot sumps of Nevada's Comstock, sold an interest he had in a silver mine in Butte for $100,000 and bought the Anaconda mine for $30,000. The Anaconda was then unimpressive. Its shaft was only sixty-five feet deep, and while it seemed a promising silver property, the gamble was substantial.

In his development of the Anaconda, Daly, too, had to seek capital elsewhere. He found it in San Francisco in the personages of James Ben Ali Haggin, George Hearst, and Lloyd Tevis. By 1882, when the Anaconda's shaft had penetrated the great russet hill for three hundred feet, it was obvious that the men had a copper mine instead of a silver mine. Having already spent perhaps $250,000 on what was presumably a silver mine, it is a tribute to Daly's powers of persuasion and to his partners' faith in him that they now backed him to the hilt in a copper mining venture of tremendous magnitude. By 1884 the world's largest smelter had been built at Anaconda, some twenty-eight miles to the west. A new community with a population of several thousand had sprung up there, and construction had been started on a railroad between Butte and Anaconda. In December, 1883, before the smelter was completed, the company had shipped 24,370 tons of copper ore to Swansea, Wales, for smelting for a gross profit of $1,702,400. By the next year the product of the Anaconda smelter was beginning to reach the channels of trade and, as we shall see was depressing the world's copper market.

In the meantime, Butte and other mines in the Territory were producing fabulously. In 1879, Montana produced $2,500,000 worth of gold and $2,225,000 worth of silver. By 1885 this had risen to $3,300,279 in gold, $10,060,000 in silver, $7,322,169 in copper, and $480,000 in lead. In addition, 49,846 tons of coal had been mined for a gross value of $174,460. As a consequence of this and other developing and related enterprises, Montana's population showed its greatest percentage increase in the decade of the eighties. From 39,159 in 1880 it jumped to 142,924 in 1890, an increase of 265 per cent. Never again was such radical growth in population to take place.

As was the case with mining, a swift growth occurred in the lumber industry in the eighties. As early as 1884 sawmills west of the Continental Divide were supplying the young giant, Anaconda, with 300,000 cords of wood for smelter fuel alone. At the going rate of $5.00 a cord, this represented $1,500,000. By 1888, Anaconda alone was using 40,000 feet of timber a day in the mines, exclusive of the smelter, and was contracting for over $1,000,000 in lumber per year. Add to this the fact that the Utah Northern and Northern Pacific railroads were building into the Territory and that they required ties and building lumber, and some picture of the swift development of lumbering in the Territory begins to emerge.

This new and vital industry ran headlong into federal regulations concerning the cutting of timber on the public domain. Because this, once again, reveals the conflict between East and West and points up the problems which arose from the passage of legislation bearing on the West but concocted mainly by legislators grossly unfamiliar with its problems, it is important to survey what happened in Montana.

The merchandising firm of Eddy, Hammond and Company, with headquarters in Missoula, took early advantage of railroad building and soon branched out into the lumbering business. The company signed a contract with the Northern Pacific Railroad to supply them with all kinds of supplies, including building lumber, ties, and tunnel timbers. The firm, under the direction of A. B. Hammond, E. L. Bonner, and R. A. Eddy, put a string of sawmills into operation in 1882 in Hell Gate Canyon, O'Keefe Canyon (to supply timbers for Marent trestle), and on the Clark Fork. Late in 1882 and specifically at the urging of a former Northern Pacific contractor named Washington Dunn, Eddy, Hammond and Company formed a new corporation, the Montana Improvement Company. Its principal purpose was to cut and market timber.

There were two things that were significant about this new corporation. First, the Northern Pacific Railroad held $1,000,100 of the corporation's total of $2,000,000 in stock; second, Marcus Daly of the Anaconda was one of the original incorporators, a fact which reveals that as of 1882 Daly was fully conscious of the vital relationship between mining and lumbering.

The Montana Improvement Company then set about securing its interests. It signed a twenty-year contract with the Northern Pacific to supply all of the railroad's timber and lumber requirements for the 925-mile distance between Miles City and Walla Walla junction. The company also got a rebate, sometimes amounting to half the ordinary rate, on everything it shipped via the Northern Pacific. To a considerable degree, then, the company was the creature of the railroad.

But in 1878 the government had passed the Timber and Stone Act. It was the purpose of this legislation to prevent exploitation of the public domain. Essentially, the act provided that timber could be cut for "domestic" purposes only but that it could not be cut for commercial purposes. All this presupposed, of course, that a survey had been made of the area and that it was therefore readily ascertainable which sections were private and which were public. Such was not the case.

The need for lumber was not only pressing; it was of the essence of things. It is not too much to say that by the middle eighties Montana's economy would have collapsed completely had the lumber industry curtailed its operations significantly.

Between 1882 and 1885 Henry M. Teller of Colorado was secretary of the interior. Teller, aware of the problems of western communities, saw fit to interpret the acts applying to the cutting of timber very liberally. His land commissioner, N. C. McFarland, had taken note of the activities of the Montana Improvement Company and had taken action to clamp down. This immediately brought derisive comment from Montana's delegate to Congress, Martin Maginnis, who wrote

Teller, "Certainly Congress never intended to overturn the ordinary processes of civilized society in the territories and make every man his own woodchopper or lumber maker!" Teller then set forth his own interpretation of the timber acts for the guidance of his land commissioner, and there was no further trouble.

But in 1884 Grover Cleveland was elected President. Cleveland was highly ethical, scrupulously honest, and he was a conservationist. He appointed L. Q. C. Lamar as secretary of the interior, who in turn appointed William Andrew Jackson Sparks as land commissioner. Sparks, reading through McFarland's records, was shocked and dismayed by what he found there. He reported to Lamar in 1885, "depredations on the public timber are universal, flagrant and limitless," and he singled out the Montana Improvement Company for special censure. Suits, both civil and criminal, were instituted against the company by the government.

The matter dragged through the courts until 1889, and on every occasion the government took a beating. Not only were the wealthiest Montana businessmen openly hostile to the government's case, but the press of the Territory was universally caustic in pointing out the absurdity of such legislation. The lumber people won the day, but, as we shall see, the rupture this brought about in Montana politics was severe.

Thus freed of governmental regulation, the lumber industry prospered. Daly, frightened by the close call of the Montana Improvement Company, set about creating his own lumber department. W. A. Clark did likewise. The small mill became increasingly a thing of the past as lumbering in the 1890's moved into an integrated phase which was to last until after World War II.

Montana as of 1890 had a population of approximately

143,000. The great bulk of this population was concentrated in the western valleys. The plains to the east were still more a hindrance to travelers than a haven for settlers. As we have seen, the plains were cattle country. They had yet to attract the farmer in large numbers, and their suitability for wheat had not been recognized. The Territory was overwhelmingly dependent upon mining, which had produced by 1890 a gross wealth of $39,615,012. Copper led among the metals with $17,625,020. Silver was second with $16,537,500, and gold third with $3,300,000. Lead and coal produced in that year were worth about $2,500,000.

We have no way of ascertaining, of course, what proportion of the wealth of this extractive industry was retained in the Territory, but non-Montanans held large blocks of stock in nearly every mining enterprise of significance by 1890. While it is true that such enterprises created new communities and sustained them and that part of the wealth produced stayed in the area in the form of wages and other local expenditures, the trend toward a disproportionate balance of "kept wealth" was significant at an early time.

By 1892, Butte, in particular, was on the crest of a boom. That year Butte's copper surpassed Michigan's for the first time—by 56,877,000 pounds. There was full employment, wages were excellent, and Butte's millionaires were numerous enough to require their own social club—although they took increasingly to finding their recreation in the East or on the West Coast.

In view of the nonresident investment trend, another and concurrent development was of particular significance. As a consequence of the panic of 1893, the Anaconda Company ceased to be a close corporation. It was reorganized in 1895, and the shares which belonged to George Hearst were put on the open market. A London syndicate purchased $7,500,-000 worth. A little later another 270,000 shares were purchased by Londoners at $25.00 a share. Nearly one-half of the stock of Anaconda was now owned by Londoners. The stock was not popular in England, however, and it rapidly found its way to Boston—still the copper headquarters for the United States. Boston, in the meantime, was moving directly in on Butte. Interests there purchased two large Butte mines, the Boston and Montana and the Butte and Boston. By 1895, therefore, Boston brokers and investment houses had a large stake in affairs at Butte—larger, indeed, than contemporary Montanans seemed to realize.

Then, beginning in 1897, a significant series of consolidations in the copper industry presaged a change in the entire basis of ownership. In the early spring of 1897 the Boston and Montana Company and the Butte and Boston Company effected a consolidation. In the same year, William Andrews Clark filed incorporation papers and brought his diverse corporate interests under one head.

This trend toward consolidation was not confined to Montana. Indeed, it was one of the hallmarks of American industrial development at the turn of the century. What lent it its particular significance in Montana was the fact that the consolidations were largely brought about by nonresidents. These consolidations were not sinisterly conceived in most cases but were initiated because they meant greater managerial efficiency and a cut in operating costs. As a by-product, however, it was also true that the process made control of all kinds easier. The reins could be more securely held, and there were fewer of them. This was to have vast significance in the future.

The process caused some concern in Montana. Stockholders in the area were almost always minority stockholders. But at least in one case they proved recalcitrant. Litigation was initiated which placed the matter before Montana's Supreme Court. The court held against such consolidations and stated that stock transfers from one company to another were illegal without the consent of minority stockholders.

In January, 1899, the legislature took a hand in the matter, and it did so when crucial developments were on the near horizon. House Bill No. 132 provided for the legality of stock transfers without minority consent, and it was introduced with tremendous power behind it. With the introduction of this bill Montana had a glimpse into the labyrinth behind some of the consolidations, and Montanans learned for the first time that Standard Oil was in some measure involved.

Concerning House Bill No. 132, W. A. Clark wrote to his close friend J. S. M. Neill: "It is a matter of great concern to me. The First National Bank of New York, the Northern Pacific Railroad Company, Senator Carter and the Standard Oil people are all working hard to get this bill through and I am sure it will be very much to my interests if they succeed."

Why was Standard Oil interested? Because they were planning to buy the Anaconda Company, and other Butte properties, and consolidate. With a great New York bank, a great railroad, and a great oil company aligned in concert, there was little doubt but that the bill would pass. It did, handily, guided through by the Anaconda Company's own attorney, E. D. Matts.

This show of power alerted the governor, R. B. Smith. He vetoed the bill, calling it "vicious." He made it clear that he deeply resented Standard Oil's intrusion into Montana politics, that he saw bad things for Montana in a Standard Oil–owned copper combine, and then, in a peroration as vigorous as it was mixed in metaphor, he concluded with the statement: "If you do not assert your independence now and defeat this measure, it will be too late when the tentacles of this octopus have fastened their fangs on the strong limbs of this fair commonwealth." But the bill passed easily over the Governor's veto. Anaconda became the Amalgamated Copper Company, owned and controlled by Standard Oil and financed by New York's National City Bank.

In the incredibly short space of two decades—1880 to 1900—Montana had gone from near wilderness to booming industrialism. But it neither owned nor controlled what it was. If all the Bakers, Powers, Hausers, Clarks, Hammonds, and Dalys had pooled what they themselves had wrested in wealth from Montana, it would still not have been enough to develop what they all could see was waiting for development and which, the nature of wealth and man being what they are, would not submit to delay.

VIII

BUTTE TO PARIS AND RETURN

THE KEWEENAW PENINSULA, a thumb of land that pokes into the cold waters of Lake Superior, had been producing copper since 1845. It was the only place on earth where pure native copper was found in commercial quantities. Not until the 1850's had mines on the peninsula even bothered to reduce low-grade ores. During the Civil War, Michigan miners, who previously had had their ore smelted in Wales, set up their own smelters and broke the monopoly previously held by Swansea. All Lake Superior copper was sold by Calumet and Hecla through a pooling agreement which was renewed with each mine every year. The entire Michigan copper enterprise was financed largely by Boston financiers, and Michigan's pre-eminence in the world of copper was considered unassailable.

In the early eighties technical journals began to carry reports of the superiority of copper for wire, overhead telegraph lines, and roofing. At precisely this time the new electrical industry was emerging. The lamps and candles of the cities gave way to electric lighting systems, and the electric motor was suddenly removed from the scientist's laboratory and put to work on a commercial basis.

BUTTE BEGAN to produce copper just as this revolution was taking place. The immensely increased demand for copper, which lifted it quickly out of the high sub-luxury class of metals, was not lost on Marcus Daly and his partners. Indeed, it was precisely why they took what, at the time, appeared to be a vast gamble and put some $4,000,000 into a promising mine between 1882 and 1884.

But when their gigantic smelter had been completed and their product was being pushed into the channels of trade, they ran into the stone wall of Calumet and Hecla. Michigan, after all, was used to setting prices, and with water transportation at their door, pure native copper to mine and smelt, and heavy Boston financing, they felt confident that they could handle their new western upstart. After all, Montana ore was mid-grade, not pure; Butte was remote and off the beaten path with miles of expensive overland transportation confronting it; and no one knew much about Anaconda's financing. Initially, such publications as the *Engineering and Mining Journal,* the most reputable of the mining trade journals, stated that the western venture, however auspiciously begun, could never hold out when Michigan chose to drive the price of copper down. Butte, said the *Journal,* had too narrow a margin of profit because of its irreducible basic costs to compete with Michigan.

The *Journal* and the Michigan miners, however, overlooked two things—the tremendous increase in the demand for copper and the fact that Daly and his partners did not propose merely to mine and smelt copper but to do so on a tremendous scale. The key lay in mass production.

Between March of 1883 and the early spring of 1886, Montana and Michigan (principally Anaconda and Calumet and Hecla) engaged in a vicious price war. Michigan drove the price of copper from eighteen cents a pound in 1883 to ten cents a pound in 1886, believing firmly that each cut in price would close the Montana mines. Except for one shutdown to install new equipment, Anaconda did not close. Most of Butte's smaller operators did, sitting back to await the outcome of the battle of the titans. But Anaconda produced prodigiously; so prodigiously, in fact, that in 1885 all seventeen of the Lake Superior mines produced 77,000,000 pounds of copper, and the Anaconda mine alone produced 36,000,000 pounds.

By 1888, Anaconda was producing copper on a massive scale and for a profit at ten cents a pound. Michigan had lost the price war, and its monopoly on copper as well as its capacity to set the price was lost. It is a tremendous tribute, particularly to Marcus Daly, that this kind of acumen and vision prevailed.

But the story does not end there. There was in Paris a bald-headed little man who bore the somewhat improbable sobriquet of Hyacinthe Secretan. Secretan was a speculator who, a few years before, had nearly cornered the world tin market. The lessons implicit in the Montana-Michigan price war were not lost on M. Secretan. The price of copper was now depressed, artificially so. The demand for copper was not only great, it was increasing daily. This should have led to a price increase. Instead, the price war had led to a decrease. Secretan decided that the moment was propitious for a corner on the world's supply of copper.

His procedure, at least on paper, was simplicity itself. He formed a syndicate of sixteen European capitalists. This was an informal group, unincorporated and not legally responsible. It had some of the Paris Rothschilds in it, the *Crédit Lyonnaise*, the *Bank de Paris et des Pays-Bas*, and the German house of *Bleichroeder*. The *Comptoir d'Escompt*, France's second largest bank, acted as the Syndicate's banker, and a separate entity was established, the *Société Industrielle Commerciale des Metaux de Paris*, which was to conduct the actual business. Secretan became the *administrateur-directeur* of the *Société* and immediately borrowed $13,500,000 from the Syndicate of bankers.

He now made contacts with every copper mine and company of any significance in the world. He approached them with a contract guaranteeing them thirteen cents for the copper they produced instead of the ten cents they were getting. There was, it is true, a limitation on production, but it was pro rata.

The copper market was depressed. The copper companies were hurting. Secretan's proposition was impressive. By late 1888 he had all the mines in the world under contract, including Anaconda. Marcus Daly and his partner, James Ben Ali Haggin, were in disagreement about the "Syndicate," as the entire setup came to be called, and Daly, who had sparkplugged the great production campaign of 1883–86, was constitutionally opposed to curtailed or controlled production. Haggin, thinking of what the additional three cents per pound would mean and believing that the Syndicate was stable and well financed, was for signing the contract. He prevailed.

Secretan now bought copper through the *Société* with the money he had borrowed from the Syndicate. In return he gave the Syndicate the copper he had purchased as collateral. Then he sat back to await the demand. He controlled all the world's copper. They had to come to him, and he knew that they had to have copper. The price was now a matter of his option.

But the "law" of supply and demand is no law at all. There are, as Secretan found to his sorrow, too many variables. Secretan had to honor his contracts and buy copper. The trouble was that he could not sell it. Users of copper were accustomed to a ten-cent or eleven-cent price. When the price was quoted in the neighborhood of twenty cents, copper users simply did not buy. They began to substitute zinc and iron. More important, they bought junk copper, a source which Secretan could not control. Copper utensils, jewelry, and knickknacks, worthless when copper was at ten cents, became worth a good deal with copper at twenty cents. In other words, Secretan overestimated the demand and forgot the junkman. It was his ruination. On March 4, 1889, one Denfert Rochereau, a director of the *Comptoir*, committed suicide. The news of the Syndicate's collapse leaked out. A run developed on the *Comptoir* which was only saved from closing its doors when the Bank of France came to its aid with a loan of 120,000,000 francs.

For a month or so the entire world copper market trembled on the brink of disaster. The French bankers had 400,000,000 pounds of copper which Secretan had given them as collateral. The market price of copper was then seven and one-half cents. They had paid thirteen cents. It would take the world more than a year, with no mine or smelter operating, to use up that much copper. If the bankers panicked and dumped their copper, it would ruin the copper industry.

Haggin of Anaconda and Quincy Adams Shaw of Calumet and Hecla embarked at once for Europe and a series of meetings with the bankers. The latter agreed to let their product into the channels of trade slowly. The former, speaking for the copper industry, agreed to peg the price of copper at twelve cents.

What was the significance of all this for Montana? It was great. In the first place, the Montana-Michigan price war had started it all. In the second place, with the state's economy heavily dependent on the price of copper, any fluctuations in that price were of vital moment in Montana. When, during the price war, the Butte mines shut down momentarily in the winter of 1886–87, there had been real hardship in Butte and elsewhere.

But of greater importance still was the fact that American financiers had watched Secretan's shoestring operations with great interest. Quite clearly, copper was something that lent itself peculiarly to manipulation, and because of the inevitability of steadily increasing demand, it was a market wherein great profits could be made. An astute contemporary economist, Benjamin Andrews, writing in the *Quarterly Journal of Economics* after the Syndicate's collapse in 1889, said of the copper situation: "To a regular trust it must and will come at last. Nor has aught taken place to indicate that a copper trust organized like the Standard Oil Trust, with its energy and its relentless methods, would fail."

When Standard Oil itself moved into Montana, its officers in New York were thoroughly conversant with all that had happened to Secretan, and months of intensive study had been given to the copper market. Anaconda's marvelous production record and the obviously appreciating demand for copper (in spite of the market's momentary glut) all pointed toward a sound and profitable enterprise. But no one in Standard Oil bothered to study Montana and what was happening there. True, they had studied production statistics; they had carefully inspected the mines and the smelter, but they had ignored the fact that politics in Montana had long since put itself exclusively at the disposal of warring copper magnates. Politics could not be divorced from business, and Standard Oil was to find that out to its own sorrow and Montana's deeper grief.

In 1888, Montana was still strongly Democratic. The party was the only really virile political force in the Territory, yet its nature had changed greatly in the preceding twenty years. Its strength was no longer attributable to the Southern element in the population but rather to the fact that the new industrial leaders had chosen the strongest vehicle available for their own pragmatic purposes.

The "Big Four" in the Democratic party, W. A. Clark, Marcus Daly, S. T. Hauser, and C. A. Broadwater, had little in common personally, but they had a great deal in common with respect to business affairs. All were moving toward wealth and power with extraordinary vigor in the new fields of heavy mining, banking, railroad building, and allied enterprises. All were carving empires out of essential wilderness. The decade of the eighties saw each of them plunge into politics because it was swiftly becoming apparent that both at home and in Washington they needed the protection and the preference that political strength could give their enterprises.

We find, for instance, that W. A. Clark was the president of the abortive constitutional convention of 1884 and that his fellow representative from Silver Bow County was Marcus Daly. When it came to the section of the proposed constitution dealing with taxation, Clark, backed by Daly, made an impassioned plea for a clause in the constitution which would exempt mines from all save a "net proceeds" tax. The miners, quite naturally, backed Clark to the hilt. There did develop a conflict between the miners and the cattlemen in the convention of 1889 with regard to this tax clause, but it was not, as has commonly been assumed, a "conspiracy" on the part of the miners. It was simply that men like Clark, Daly, Hauser, and others were acting through political means to secure maximum benefits for themselves and their businesses.

In November, 1888, Marcus Daly and W. A. Clark had a falling out which split the party asunder. This started a twelve-year feud which, in turn, was the fulcrum on which the entire political structure was precariously balanced for more than a decade. The Clark-Daly feud has been widely misinterpreted and oversimplified by those who have interpreted it as a series of individual and unconnected aberrations. Yet from 1888 to well into the first decade of the twentieth century there is a progression of political cause-and-effect anchored deep in economic developments, all of which were of tremendous importance to Montana. Therefore it becomes necessary first to examine the nature of the antagonists, second to chronicle the events as they transpired, and then to examine the constant underlying factors.

William Andrews Clark had come to Bannack, Montana, in 1863, hard on the news of the discovery of gold. Not yet affecting the beard which in later life covered a sharp chin, Clark was described by a contemporary in Bannack as "a little, red-headed man with a pack on his back . . . he wore a red shirt, an old army coat with one of the tails burned off by too close a proximity to the fire." He was a small man with a somewhat ferret-like appearance, except that his eyes were direct and rather pale. He had a high, thin voice which never lent itself to oratory, even though in later years it was frequently put to oratorical uses.

Originally from Pennsylvania, he had attended Laurel Hill Academy and spent two years at Ohio Wesleyan where he studied law. He taught school in Missouri from 1856 to 1860 and then, after a brief interval, headed west.

The Bannack to which this unprepossessing man came in 1863 was suffering from its plague of road agents. The camp was as tough a settlement as the West produced. Into it Clark carried only his pack and three books: *Poems by Burns*, Hitchcock's *Elements of Geology*, and *Parsons on Contracts*. This is some slight indication of the man's character. Only a man with an eye to the future would carry into the wilderness a law book and a geology book. Burns represented studied recreation, and Clark's recreation remained studied all his life.

But this rather taciturn and fastidious little man was neither appalled by nor fearful of the riot that was Bannack, and he set about making a place for himself without delay. He was quick to see that mining in Bannack was not the road to success, but that merchandising was. A dollar never left his hand but that it returned with another stuck fast to it. Gradually he expanded his activities to Virginia City, and then, in 1867, he obtained a contract to transport mail from Missoula to Walla Walla.

Clark's detractors, and they are nearly legion, are prone to forget his early years in Montana. They fail to measure the extent to which the elements conspired against him. He moved through the erratic and violent frontier life with implacable determination. He asked for no quarter and gave none, but he had no initial advantage over his fellow men save that which sprang from his intelligence and his determination.

By 1872 he had started to purchase mining property in Butte. Struck by the possibilities in that camp when other men were discouraged by the depletion of the placer ground and the bothersome presence of silver ore, Clark took several months off and went east to the Columbia School of Mines for a cram course in mineralogy.

Upon his return from New York he concentrated on his properties in Butte. In 1875, he obtained the Dexter Stamp Mill when one William L. Farlin defaulted on a mortgage. By the time Marcus Daly arrived at Butte in 1876, Clark was well on the road to wealth. He now owned a bank in Deer Lodge and a considerable amount of real estate.

After Daly had probed down into the great hill and struck copper, Clark, too, went into copper. Clark and Daly grew together and pulled Butte after them. Clark remained constrained, even cold, and perhaps because he had a measure of contempt for his fellow men, he never inspired adulation that soon became Daly's. But he did inspire respect—the more to be noted because it was often grudgingly given.

By the turn of the century Clark was a power. He owned thirteen paying mines in Butte, and he owned extensive mining property in Coeur d'Alene, Idaho, as well as 95 per cent of the stock in the United Verde Copper Company in Arizona. He was treasurer of the Butte City Street Railway Company, a large stockholder in the Butte Electric Light Company, owner of the Butte *Miner,* vice-president of the Colorado Smelting and Mining Company, president of the Rocky Mountain Telegraph Company, and treasurer of the Silver Bow Water Company.

Marcus Daly, as we have already seen, arrived in Butte in 1876. He had been born in Ireland, had come to New York in 1856, and had remained there for five years. He had mined in Calaveras County, California, and had become a foreman at the Comstock in Nevada. In 1870, he appeared in Salt Lake City and soon became the foreman of the Emma Mine at Alta, Utah. The following year he went to work for Walker

Brothers, miners and bankers of Salt Lake City. He managed a property then being operated on Lion Hill for Walker Brothers and also served as a kind of roving prospector for them. Between 1873 and 1876, Daly did a lot of prospecting and made many mining contacts, one of whom was George Hearst (father of William Randolph). Hearst was associated with San Francisco's James Ben Ali Haggin and Lloyd Tevis. These men were tremendously wealthy, having made bonanza real estate transactions and having branched out into mining all over the West.

In 1876, Walker Brothers sent Daly to Butte to examine a silver mine, the Alice. When the Walkers bought the mine, Daly became its manager and took a one-third interest in it for himself. We have already seen that he sold his interest in the Alice in 1880 and bought the Anaconda and that Anaconda's subsequent financing was through Haggin, Hearst, and Tevis.

Daly, unlike Clark, was uneducated. But he had great charm and wit. He was of medium height and had a stocky figure. He talked the miners' language, and they understood him and he them. Even though his spontaneous generosity and quick wit have become almost legendary in Montana, the fact is that behind his open geniality was not only a penetrating intelligence but a fiery temper and an implacable determination equal to Clark's. While he never forgot a favor, neither did he forget an affront. He could readily be as merciless as he was kind. Like Clark, Daly was a powerful man by the turn of the century.

In the early summer of 1888, W. A. Clark decided to run for territorial delegate to Congress. He won the nomination handily, and because in Democratic Montana such a nomination was tantamount to election, Clark packed his bags and made ready to leave for Washington after the routine election in November.

But when on November 10 all the returns were in, lo, Clark had been defeated by a young and comparatively unknown Republican, Thomas H. Carter—and by a thumping 5,126 majority. Clark was not naïve, and he perceived at once that Daly had had a hand in his defeat. The national campaign in 1888 had revolved around the tariff, but Montana's six largest wool-producing counties, where a tariff party would show its greatest strength, voted almost solidly for Clark. He lost the election in Butte, Anaconda, and the lumber counties of the west where, indeed, he should have been strongest.

On November 10 he wrote a bitter letter to Martin Maginnis, a fellow Democrat who had campaigned ardently for him. "The conspiracy," he wrote, "was a gigantic one, well planned and well carried out . . . [but] the day of retribution may come when treason may be considered odious. . . . For the time being, I retire politically."

Clark's paper, the Butte *Miner,* cried out that he had not been defeated by Republicans, that at least one thousand Democratic votes in Silver Bow County had been sold to the Republicans, and that it was not a matter of the tariff or personality but was the consequence of "potent influences which are well understood and deeply deplored by the best thinking citizens of this county." The *Miner* did not name Daly as the culprit. But the Great Falls *Tribune* was less cryptic. "No," wrote Jerry Collins, its editor, "it was not the tariff that defeated Mr. Clark—it was treachery with a big T . . . . As to Marcus Daly's part in this perfidious business, his apathy during the campaign and the vote in Anaconda and Butte tell the story. Comment would be idle."

But widespread comment there was. Not only had the

Daly strongholds of Butte and Anaconda gone Republican; so had the counties where the Montana Improvement Company and the Northern Pacific Railroad employed many men. Obviously Hammond, Bonner and Eddy of the Improvement Company were somehow involved. Yet all were Democrats.

The "Big Four" acted in concert no longer. Clark had been deserted not only by Daly but by Hauser and other strong Democrats. For the next twelve years, and in the most bizarre way, political action reverted again and again to the events of November, 1888. In all the charges and countercharges there early emerged one voice of concern with respect to the principle involved. Lee Mantle, a friend of all the men involved and owner of the *Inter-Mountain* of Butte, commented:

> There is the evil. Messrs. Daly, Hauser, Clark, and Broadwater are not leaders in their party. They are autocrats of the strongest type . . . . The theory of the millionaire employer that he can command the suffrage as well as the services of the employed is bad.

Soon Clark was getting explicit with his charges. His *Miner* for November 28 carried a reprint of a story he had given to the St. Paul *Pioneer Press* on his way east:

> There was a combination against me which could not be defeated. On Saturday the foreman of the night shift in the Anaconda Mine ordered his men to vote for Carter. The day shift on Sunday also received the same orders, and five bosses were stationed at one of the polling places to see that the orders were carried out. The employees of the Missoula Mercantile Company [Montana Improvement Company] received similar orders, and their employers saw to it that they obeyed . . . . The employees of the North-

ern Pacific Railroad in the territory numbered about 2,000.
They were under instructions to vote for Carter.

The duration of Clark's bitterness is demonstrated by the
fact that twelve years later, in 1900, he was still brooding
about it. When he ultimately did get to the Senate, he was
forced to resign on the basis of bribery charges brought by
Daly. In his speech of resignation he returned again and again
to his defeat of 1888. At one juncture he said:

> At the opening of the polls his [Daly's] employees came
> flocking down the hill with Democratic tickets in their
> hands except that the name of the Republican nominee
> was pasted over mine. The Australian ballot system had
> not then been established and there were shift bosses at
> the polls who knew the men and made them show their
> tickets before depositing them.

Even when in 1900 Daly lay dying in the Netherlands
Hotel in New York City, Clark reverted to the election of 1888.
After reviewing Daly's perfidy for a reporter from the New
York *Herald,* Clark finished by saying: "Marcus Daly is now
dying, the victim of his own spleen. He is the most violent
tempered man I have even known."

Did Daly, Hauser, and the other important Democrats in
Montana defeat Clark? They did, and there is abundant evidence that while Clark overdid his descriptions of the manner
in which voting was controlled, it was controlled. Men in the
mines and woods camps were given to understand that they
should vote for Carter. Whisky and cigars were passed out
liberally. In some cases, men were undoubtedly afraid for
their jobs.

The question arises as to motive. Unfortunately Montana writers and historians have evolved a series of romantic stories purporting to explain the events of 1888 on the basis of a Clark-Daly falling out prior to 1888. But there was a compelling reason for Daly's actions.

The appetite of Butte's mines for lumber, stulls, fuel, and timber products was now voracious. We have already seen that Montana lumbermen (particularly those of the Montana Improvement Company) were under indictments both civil and criminal for depredations on the public domain. It has been pointed out that the Northern Pacific Railroad had equal need for lumber and that it also owned more than 50 per cent of the stock in the Montana Improvement Company. Practically all the men involved in these enterprises were Democrats. Hammond was even a Democratic national committeeman, but as the summer of 1888 waned, it became quite obvious that the political situation for the Democrats on the national scene was a precarious one. The beleaguered Montanans found themselves at odds with President Cleveland's Interior Department, Democrat though Cleveland was. And now, should a Republican administration come into power nationally, they could foresee no relief. Indictments were already being processed. They desperately needed a friend at court. But what good could Clark do with a Republican administration? Further, even though Clark's interests were to some extent theirs in that he owned mines, he had not been outspoken regarding the suits. Here was young T. H. Carter, smart and very ambitious but with no real chance of winning . . . unless . . . .

Hammond and Bonner approached Daly. They convinced him that it was in his own interests to support Carter and defeat Clark. These three, and all that they represented, were then joined by the Northern Pacific Railroad. Clark was defeated.

From that day forth the two men were bitter enemies, and because by this time they were very wealthy and powerful, their enmity continued to permeate all political activity. The state was soon divided into Clark and Daly camps. There was no room in the middle. The next battle took place in 1894, when an election was held to determine whether Helena or Anaconda should be the permanent capital of the new state.

"Capital fights" were relatively common in the West, and they were usually lively. Few, however, were quite the show that Clark and Daly put on; Clark for Helena, Daly for Anaconda. One estimate placed the amount spent in the campaign at about $1,500,000. Of this sum Clark later asserted that Daly spent over $1,000,000, but Daly denied it. He estimated that the Anaconda side spent about $350,000. When being queried about Montana elections by a United States Senate committee, the blandness with which S. T. Hauser talked about finances brought forth the incredulous question: "Do I understand you to say that in these Montana elections a million dollars would go for legitimate expenses?" To which Hauser replied: "It would depend on what you call legitimate expenses. I presume [in the] East some of these expenses would hardly be considered legitimate, but there is none of it for the purpose of actually buying votes."

Clark, however, was in no doubt but that Daly and the Anaconda forces were engaged in dark business during the capital fight. He told the Senate committee:

> Conditions were such in Montana—everything in the way of elections there, where this company has had domination,

The treasure of timber: a view of the Fort Owen lumber mill
in 1865.

"Cut-out and get-out": shortsighted policies left empty towns
and silent sawmills.

Courtesy the Forest Service; photograph by K. D. Swan

has been of such high-handed character—that nobody could expect any recognition whatsoever unless he bowed his knee and crawled in the dust to these people . . . . They own the political machinery of the country—or a good deal of it.

If Daly and/or the Anaconda Company did own the state's political machinery as of 1894, the capital campaign was poor testimony to its efficiency because Helena won the election, 27,028 to 25,118. "Three Cheers," trumpeted Clark's Butte *Miner*, "The People Are Supreme! The Citizenship of Montana is Vindicated! Tyranny has reached its Waterloo!"

It was probably the theme of tyranny, or the threat of it, that defeated Anaconda. The Clark forces hammered at it unmercifully, and there was really no effective argument against it. "Are the voters of Montana," said an anti-Anaconda pamphlet, "now ready to turn over in perpetuity the legislative, executive and judicial departments of government to struggle and gasp in the restricting coils of the Anaconda Company?"

Clark's *Miner* carried statistics purporting to illustrate the extent of Anaconda's subservience to the company. It noted that of the 1,812 city lots, the company owned 926. Out of every 500 corner lots, the company owned 300. Thousands of little copper collars were manufactured by the Clark forces and were distributed with the admonition that a vote for Anaconda was a vote for the octopus. All this was effective because the germ of truth was in it. Anaconda was clearly a company town.

Anaconda's propaganda was limited to innuendoes that Helena was "importing" voters, that Helena discriminated against Negroes, and that Helena residents were too "culture conscious." The Anaconda forces put on giant torchlight parades, bought and gave away barrel after barrel of whisky in Butte, and even passed out five-dollar bills in the streets. It was in Butte that the Clark and Daly forces met on "neutral ground." For weeks the city echoed to dynamite blasts, the night was made bright with torches, and bands coursed up and down its hilly streets. But Anaconda could not circumvent the belief in the minds of many residents that state government should be as far removed as possible from the center of corporate influence.

While Helena won and while, in a sense, that fact could be interpreted as a repudiation by a wary populace of corporate participation in local government, the victory of political rectitude was more apparent than real for in the fight over the capital more than one million dollars was poured out indiscriminately. Whether it went to buy votes directly or indirectly is of little moment. The edge of political integrity was dulled to the precise extent to which the capital fight encouraged popular acceptance of the alliance between the dollar and the vote. Twice now, in the battle between Clark and Daly, votes had been paid for, swung, and used for particular purposes.

By 1894 a certain cynicism marked the attitude of some Montanans. S. T. Hauser remarked to the Senate committee concerning Montana elections: "It is pretty nice to get the saloons . . . . We simply hand them money to give the boys a drink. If you get them on your side it is quite an element." When asked how the barkeep used the money, Hauser replied: "He probably, instead of using it for drinks keeps a large percentage of it."

Clark's statement before the same committee is also revealing: "Many people have become so indifferent to voting there by reason of the large sums of money that have been expended in the state heretofore that you have to do a great deal of urging, and it takes a lot of men to do it, to go around among them and stir them up and get them out."

And there was, subsequent to Clark's and Daly's second clash, a general uneasiness abroad—an uneasiness reflected in the fact, for instance, that in 1895 the legislature passed a law defining crimes against the elective franchise which limited in purpose and amount the expenditures which could be made in any elections, either by a political committee or a candidate. With the capital campaign in mind, the lawmakers set the limit at $1,000 per committee for each county.

Former Vigilante and United States Senator Wilbur Fisk Sanders, who had come to Montana in 1863 found himself out of step with the times by 1895. Writing to his old friend James Fergus, he remarked:

> There must be observed painful dilutions of our political and moral life since the great influx which has separated the life of adventure from the scramble of greed. It is a dull vision that does not see great changes in Montana. In our politics it is not thought necessary that legislators should comprehend the principles of government . . . . I desire representatives who in the legislative assembly could not be hoodwinked or bribed . . . but the weaklings are not of that quality.

Sanders saw changes taking place, and events, indeed, had passed him by. But the changes wrought by wealth, corporate power, and the use of politics for economic purposes had just begun.

IX

THE WAR OF THE COPPER KINGS

O N JANUARY 10, 1899, the galleries of the Senate chamber in Helena filled early. A crowd gathered outside the Capitol in spite of the brittle cold. Not a seat in the Senate was vacant, and in the Statehouse corridors there was constant bustle. The Senate was electing a United States senator.[1] W. A. Clark was a candidate, and Marcus Daly was out to defeat him.

Rumors of bribery had been bandied about in Helena for weeks. Whether from desperation or contempt, W. A. Clark was making no real effort to hide the fact that Clark money was available. By this time Daly had his own newspaper, the Anaconda *Standard*. Since 1894 it had become one of the best papers in the Pacific Northwest, with *Standard* reporters in all principal Montana cities as well as correspondents elsewhere. Under the able editorship of John H. Durston, the *Standard* was as much Daly's personal organ as the *Miner*

[1] Until 1913, United States senators were elected by state legislatures, not by popular vote.

was Clark's. Daly had spent over one million dollars developing the *Standard* and, even though it was younger, its circulation was as large as, if not larger than, the *Miner's.* Both papers now became the exclusive servants of their masters in the fight over the senatorship.

Although Daly himself was ill in his quarters in the Netherlands Hotel in New York, his Montana machine slipped smoothly into action. On November 10 the *Standard* started things off with this statement:

> This watchword lately made potent against boodlers in Chicago, ought to be blazoned over the main entrance of the temporary capitol[2] at Helena: "Make it hot for men who take bribes and hotter still for men who give bribes."

The *Miner* was content to remark ominously that there appeared to be "some shady characters on hand." Again, when the Daly faction in the Senate succeeded in pushing through the establishment of a joint committee to investigate rumors of bribery before the balloting began, the *Standard* remarked, "now greasers and bribegivers will be compelled to face the music."

The first balloting found no one with a majority. But before the second ballot could be taken, a report was demanded from the bribery investigating committee. State Senator Fred Whiteside then rose from his seat and in the electric silence asked the joint assembly for recognition. Then he produced four envelopes, and from them he took $30,000 in currency. He held the money aloft and loudly announced that it had been given him by the agents of William Andrews Clark for the express purpose of buying his vote and the votes of four other men whom he named.

[2] The *Standard* always referred to Helena as the "temporary capital."

Pandemonium broke loose at this announcement. The press table was quickly emptied; there was a sudden exodus from the floor and from the galleries. The *Standard* for January 11 ran a banner headline:

CLARK BRIBERS CAUGHT RED HANDED
THIRTY THOUSAND DOLLARS OF THE
BOODLE FUND UP IN FULL VIEW
CONSPIRACY'S FOUL SECRET LAID BARE.

The *Miner*, however, was not struck dumb. Its issue for the same day trumpeted:

A DAMNABLE CONSPIRACY
DALY CROWD SPRING THEIR
PROMISED SENSATION
BUNGLING WORK AT THE OUTSET

The *Miner* went on at length to explain that it was a Daly plot, that it was Daly money which had been planted by Whiteside to defeat Clark. In the meantime, a grand jury had been chosen to investigate the whole business, while the balloting continued in the midst of furor. Between January 11 and January 24, Clark gained steadily. On the latter date, excited almost to a lather by Clark's steady gains, the *Standard* carried this notice:

TO EVERY MAN WHO IS GETTING READY TO SELL OUT TO W. A. CLARK, GREETINGS. WHEN YOU MAKE YOUR DEAL, GET THE REAL STUFF—CASH IN HAND —IF YOU'RE GOING TO BE A CRIMINAL, BE IT IN STYLE. DEMAND CASH EVERY TIME.

When, to the amazement not only of the *Standard* but of a great many Montanans, the grand jury reported that there was insufficient evidence to return an indictment, the *Standard* howled:

THEY SIMPLY FELL DOWN FLAT
HELENA'S GRAND JURORS DIDN'T HAVE
THE PLUCK TO FIND ANYBODY GUILTY
IT WAS A DARK DAY OF WRATH.

The jubilant *Miner* stated that now Clark's vindication was complete. The conspiracy had failed. Again it accused the Daly faction of having planted the money.

Then, after eighteen tension-filled days of balloting, W. A. Clark was elected to the United States Senate. The estimated cost of the campaign for Clark was over $400,000; Clark subsequently admitted to a cost of $272,800 before a United States Senate investigating committee. Thus, at long last, W. A. Clark reached the Senate and won his second round in his battle with Daly.

But Daly, even though ill in New York, was infuriated. He had no intention of capitulating. He later told the Senate committee, "the crime of bribery is bad enough, gentlemen, but to try to fix that on some innocent people was worse." Daly demanded that the United States Senate Committee on Privileges and Elections conduct an investigation with respect to W. A. Clark's election. In the meantime, he sent his minions scurrying about Helena to unearth whatever evidence they could of bribery. Daly's own faction in the legislature petitioned the United States Senate. Although he later denied it, there is evidence that Daly also called in the Pinkerton Detective Agency and instructed them to get the evidence.

The actual hearings by the Committee on Privileges and Elections took place with the convening of the fifty-sixth Congress in 1900.[3] The committee heard exhaustive testimony from both Clark and Daly factions. In the three thick volumes of the committee's ultimate report a sordid yet compelling picture of power and bribery emerge. The committee determined beyond all reasonable doubt that W. A. Clark had been guilty of bribery, and it unseated him. It concluded that the $30,000 had not been Daly's but was actually offered by Clark's agents for the purpose of purchasing votes. While the indictment of Clark was clear, Daly and his forces did not emerge unscathed. In spite of the rather general nature of Clark's accusations and his penchant for violent overstatement, Clark and those who testified for him did succeed in bringing to light some revealing details of the consequences of corporate participation in political affairs. Clark based his testimony on the theme that he had run for the Senate to end Daly's one-man policy of "rule or ruin" and to fight against the power of the Anaconda Company to command the political loyalty of its employees. He reiterated again and again that the company bought votes outright, that it intimidated its employees both in the mines and in the woods (the Anaconda Company had vast lumbering operations of its own by 1900), that it hired transient voters and vote repeaters, and that "it had been very subversive to good government in that country."

Daly stated bluntly that his motives were not altruistic with respect to his fight against Clark, that Clark had bribed the legislature and blamed him for it, that he had then de-

---

[3] All quotations from *Report of the Committee on Privileges and Elections of the United State Senate, Relative to the Right and Title of William A. Clark to a Seat as Senator From Montana* (56 Cong., 1 sess., *Senate Report No. 1052*, 3 vols.).

manded an investigation, and that he had never bought a vote in his life, nor had the Anaconda Company.

The committee trapped at least nine of Clark's witnesses in outright lies and revealed an embarrassing relationship between their sudden affluence and the timing of their votes for Clark in the legislature.

A minority of the committee, while they agreed with the majority that Clark should be unseated, deplored Daly's methods of investigation. Daly had hired A. J. Campbell to dig up evidence against Clark. Affidavits were bought at $100 apiece. Daly also instructed Campbell to buy newspapers to turn public sentiment against Clark. Letters from Clark's supporters were filched, steamed open, copied, and then resealed. Campbell was then placed on the Anaconda Company's payroll at $5,000 a year.

The entire committee expressed horror at the amount of money which had been poured into politics in Montana in elections from 1888 onward and expressed its concern with respect to the general aura of corruption in Montana.

When the committee's report was made public, no one in Montana was much surprised, and few were elated. Except for those papers owned either by Clark or by Daly, public sentiment is perhaps implicit in the remarks of the smaller newspapers removed from the actual scene. The Butte *Inter-Mountain* remarked disgustedly that it was a case of the pot calling the kettle black. The Townsend *Star* said that it was simply a matter of a "thief being caught by a gang of thieves." Some fifty of the nearly sixty Montana daily and weekly newspapers viewed the matter either with weary resignation or caustic contempt. The picture of virtue versus evil, clear and simple, emerged only in the particular organs of Daly and Clark.

On May 15, 1900, W. A. Clark made his speech of resignation to the Senate. He poured out his resentment of Daly and the company for more than half an hour and finished by saying: "I was never in all my life, except as by such characters as are now pursuing me, charged with a dishonorable act, and I propose to leave my children a legacy worth more than gold, that of an unblemished name."

Honorable or otherwise, Clark was even at that moment plotting a new move so bizarre as to be almost unbelievable. In his peroration to the Senate, Clark read a letter of resignation which he said he had mailed to the Governor of Montana on May 11, four days previously. Actually he had written the letter many days before and sent it to his dutiful son, Charles, then in Helena. Charles was waiting to launch a series of activities designed to place his father back in the Senate irrespective of the fact that he had just been unseated.

The Governor of Montana, Robert B. Smith, was an impecunious politician whose chief claim to fame was that he was immovably anti-Clark and pro-Daly. He was also, however, in debt to one Miles Finlen. Through the offices of Thomas R. Hinds, a shrewd politician and a Clark man, Governor Smith was lured out of the state. Hinds, whom Smith had no reason to suspect, told the Governor that Miles Finlen (who had employed Smith in legal matters before) wanted the Governor to go to San Francisco to examine the title to a valuable piece of mining property, and Hinds gave the Governor a check for $2,000. Here was a way to liquidate his debt to Finlen. The Governor suspected nothing. He was aware that the lieutenant governor, A. E. Spriggs, was a Clark man, but Spriggs was out of the state attending a Populist convention at Sioux Falls, South Dakota. So the Governor left for San Francisco, leaving State Senator Edwin Norris, a Daly man, as acting governor.

Soon after the Governor's departure, a wire from Charles Clark reached Lieutenant Governor Spriggs at Sioux Falls. Spriggs at once left Sioux Falls and hurried back to Helena. Here he relieved Senator Norris as governor. Charles Clark then handed Spriggs his father's letter of resignation, which he had held for just this moment, and Spriggs immediately appointed William Andrews Clark to fill the vacancy left by William Andrews Clark in the United States Senate.

One can imagine Governor Smith's state of mind when, on the following day, he was informed of events in Montana. He at once left San Francisco and set out for Helena.

In an interview with a reporter in Ogden, the Governor gave evidence of his agitation:

> This man Clark has been convicted in the United States Senate of perjury, bribery and fraud and it is an insult to send him back to that body . . . it was another one of the tricks, perjuries and crimes resorted to by Clark and his minions to fasten him on the state as a Senator.

The Governor stormed into Helena and at once rescinded the appointment. He informed Clark that it was tainted by "fraud and collusion." He also telegraphed the president of the United States Senate to the same effect. Although Daly himself was in Europe, his machine swung into action. Telegrams and petitions poured into the Senate from Butte, Anaconda, and Helena.

On June 9, 1900, Daly arrived in New York from Europe. On June 10, Clark returned to Butte from New York. Daly had planned to come directly to Montana to rejoin the old issue with Clark, but the German spa had worked no cure on an ailing heart, and he was forced once more to go to bed in the Netherlands Hotel.

With Senator Chandler, chairman of the orginal investigating committee, threatening to reinvestigate Clark, Clark again resigned with a blast at the United States Senate. Chandler, thoroughly nonplused and confused by Montana political developments, could only rise and say to his colleagues:

No rogue e'er felt the halter draw
With good opinion of the law.

The feud, however, had not run its course. Something new was soon to be added.

Standard Oil purchased the Anaconda Company in 1899. There had been much speculation in Montana during February and March of that year about rumors in connection with the sale. When it was formally announced on April 27, Montanans were informed that the Amalgamated Copper Company had been incorporated at Trenton, New Jersey, that Amalgamated was a holding company only, that Marcus Daly would remain the president of the Anaconda Company, but that Amalgamated officers were Henry H. Rogers, the real power of Standard Oil, William G. Rockefeller, and Albert C. Burrage. New York's National City Bank was represented by James Stillman.

It was, however, with relief that the Butte *Inter-Mountain* noted the presidency of Marcus Daly. On April 28, the *Inter-Mountain* editorialized: "Now the anticipated evils of the copper combine may not be realized." A few days later, in a kind of whistling-in-the-dark follow-up, the *Inter-Mountain* added, "After all, trusts and combinations of capital will not change the conditions that now exist insofar as questions of personal independence are concerned, but will merely enlarge the army of employees under one management." Then, with a sort of "oh, the devil with it" conclusion, the paper about-faced a few days later and remarked: "This paper has never endorsed the trust as a business proposition. It has merely recognized the indisputable fact that we are confronted, as Cleveland might put it, by a condition, not a theory."

The *Inter-Mountain* was clearly reflecting the full measure of uncertainty in Montana. Approximately three-quarters of the wage earners of the state were dependent on Anaconda's now varied enterprises. What happened to Anaconda mattered a great deal to almost the entire populace—a fact that must be emphasized if succeeding events are to be seen in their true perspective.

The initial subscription to Amalgamated stock in New York witnessed a "watering" of considerable magnitude. These complex and ruthless eastern stock maneuvers have been graphically described by an insider, Thomas W. Lawson, in his massive book, *Frenzied Finance: The Crime of Amalgamated.* The details need not concern us here save to note that such speculation augured ill for Montana. The matter was so complex, however, that stock quotations in Montana had little meaning. The *Inter-Mountain* interpreted the stock activity as a "freeze out" in which "small operators and buyers on the margin" were pinched in the "interests of large stockholders." The paper was substantially correct except that it had no idea of the magnitude of the business. Butte's *Western Mining World* dismissed the matter with the comment, "The flurry of copper stocks has but little interest to the citizens of Butte. The number of our people who dabble in coppers on the Boston market is small. . . . Thus the manipulations of these shares have but little interest to Butte people . . . the capers of the Bears and Bulls are of no vital concern at this end." This naïveté is difficult to understand unless it was, in fact, a representation of wishful thinking. In any event, Montanans were soon to be disabused of any idea of "nonparticipation." The local political schisms to which they had long since become accustomed—which, indeed, they regarded either with weary resignation or fond indulgence—were now of immediate concern to outsiders who had a stake of many millions of dollars in the turn of political affairs and who were already engaging in stock maneuvers in New York of unparalleled magnitude based solely on the acquisition of Montana property.

These developments left W. A. Clark in something of a quandary. His enemy had sold out, and if he were to strike at Daly now, he would strike also at a great foreign corporation with unlimited resources and vast power. But a seat in the United States Senate, in spite of all that had happened, was an obsession with Clark. He proposed to get it, Amalgamated or no Amalgamated. He had two things in his favor —the fact that Daly was now mortally ill in New York and the fact that a young man by the name of F. Augustus Heinze had recently come to Butte.

Thomas W. Lawson in *Frenzied Finance* described Heinze as "a notorious character who, like the spot upon the sun, looms up in all American copper affairs whenever they appear in the full vision of the public eye." Joseph Kinsey Howard, in *Montana: High, Wide, and Handsome*, spoke of him as "this gay, handsome, industrial desperado and demagogue" and called him "the most adept pirate in the history of American capitalist privateering." This last description may be a bit superlative, yet it is difficult to deal with Heinze without using superlatives. Even his bitterest enemies granted him charm, wit, courage, and a peculiar power over the miners of Butte. They granted all this even while asserting his unmitigated rascality. Probably posterity has granted him good motives where none in fact existed. But for a moment he stood up alone in front of the great juggernaut of Standard Oil and stopped them. It is not surprising that he should have become in legend a kind of knight on a white charger.

Heinze came to Butte in 1889 at the age of twenty and immediately went to work as a mining engineer, having graduated from the Columbia School of Mines. At a salary of $100 a month, young "Fritz" went to work for the Boston and Montana Consolidated Company, and in their mines he learned, and learned thoroughly, the complicated and jumbled vein system in Butte.

Two years after he had come to Butte, he inherited $50,000 which enabled him to go to Germany to study mining and smelting methods. Upon his return to America, he went to work in New York as an assistant editor of the *Engineering and Mining Journal* where he became thoroughly familiar with the marketing end of the copper business. Having thus equipped himself he returned to Butte where he purchased the Rarus mine adjacent to a Boston and Montana property, the Michael Davitt.

Now Heinze began to push himself into the arena so long occupied by Daly and Clark. Mr. A. S. Bigelow, president of the Boston and Montana, however, was the first to feel the push. Word reached him in Boston that Heinze, operating through his Rarus, was encroaching upon Boston and Montana ore bodies. Quite naturally Bigelow sought an injunction.

David had not challenged Goliath, however, with only

sling in hand. Bigelow was a Bostonian. He did not know Montana save through the checks that came from there, he did not know mining law, and above all, he did not know that Heinze had taken a page from Daly's and Clark's book and had carefully prepared himself politically. But where as Daly and Clark had concentrated on the legislature, Heinze concentrated on the judiciary in Silver Bow County (Butte). To put it bluntly, he bought it—first one district judge and later the second.

The "fearfully and wonderfully made" federal mining law contained a clause known as the "Apex Law," which held that if a vein of ore "apexed" or broke surface on any given surface claim (i. e., a patented surface area at least 1,500 feet long and 600 feet wide), the claim locator had the right to follow the vein any distance underground as long as he remained within the 1,500-foot length of his claim. There was no restriction at all on the lateral variation of the vein underground. This law made sense in mining districts with clearly defined vein systems, but in Butte, where faulting had created an incredible underground jumble, and man with a mind to do so (and with a court at his disposal) could cause untold trouble and confusion.

How the battle might have gone if confined to Bigelow and Heinze is an interesting speculation, but academic, because the Bigelow interests were absorbed by Amalgamated and Bigelow's battle became Standard Oil's. The latter inherited F. Augustus Heinze. The burr in their side became more annoying still when Heinze came into possession of Miles Finlen's Minnie Healy mine. Heinze's title was in question, but that did not bother Heinze. He held that Amalgamated's rich Piccolo and Gambetta veins apexed on the Minnie Healy claim, and he was perfectly willing to go to

Anaconda, Neversweat and Mountain View Mines, Butte, Mont.

Three copper giants: Anaconda, Neversweat, and Mountain
View mines in Butte.

Levels of affluence: the Berkeley Pit in Butte, the latest mining development in the area.

court on the matter while he industriously mined Amalgamated's copper. If necessary, and it became so, Heinze was willing to make his point with rifles aboveground and a dynamite war in the drifts and crosscuts underground. Meanwhile, in a burlesque of judicial dignity, William Clancy found in Heinze's favor with monotonous regularity. These were cases in equity, and hence there was no jury.

In the meantime, W. A. Clark had watched Heinze with interest. Clearly, here was a man who could be useful. Clark had money, and he wanted a seat in the Senate. He wanted to humiliate the Anaconda Company and Marcus Daly. Heinze needed money, and he had the actual means of causing Daly and Amalgamated much trouble. A Clark-Heinze alliance came into being. To Clark's *Miner* there was now added the vitriolic voice of Heinze's *Reveille,* edited by the caustic and brilliant P. A. O'Farrell. In a state where invective had long characterized the press, the *Reveille* was egregious.

The first move on Clark's and Heinze's part was to grant their miners the eight-hour day, thus whittling at Daly's popularity. Then they took to the road, where Heinze's remarkable gift for oratory was put to full use. Everywhere they planted suspicion of Standard Oil. "Your enemies," cried Heinze, "are a combination of ruthless pirates who have trampled underfoot every law of God and man in building up the Standard Oil Trust. These people are your enemies and mine, fierce, bitter and implacable." But Heinze was too clever to attack Daly directly. He pictured Daly as a captive "in this great conspiracy." "I know not," he told a huge audience in Butte, "by what soft blandishments Mr. Rogers persuaded Mr. Daly to join this unholy alliance. I know it was totally and absolutely opposed to the traditions which served in the past to guide Mr. Daly."

Clark and Heinze accelerated their campaign. Gradually they won over the Democratic machine by sheer persistence and constant work. Then they set about electing a pro-Clark legislature in the fall. With Daly ill, Amalgamated was somewhat slow to counterattack. They set up a $1,500,000 war chest and bought newspapers all over the state, turning them into anti-Clark organs. They struck back through the *Standard* and their new papers, and they began, through Daly's weakened machine, to take political action.

The months of September and October, 1900, saw the biggest and most flamboyant political shows yet. There were fireworks, parades, rallies, and picnics. The whisky flowed so generously that absenteeism in the mines was a chronic problem. Day after day the press on both sides carried stories of bribery, fraud, conspiracy, plots, and counterplots.

On November 5, 1900, the following message from Marcus Daly appeared in a box on the front page of the *Standard:*

> The election will decide whether justice will be honestly and fairly administered and rights given the protection provided for by the laws, whether employment is to be secure, and it will also show plainly whether men whose plans and enterprises mean so much for our towns and the state shall be encouraged or treated as enemies. You have fought well—the voters will not go back on their own best friends and interests at this time.

Seven days later Marcus Daly died in his suite at the Netherlands. "A Mighty Oak Has Fallen," said the *Standard,* and even the *Miner* paid tribute to him the following day. Daly died with the full knowledge that the legislature which was elected on November 7 was overwhelmingly pro-Clark and that at long last his enemy would go to the Senate.

With Daly's death, the only personal and understandable relationships between Montanans and the great trust vanished. They had, in effect, put W. A. Clark in the Senate, and he was now packing his bags to go to Washington. In the void left by Daly's departure from the scene stood F. Augustus Heinze.

W. A. Clark, a conservative at heart, had entered his alliance with Heinze because of the pressure of immediate exigencies. He had no real quarrel with Amalgamated, and he was a manifestly practical man. Moreover, it was probably clear to him that he would need Amalgamated in the future far more than he needed Heinze. The disintegration of the Clarke-Heinze combination was a natural development.

"What should be done with this man William A. Clark who has gone over to your enemy, body, soul and bank account?" asked the *Reveille* after Clark had gone to Washington. Before long, evil caricatures of Clark were appearing regularly in the *Reveille*. The paper called him "contemptible" and "cowardly," and cartoons invariably depicted him in the salacious company of the "Kerosene Crowd."

The *Reveille* was now alone against the field. There was perhaps portent in the fact that as it grew more shrill and venomous, Clark's *Miner* and Amalgamated's papers, including the *Standard*, grew more sedate.

But Heinze had more than P. A. O'Farrell and the *Reveille*. In the "Table of Cases Reported" for 1901–1902, Heinze is listed as being involved in fourteen separate cases before the Supreme Court alone. The lower courts in Silver Bow County were clogged. At the height of this litigious period, Heinze had thirty-seven attorneys on his staff who were at one time involved in nearly one hundred law suits. He still had the egg-bespattered Clancy, and now he had the second district judge in Silver Bow County, Edward W. Harney. The immensely complicated suits were carried on at an average cost of about $1,000,000 a year for attorneys' fees and involved mining property evaluated at close to $200,000,000.

Amalgamated had considered Judge Clancy hopeless. He was irrevocably committed to Heinze, he made no bones about it, and his ignorance was as overwhelming as was his dedication to Heinze. Harney was quite another matter.

H. H. Rogers, Lawson, Burrage, and Stillman were no strangers to ruthlessness. But momentarily they stood confounded by the situation in Montana. They were used to high financial maneuvers, massive squeeze plays, mergers, combinations, and impersonal dealings. But how did you deal with a corrupt district judge in the tough city of Butte with eggs in his beard and larceny in his heart? How did you deal with the man who owned the judge—who not only had you tied up in millions of dollars' worth of lawsuits but stole your ore between times and was perfectly willing to meet you with rifles at the gallows hoist or in a dynamite war at the nine-hundred-foot level? And how did you deal with a man who had an almost hypnotic power over the very miners who dug the ore in your own mines, who reached these men through the power of his oratory and the venom of his press?

Amalgamated paused, but then it did the practical thing: it tried to buy one of Heinze's judges away from him. Heinze had once written his mother in response to an admonition from her: "My dear Mother, I cannot fight a band of robbers by singing hymns and sprinkling holy water." He was quite right; nor did he overestimate Amalgamated's charity. It had none.

As the fight progressed, *Leslie's Magazine* pointed up the problem, peculiarly moral in nature:

It is to be hoped that Mr. Heinze can be curbed by law without being crushed, even though he represents a type of businessman both predatory and parasitic. For he has made a more effective resistance to the deadening influence of Standard Oil domination than any other kind of man could possibly have done. His course has been without moral justification, but not wholly without excuse. Indeed, the most depressing feature of the conflict to an unprejudiced onlooker is the fact that had he been a more scrupulous man, he would long since have been wiped off the slate . . . . He has been willing to play the game unfairly and win on a foul.

In any event, the first in a long string of casualties, the last of which was to be the "sovereign" state itself, was a mild-mannered, not quite honest district judge named Harney who had made the mistake not only of being bribed by Heinze but also of having an illicit liaison with a not so innocuous public stenographer in Butte by the name of Ada H. Brackett. Mrs. Brackett, it seems, had other liaisons too. She lived in a small house rented to her by an agent of Heinze's, and she and Judge Harney were often together there. But she sent notes to the Judge via a lawyer friend of hers, George B. Dygert, who also happened to be a friend of one D'Gay Stivers, who, in turn, was a lawyer for Amalgamated. Thus, the correspondence between Mrs. Brackett and Judge Harney came into the hands of Amalgamated detectives; the letters were opened, copied, and replaced. These "dearie letters," as they came to be called, gave Amalgamated ammunition because Mrs. Brackett quite clearly sought to influence the Judge in Heinze's behalf. Amalgamated, through its detectives, compiled additional information that Harney had been bribed outright by Heinze. While the information was somewhat dubious, it was sufficient for Amalgamated to proceed. When Harney found in Heinze's favor in the Minnie Healy case, Amalgamated acted. The company wanted a retrial or, failing that, they wanted Harney to resign.

On the night of August 5–6, 1901, in the Thornton Hotel in Butte, D'Gay Stivers and A. J. Shores, Amalagamated attorneys, as well as Charles Clark (W. A.'s son) and Mrs. Brackett, held an all-night conference with Harney. The attorneys and Clark were trying to get Harney to sign an affidavit that he had been bribed by Heinze. They were trying to get Mrs. Brackett to put additional pressure on the Judge. They told Harney that Amalgamated was after Heinze not Harney, but that Harney was going to be ruined in the process. They told him that they already had affidavits exposing his relationship with Mrs. Brackett and other affidavits proving that Heinze had bribed him. Since he (Harney) was going to be ruined anyhow, the point was whether he wanted to be ruined a rich man or a poor man. By the subsequent admission of Charles Clark (in disbarment proceedings against Stivers and Shores), Amalgamated made Harney a flat offer of $250,000 to sign an affidavit that Heinze had bribed him.

In spite of concerted pressure all night long and the offer of $250,000, Harney refused. If Heinze had, indeed, bribed him, he stuck by Heinze. If Heinze had not bribed him, the Judge had more integrity than Amalgamated suspected.

Amalgamated filed its affidavits and also initiated impeachment proceedings in the legislature. Harney countered with disbarment proceedings against Shores and Stivers. In the mass of printed material constituting the evidence presented in these legal actions there is no question but that

Amalgamated's offer was actually made and that Harney turned it down. It is less demonstrable that Heinze had directly bribed Harney or that Mrs. Brackett was directly paid by Heinze. Shores and Stivers were ultimately acquitted largely on the basis that they were not offering a bribe but were offering to pay for evidence. Harney was not impeached.

The Harney matter is important only because it demonstrates the lengths to which the parties to the argument were willing to go and because it shows clearly that Amalgamated now realized that it had to control the Silver Bow judiciary, by fair means or foul. With no real substance behind him, having been deserted completely by Clark, who, indeed, was now in the Amalgamated camp, Heinze was in fair train to force the world's largest and most powerful trust to do business on his basis or not at all—in truth, to pay him vast tribute simply because he had the judiciary in his pocket. In the meantime, actual underground warfare was going on. Heinze was not content merely with legal battles. He made secret crosscuts into rich disputed ore bodies. On several occasions his men actually broke through into Amalgamated workings. Then Amalgamated and Heinze men fought each other with steam and hot water, dynamite and slaked lime. There were two fatalities, and a good many men were wounded.

Both Heinze and Amalgamated began to broaden the base of their political activity. Amalgamated began to extend its influence to nearly every state and county official, with particular emphasis on legislators. In this latter endeavor it had the help of Clark, an old hand at getting legislators. But Amalgamated did not ignore judges, sheriffs, county commissioners, and assessors. It began to develop a vast, state-wide political network. Heinze had remarkable political power in Silver Bow County, based fundamentally on the hold he had over the miners themselves. Even though 75 per cent of these men worked for Amalgamated, Heinze was enormously popular with them. But outside the county, Heinze could not compete with Amalgamated. He simply did not have the resources. Also, Amalgamated was now using its state-wide newspaper network in the battle, and Heinze had only the *Reveille*.

Heinze was repeatedly on the edge of financial ruin. On occasion he drew drafts for large amounts on New York banks, barely covering them in time with revenue from stolen ore. Amalgamated apparently never guessed how immediate his stringency was. His was a very bold game of bluff.

The conflict extended far beyond Butte. As one contemporary put it, "This internecine warfare, coming after the Clark-Daly feud, seemed for a time to disintegrate the whole civic life of Montana. It brought discord into social affairs, broke up business relations, strained family ties."[4] And through it all Heinze was immensely cool and collected.

By October, 1903, Heinze's tactics had become so aggressive and his activities were causing Amalgamated so much damage that the trust decided to act. For three years they had actually prepared for the ultimate crisis. Their political influence was very great. They controlled the sources of news by their control of the papers. They could paint the picture the way they wanted to. However the miners in Butte might feel about Heinze, the vast majority of them were paid by Amalgamated. And there were thousands of smelter workers, woods workers, mechanics, engineers, newspaper people, and office people who, with their families, were dependent on Amalgamated.

On October 22, 1903, the company announced the complete shutdown of all its enterprises in Montana except its

4 Christopher P. Connolly, *The Devil Learns to Vote.*

newspapers. Ten thousand men were laid off the first day, and within a week an estimated four-fifths of the wage earners of the state were unemployed. The Boston *Beacon,* always interested in copper affairs, remarked: "Twenty thousand men have been thrown out of employment. The effect of this act is to bring home to the body of the people, their dependence on the good will of the trust."

It is difficult to analyze the reaction of Montanans in the month of October, 1903. They had long been conditioned to strife, political warfare, corruption, and the open manipulation of political machinery for personal ends. But all this had passed by the average Montanan. Whether he was weary of it, sickened by it, or indulgent, he was at least used to it, and it was of no great moment to him. As is so frequently the case, the average Montanan probably simply ignored the whole business—at once the privilege and perhaps the sickness of citizens in a democracy. But there is evidence that the shut-down of October and the sudden economic paralysis that followed came as a profound shock to practically every Montanan. This was no mere strike or shutout; it was the bludgeoning of an entire state. It affected merchants, tradesmen, clerks, teachers, salesmen, housewives, carpenters—everyone.

In company newspapers they read the involved story of Amalgamated's fight with Heinze; they heard, many of them for the first time, of a thing called the "Apex Law." They were given to understand that F. Augustus Heinze (of whom doubt-less many of them had never heard) was the root cause of the trouble. They read statistics demonstrating how much Amal-gamated had lost because of Heinze's crooked activities, but it is doubtful that any of this mitigated their shock or lessened their sudden and apprehensive realization that they were utterly dependent on the good will of one giant enterprise.

On the periphery, small independent newspapers reflected the state of mind. "Let us be thankful," said the Lewistown *Democrat,* "that Fergus County is not in the coils of the Anaconda monster." The tiny Flathead *Herald Journal* asserted that "a deep, dark, damnable game is being played." "It is a pity," said the Livingston *Post,* "that there is not a daily paper in Montana which can be depended upon to give the exact facts as they occur." The Bozeman *Avant-Courier* complained, "the leading daily papers are absolutely owned, directed and sustained, at enormous expense, either directly by the Amalgamated syndicate or indirectly by the mining corporations it claims to own or control."

Heinze's *Reveille* was stirred to a frenzy. "Once More," it cried, "H. H. Rogers Resorts To The Mailed Fist In Montana." And Heinze himself took to the stump. Addressing nearly ten thousand grim miners from the steps of the Butte courthouse, he thundered:

> If you want to join hands with the Amalgamated Copper Company and the Rockefellers and Rogers in driving me from the state of Montana, very well. It is your business. If you do, you will rue the day until you leave the state, because I will not be gone from the confines of Montana a twelve-month before you get the same order which you got a few days ago closing down all the mines.

On the last day of October, Amalgamated laid down its terms. It demanded that a special session of the legislature be called to pass a "Fair Trials Bill" permitting a change of venue if either party to a civil suit considered the judge corrupt or prejudiced. Then, and only then, Montana could go back to work. It was as simple as that. Petitions began to flow into the capital, some undoubtedly Amalgamated-sponsored, others genuine, asking for a special session and relief. The popular Democratic governor, Joseph K. Toole, who, if anything, had been anti-Amalgamated, turned to his party leaders for advice. He knew full well that this was an unprecedented coercion of state government, and his resentment was quick and bitter. But faced with an intolerable situation, he had no recourse. The special session was called. The legislators, peculiarly docile, trooped to Helena and quickly passed Amalgamated's bill.

While they were sitting (but outside the legislative corridors), there was a last flicker of resistance. Six hundred and fifty delegates from every county in the state assembled in the capital city to protest in the name of a new antitrust party the fact of corporate participation in state and local government. But while the hurriedly assembled convention deliberated, the legislators passed the Fair Trials Bill and quietly left Helena. Amalgamated gave the signal, and Montana went back to work.

F. Augustus Heinze lingered in Montana for a while, but the "War of the Copper Kings" was over. In 1906, Heinze sold out to Amalgamated for $10,000,000, a sum which represented his nuisance value. Some eighty lawsuits still pending in the courts were thus dismissed. Heinze himself went to New York, where he sought to meet H. H. Rogers on the latter's own ground in banking and the speculative copper market. In 1910, beaten and outmaneuvered, his bank failed, and in that same year he died, broke.

The *Reveille* was purchased by Amalgamated and was closed down. Now there was no voice at all, not even the voice of "an industrial desperado." Amalgamated then set about buying the properties of W. A. Clark and the few others that remained on "the hill." With Clark's property went the

Butte *Miner.* In 1915 the holding company, Amalgamated, dissolved itself, and once more the operating company, Anaconda, took over. Anaconda today has no Standard Oil connection.

X

SOUND AND FURY
—AND ONE SMALL TAX REFORM

IN A VAST BURST of activity Americans had increased the national wealth from seven to eighty-eight billion dollars between 1850 and 1900. The frontier was gone; there had been profligate use of natural resources and of the public domain. Both government and business had been dedicated to an immutable policy of laissez faire. Industrial accomplishments had been wondrous.

But no thoughtful American at the turn of the century could look with either complacency or resignation at his economic, social, and political institutions. For all these marvels had been wrought at a cost which now became manifest. The farmer was on the edge of peasantry; industrial development had been inspiring to say the least, but the process had depressed large segments of society; depressions were monotonously cyclical; there was chronic unemployment, a gross imbalance of wealth, and an increasing industrial arrogance. So there arose a new consciousness of man's inhumanity to man, a sudden awareness of economic and social inequity, and an abhorrence of rapidly developing class distinctions. A reform movement swept America. Its roots lay in economic factors and economic abuses. It produced Theodore

Roosevelt, Woodrow Wilson, and La Follette of Wisconsin, and such men as Pingree of Michigan, Tom Johnson of Ohio, Altgeld of Illinois, and Hughes of New York.

Since 1903, Montana had been politically quiescent. Indeed, there had been a kind of political stupefaction. Now the prairie gale of discontent blew in from the East, and Progressivism swept into Montana. It was given body by three Montanans: Joseph M. Dixon, Burton K. Wheeler, and Thomas J. Walsh.

J OSEPH M. DIXON had come west from North Carolina and settled in Missoula in 1891. There he studied law, ran successfully for county attorney, and was elected to the state legislature. In 1903 he ran for Congress and was elected. He spent two terms in the lower house and then, in 1907, was elected to the Senate. All during this period there was little remarkable about Dixon save that he exhibited a penchant for oratory and was unusually alert to the desires of his constituents. But he was both perceptive and intelligent, and, in the Senate, he could not remain aloof from the quickening tenor of Progressivism. The ferment in the nation reflected itself most powerfully, perhaps, in political circles in Washington. Dixon was responsive. He began with ever increasing frequency to depart from the Republican fold, and by 1910 he was marked as a maverick and as "unsound" on such pending legislation as a graduated income tax and railroad regulatory legislation. He found himself anathema to Senate Republican leadership and to President Taft.

In the meantime, a liberal Democrat, T. J. Walsh, was causing some consternation back in Montana. Walsh had arrived in Helena in 1890 after a jump from Wisconsin to South Dakota. A graduate of the University of Wisconsin Law School, Walsh was extremely serious, almost broodingly so, but he had a penetrating intelligence and a thoroughness which was remarkable. He had little of Dixon's personal appeal because he was austere, even cold, and very precise. In a short time he became a lawyer's lawyer. He was nobody's man. And this, in Montana, was itself a disconcerting quality for a man with political ambitions to exhibit.

U. S. Senators were still being elected by the State Senate at this time, and in 1910–11 Walsh made his bid for the Senate. The balloting went on for two months, with T. H. Carter, Walsh, and W. G. Conrad all contending. None could muster a winning vote, and at last both Walsh and Conrad withdrew in favor of Henry L. Myers. Throwing their support to Myers, they managed to defeat Carter, who had been in Washington since 1888 and was, at least in their minds, irrevocably associated with "the interests" in Montana. Walsh felt that Carter "had voted consistently against every reform demanded by the people . . . ." In this long battle Walsh had been particularly grateful for the support (in the legislature) of young B. K. Wheeler from Silver Bow County, who had defied Amalgamated with his support. He and Wheeler became fast friends in 1911. Walsh's gratitude is understandable because B. K. Wheeler risked his entire career by defying Amalgamated. He was, after all, from Butte.

In the meantime, Dixon was feeling the chill in Washington and was beginning to realize that he, too, would have to contend with "the interests" in Montana the next year. Walsh had been pleased with the election of Myers. As he expressed it, he was "delighted" because of his dislike for Carter. Dixon did not share his sentiment. He felt that "the Amalgamated

Copper Company and the Carter influence undoubtedly were in league to have the second senator named in my own back yard [Dixon was from Missoula, Myers from Hamilton, only sixty miles away] to make it embarrassing for me two years from this time." But there was little Dixon could do to mend his fences, if, indeed, he even considered it. About the time that Myers arrived in Washington, Dixon wrote:

> I am afraid that the trouble with some of our leaders lies in the fact that a revolution is on in this country between the ordinary citizenship and the big interests, and they have not recognized the new condition that has arisen . . . . The great handicap to real representation in government affairs by the people themselves is the ease with which the great corporate interests can control conventions and legislatures.

Already Dixon was stumping hard for the direct primary and was, moreover, making his views on this and other matters well known in Montana. In 1911, the Montana legislature anticipated the federal constitutional amendment of 1913 and provided, in effect, for the direct election of Montana senators.

In 1912 the ticket for United States senator could hardly have pleased Amalgamated. Nominating had taken place in conventions, and control of the State Senate was no longer of moment. There were three candidates: Walsh, Dixon, and Henry C. Smith, a Republican. Dixon had dropped all pretense of Republicanism and was running on the Progressive ticket. Smith was a weak candidate, and Amalgamated had to choose the lesser of two very positive evils. The campaign was a bitter one, with Dixon stumping as much for a direct primary law as for himself. The Progressive platform was bitterly anti-company, even to having the slogan "Put the

An uncommon politician: William Andrews Clark reduced
the affairs of state to a feud between himself and Marcus Daly.

In the war of the "copper kings," Marcus Daly spent millions
in his efforts to defeat William Andrews Clark.

Amalgamated Out of Montana Politics" inscribed on its stationery. When, at last, the returns were in, Walsh had defeated Dixon, 28,421 to 22,161. The Republican, Smith, polled 18,450 votes.

Dixon was defeated not only by the opposition of Amalgamated but by a series of circumstances: The Progressives did not have the party organization of the Democrats; Dixon had managed Roosevelt's Bull Moose campaign and had divided his efforts. In addition, Walsh had clearly foreseen that if Montana Democrats were to win, they must, in keeping with the tenor of the times, devise a liberal platform and policy at their convention. At his insistent urging, they did so, thus keeping the liberal vote which otherwise would have gone to the Progressives and Dixon. Walsh went to the Senate in 1913 and remained there until shortly before his death in 1933. In a sense he left the Montana scene. After breaking the "Teapot Dome" case, he became a national figure, and even though he was several times in danger in Montana, because of company opposition, he walked the tightrope of senatorial liberalism and local conservatism with consummate skill. He supported Wilson without fail; he opposed the protective tariff and in general placed himself on the side of liberalism with consistency. But he had his troubles at home, and initially they stemmed from his obtaining the appointment of Burton K. Wheeler as United States district attorney for Montana. Thus, with Walsh in Washington and Dixon girding his loins for the next round, we turn to a consideration of Burton K. Wheeler.

Organized labor had collapsed in Butte in 1914, and unionism throughout the state was weak and vacillating. As the clouds of war gathered, I. W. W. agitators found fertile ground among the demoralized labor elements in Montana, especially in the mines and woods camps. As for the rest of labor in Montana, it was not sufficiently organized or powerful to count. The war in Europe produced an increasing hysteria at home. These were the days of "book burning," of suspicion, and of talk of spies and espionage. Into an atmosphere of hate and suspicion came B. K. Wheeler. Adding to the tenseness of the times was the fact that in a triangular contest between the Butte Miner's Union, the I.W.W., and the company, the latter had won, but there had been violence and bitterness. The trouble reached a fever pitch when on June 9, 1917, a terrible fire in the Speculator mine (not a company mine) killed 162 men and injured scores. Now the I.W.W. swung into action, calling for a strike and labelling working conditions "intolerable." The company's Butte *Post* attributed the agitation to "Socialist—I.W.W. animus and purpose." Four days after the tragedy the *Post* editorialized:

> No grievance of the workers in the Butte mines has been brought to the attention of the operators, and we believe that none exists . . . . The working conditions in Butte are better than the average and compare favorably with those of any other camp . . . . The miners of Butte will not permit a comparatively small band of cowardly agitators and non-workers to deprive them of their livelihood and drive them from their homes, but such protection as they require will be furnished them.

From this time on the situation deteriorated rapidly. One Frank Little, an I.W.W. agitator, was particularly militant, and the *Post* began attacking Little as a traitor and a fiend. On August 1, 1917, Little was dragged from his room in the Steele Block by six masked men and was hanged from a railroad trestle on the outskirts of Butte. The *Post* called this regrettable but referred to it as "vigilance activity." The Butte *Bulletin*, a newly arisen labor organ edited by the brilliant and caustic W. F. Dunne, said that "every man, woman and child knows that Company agents perpetrated this foulest of all crimes." The murder of Little was never solved. Neither was it forgotten.

In an atmosphere of pending violence, hatred, espionage, and crisis the United States district attorney, B. K. Wheeler, kept his head. For nearly a year Wheeler had been castigated by the press for his failure to "prosecute aliens" and for his failure to incarcerate the I.W.W. and clamp down the long arm of federal law on the mines and woods camps and on the newly arisen and radical Nonpartisan League.

But Wheeler stood implacably firm. "There is such a thing as treasonable utterance in common parlance," he said, "but as a matter of law there is treason, but there is not any such crime as treasonable utterance . . . there is no such thing known to the law." It was, said Wheeler, no crime to be a Socialist or a Radical, however strongly "the interests" felt about it. He would prosecute criminals, he would prosecute any alien who violated the specific provisions of the Espionage Act of June 15, 1917, but he would not run around prosecuting people with German accents or people against whom the charges turned out to be the stuff simply of radicalism. As for the I. W. W., Wheeler pointed out that some twelve thousand miners went on strike after the Speculator disaster. "They were substantial citizens, workmen in Butte . . . . I know a lot of them and the vast majority of them were not I. W. W.'s." Wheeler estimated that there were perhaps five hundred actual I. W. W.'s in Butte at the height of the trouble.

This rock-like man had already garnered the company's opposition when he supported Walsh in 1911. But conservative opposition and company concern went farther than that. Wheeler was patently a liberal and a man who could neither be bought or influenced. Worse, he had the temerity to address the Nonpartisan League, the leftish farmers' organization, quite openly and to condemn corporate control of political machinery. And there was something compelling about him on the speaker's stand. He was not fluent, his voice was harsh, almost strident, and his accent was as flat as his gestures were sharp; but Wheeler was rapidly becoming a power in labor and farm circles.

Meanwhile, in Helena, the Montana Council of Defense was meeting. Most states had such councils, designed to be watchdogs of public conduct and to see that patriotism was exhibited in full measure. The bleak and dreary records of such councils stand as monuments to the aberrations which, in war, often lead the principles of democracy into the expedients of suppression and, worse, into political coercion. On the pretense of investigating subversion in the Butte mines, Wheeler was hauled before this body. His inquisitors were primarily J. Bruce Kremer, a Butte attorney whose company connections were beyond question, and William Campbell, of the company's Helena *Independent.*

To read the record of Wheeler's inquisition today is at once depressing and encouraging—depressing, because here was a governmental body at the service of corporate interests coldly and viciously accusing Wheeler of disloyalty to his country and wrapping its own views in the flag of patriotism; encouraging, because under this barrage of bigotry and hypocrisy, Wheeler stood up to them. The Montana Council of Defense, led by J. Bruce Kremer and William Campbell, memorialized the United States Senate requesting that B. K. Wheeler not be reappointed as United States district attorney, "his presence being inimical and injurious to the best interests of this state and the peace of its people."

By this time Walsh was back in the state campaigning for re-election. He had the "hot potato" of Wheeler to deal with. His position was uncomfortable.

If the agrarian revolt farther to the east had failed to penetrate Montana in the 1890's and early 1900's, it had at last done so. The Montana Society of Equity had been organized in 1914, and by 1917 it had fifteen thousand members. It espoused many of the principles of the old Farmers Alliances that had controlled the Dakotas and had turned the Middle West into an area of political radicalism. It protested the unfavorable wheat market and the high cost of everything the farmer had to buy, and it was vehement in its condemnation of corporate control of Montana's political machinery. This organization was succeeded in 1918 by the Nonpartisan League, which was more dexterous than the Society and perfectly willing to operate within the context of either party, just as the Anaconda Company did. And by 1918 both labor in the west and the farmer's organization in the east were solidly behind Wheeler and wanted him reappointed as U. S. district attorney.

Walsh was in a dilemma. If he backed Wheeler, he would lose the support of the mining interests, who, by this time, seemed ready at least to be neutral in his case. But he would also lose the entire conservative element in the state, including the now predominantly conservative Democratic party. If he did not support Wheeler, he would lose all liberal support, both agricultural and labor.

As for the Republicans, they had plenty of liberal talent on the horizon. There were rumblings in Missoula that Dixon might run again. And there was young Sam C. Ford, who was presently attorney general. There was, too, Jeannette Rankin and her spellbinding brother, Wellington, all of whom were associated with the liberal cause.

Walsh chose to recommend the reappointment of Wheeler, and the "fat was in the fire." Wheeler at once became the major bar to his re-election and the *cause célèbre* of the conservatives. The Democratic party was split down the middle. Newspaper assaults on Wheeler reached a crescendo in the fall. Walsh was inundated with pleas from his supporters to jettison the millstone that promised his defeat. In early October, Walsh gave in and with great reluctance asked Wheeler to resign. Immediately thereafter, his prospects brightened greatly. As his law partner, C. B. Nolan, wrote him after his victory:

> The election returns show most conclusively that the Company did all that it possibly could do to bring about your election, and without the financial assistance that was given by Con Kelley [later chairman of Anaconda's Board], our situation would be critical in meeting the expense account that was contracted.

Walsh surrendered on Wheeler, and the company obviously supported him. This pattern the company followed again and again in the years to come. But in the light of subsequent events, there is no evidence that Walsh "sold out." The company was utterly practical in its politics. Walsh had not proved himself a firebrand radical in the Senate. The company, in any event, would prefer a liberal senator in Washington, D. C., to an ambitious firebrand whose political potential was obvious in the district attorney's office in Butte. In any event, Walsh yielded to terrific pressure and deserted Wheeler as a matter of practical political necessity. But Wheeler endured only a momentary eclipse.

The year 1920 was a bad one for the company because of the ground swell of liberalism. When a young university professor named Louis Levine published a book entitled *The Taxation of Mines in Montana,* which clearly reflected an imbalance between the farmer's and the corporation's taxes, he was summarily fired. But the horse had left the barn; the book was out. Worse, Dixon and a good many other people who looked into the matter found the ubiquitous J. Bruce Kremer involved in the affair. And it soon became apparent, if not to the public at large, at least to a number of informed people, that both the chancellor and the president of the University of Montana had been roughly coerced by the Anaconda Company to prevent the publication of the book. The chancellor had warned Levine that he would be "brought up on trial charges of Socialism and Bolshevism" and that he "would not get fair treatment in the press." The University had already undergone an investigation by the legislature for "red tendencies," and neither the chancellor nor the president felt they could alienate the company. Kremer brought charges against Levine before the Board of Education, and Levine was fired. The chancellor had almost pleaded with Levine not to publish the book, "lest the 'interests' crush all liberal thought in Montana." But after the book was out, it proved to be in the tradition of the classical economists, with nothing at all radical in it except that it maintained that the company was not paying its fair share of Montana taxes. An investigation by a special faculty committee and the agitation of Dixon and others led to Levine's reinstatement, but he shortly left the state for areas where independent inquiry could enjoy a more salubrious climate.

Meanwhile, Wheeler was anything but quiescent, and both Wheeler and Dixon entered the arena at the same time. Dixon's platform was the promise to seek revision of the mining taxation laws; Wheeler adopted the aims of the Nonpartisan League and the Labor League. Both men ran for governor. The company failed to split the vote in either primary and found itself in the fall with the unhappy choice of Wheeler or Dixon—both liberal, both dangerous, and both unbuyable.

Wheeler lost to Dixon, 74,875 to 111,113, and once more he retired from the scene temporarily. Why did he lose? In the first place he was the greater of two malignancies as far as conservatives were concerned. They strongly disliked Dixon, but they detested and feared Wheeler. In the second place, "Bolshevik Burt," as he was now called, was too much of a radical for the year 1920. Cigar in mouth, dented Stetson on his head, he stormed the state and poured out his long pent-up detestation of corporate machinations and control. Party label was hard to fasten on him. He espoused some of the causes of Socialism but maintained that he was no Socialist; he disowned the conservatives in the Democratic party but was often too mercurial for the liberal wing of the same party. Flat-footed, flat-voiced, he took to the stump anywhere, any time. And he lost. The support of the Leaguers was not sufficient. Walsh's law partner, in a letter to Walsh, said of the company: "They have their shift bosses here [Helena's Placer Hotel] likewise their attorneys." Furthermore, their own J. Bruce Kremer was Democratic national committeeman, and Kremer and Wheeler had locked horns before; now Kremer was opposing his own ticket.

In the long run Wheeler's defeat was fortuitous for him, because the governorship doomed Dixon. Dixon proved the

old saying that in Montana anti-company politicians seldom
lasted long—a fact to which Wheeler was one day to recon-
cile himself. Dixon is the only Montana politician, then or
since, to reach the governorship with active company opposition. And the four years of his administration were unre-
lievedly grim. Agricultural depression had heightened; the
company fought him tooth and nail and turned their newspapers over completely to the process of his excoriation. The
people heard little from Dixon himself because he had no
medium for expression. The press was controlled, and there
were no radios.

Dixon's first address to the legislative session "earned
rank," as Joseph Kinsey Howard put it, "in the undistin-
guished records of that apathetic assembly, as a great state
paper. It went to the roots of Montana's economic disorder,
yet it was temperate and so scrupulously fair."

Reading Dixon's address today, one is hard put to explain
the historical eclipse concerning him. No governor before or
since has shown such penetrating grasp of Montana's historical and economic problems. No one has so clearly and
bluntly defined them. He dealt with the deficit and recommended new and sensible sources of revenue. He pointed out
the anachronisms in both state and local government and
proposed changes which were practical. But most of all, he
concerned himself with inequities in taxation.

But the legislature did nothing, and it left Dixon alone
on the scene being, as Senator Walsh put it (and mildly at
that), "violently assailed by all the newspapers of the State
generally believed to be more or less under the influence of
the Anaconda Company."

In 1922 a legislature hostile to Dixon was elected, and
this by the Democrats themselves, who were fearful now of

Dixon's "radicalism" and who (the more cynical among them) recognized that four years of the newspapers' unrelenting campaign against the Governor would make him an unlikely victor in 1924.

In 1922, also, Wheeler emerged again, this time in the setting of a farmer and labor situation which had still further deteriorated. There was a veritable gale of discontent blowing across the state. But Wheeler had had two years to simmer, two years to witness what was happening to Dixon and to contemplate Walsh's strategic political withdrawal of 1920. Wheeler was a far better politician in 1922 than he had been in 1920. Righteous indignation would get him no place. He recognized that the wide disillusionment with Dixon would bring him liberal Republican support for the Senate and that he already had the radical labor and farmer support. All that he needed to reach the Senate was, if not the neutrality, at least the mild opposition of the company. Wheeler won the Democratic primary. In November he won the general election by a vote of 88,205 to 69,464.

Who had made the overtures, the company or Wheeler? We may never know, but the evidence points to the fact that Wheeler made them, with Walsh as intermediary. In any event, B. K. Wheeler now went to Washington, where he was to remain until 1946. By that year, time had come 'round. Wheeler receiver the ardent support of the company in a primary campaign against young Leif Erickson. Wheeler had remained in liberal favor in Washington until about 1937, when he fell out with Roosevelt over the court-packing plan. He began then to attack the New Deal and to demonstrate deep-seated conservatism. Moreover, he became one of the most vocal of isolationists. By 1946 he was an avowed conservative, and that year he was defeated in the primary in spite of strong company support.

At least, however, Wheeler's tenure in the Senate was a long one. Dixon's in the governorship was short. It is a sad commentary that both Walsh and Wheeler covertly opposed Dixon when he ran again for the governorship in 1924. This emerges devastatingly in Walsh's political papers now in the Library of Congress.[1] Both Walsh and Wheeler joined the Anaconda Company in supporting John E. ("Honest John") Erikson, a Kalispell lawyer. The fulcrum of Dixon's campaign was his Initiative No. 28 (on the 1924 ballot), which called for a basic revision in mine taxation.

At the time of the 1923 legislature a hard-pressed Dixon had nonetheless struck back. He pointed out in his message of 1923 that the production of the metal mines in 1922 had totaled more than $20,000,000, but the state had collected only $13,559 on the basis of a net proceeds tax. This, to Dixon, was a complete travesty, as, indeed, it was. But again the legislature did nothing. That apathetic body had never risen from the depths to which it had plummeted in 1903.

Dixon, however, had an ace in the hole. He prepared Initiative No. 28 for presentation to the electorate in 1924. This measure provided that mines with an annual gross production of less than $100,000 should be exempt, but it set up a graduated tax on mines which produced more than $100,000, a tax ranging from one-fourth of 1 per cent to a maximum of 1 per cent.

Now the Company made a tactical blunder. It attacked Dixon with every gun in its arsenal, even accusing him of

[1] See J. Leonard Bates, *Senator Walsh of Montana, 1918–1924: A Liberal under Pressure*, 23. See also Jules Karlin, "Progressive Politics in Montana," in *A History of Montana*, ed. by Merrill G. Burlingame and Ross K. Toole, I.

bilking the state by buying an expensive silver gravy boat for the governor's mansion. The campaign was one of the state's most virulent. The press warned labor of mine shutdowns and depression in the woods camps should Dixon win; they spoke of his tax proposals as confiscatory and said that they would not only destroy old businesses but would prevent the coming of new business. They attacked Dixon's policies and Dixon himself, and they defeated him by a plurality of almost 15,000 votes. But in their attacks on Dixon they overlooked Initiative No. 28, and it passed. Few took note, a year later, that under the new tax, called confiscatory and ruinous by the company, its net profit for 1925 was $17,540,532, nearly three times its net for 1924. And the state of Montana, instead of receiving $13,000 in tax revenue, received $300,000.

With the defeat of Dixon and with Wheeler and Walsh in Washington both involving themselves increasingly in national affairs of moment, the Progressive movement in Montana died. There were occasional spurts and starts, such as Leif Erickson's momentary primary triumph in 1946, when it appeared that there might yet be some life in the indignant liberal. But this was a matter of appearances only. For all effective purposes, the defeat of Dixon marked the end of the Progressive era. It had lasted from 1910 to 1924, and the most notable thing about it, in the end, was that, save for sound and fury and one small tax reform, it got no place. The forces of conservatism were overwhelming. On no single occasion did any spirit of rebellion infect the legislature. What on the national scene had led to reform and change that had regenerated Democratic strength, in the end amounted to nothing on the local scene. Forces which, in the nation at large, recast economic philosophy passed Montana by. Industrialists and financiers themselves, confronted with antitrust laws, an alert Congress, and a population determined to share the national wealth, recast their own attitudes and concepts and emerged into the latter half of the twentieth century with enlightened policies. Montana remained in a kind of backwash—for a second time defeated and demoralized.

There was an interaction of events in all this which cannot be ignored lest we emerge with a picture too black and too white. It is a gross oversimplification to say merely that the forces of liberalism and reform were checked by the arch-conservatism of the Anaconda Company. In the first place, there was a conservative element in Montana which opposed Progressivism quite aside from the Anaconda Company.

Moreover, Progressivism struck Montana at precisely the time that genuinely divisive and violent labor developments were taking place. The I. W. W. was not only the company's enemy but the enemy of the vast bulk of organized labor. Its essentially Marxian philosophy precluded activity which would have brought about a *modus vivendi* between labor and the company. The I. W. W.'s were political theorists, not pragmatists. They wanted no half a loaf; they wanted a complete economic revolution, and they were willing to get it with dynamite.

Thus beset with a memory and with frightening things on the contemporary scene, the company struck hard and ruthlessly at developments and men which it had cause to believe would be destructive of its interests. If liberal Montanans were suspicious of the company, the company was no less suspicious of them. They became antagonists in a vicious circle of mutual suspicion which, somehow, the swiftly moving times entrenched. Events left no time for *rapprochement.* Thus mistrust and fear became habitual and abiding.

THE HONYOCKER

XI

The ARID PLAINS of America resisted settlement longer than any other area. Indeed, in the proper sense of the word, these plains have never been settled. A great onslaught was made against them, and in some places, in islands, the population stuck. In vast areas, however, where the settler flooded in, he also flooded out—beaten, discouraged, and bitter.

In the eighties it was Dakota Territory that "enjoyed" the boom. By 1885 practically all of the territory east of the Missouri was settled, and the population was 550,000—a 400 per cent increase over 1880. Crop failures during the years at the close of the decade ended the boom, and some 50,000 of the settlers fled east or west.

Between 1880 and 1890 settlers following the Great Northern and Northern Pacific railroads pushed into eastern Montana, where there were small islands of settlement around Glendive, Miles City, and Billings, and into northeastern Montana. But in the main, the plains of eastern Montana did not feel the plow until after the turn of the century. In sum total, the story of the settlers, the "honyockers" or "scissorbills," is one of tragedy both for them and for the land. The elements that combined to make this tragedy were many and varied; some were human, some were natural. There were errors of commission and omission, and there was greed, ignorance, blindness, and fraud. In the end, however, it was a tragedy of miscalculation. It was based on an expectation that the country would behave consistently—and this in a country where extremes and inconsistency always had been and always would be the order of the day.

P ERHAPS THE FLOOD of settlers into eastern Montana was inevitable. Maybe it was in the scheme of things. Yet with the benefit of hindsight it seems incredible that so many factors could conspire simultaneously to bring them in such numbers and to bring them at the wrong time.

Had they come in slowly, in single families, over a period of years, and passed their experiences on to those who followed them, had they even been wary, it would seem that enormous human misery could have been avoided. But that is not the way it happened; and, in fact, the way it did happen was more in the Montana tradition of too much too soon with too little.

Let us first examine the honyocker, even though he is hard to typify, and then examine his life on the plains at its best. Most of these people came from the Middle Western states. There were Slav and Swedish immigrants among them, but most were native born. Very few were single. A majority had had farming experience, but a sizable number had not. Why had they moved? A poll, of course, was never taken to find out, but we can surmise that they had been none too successful where they were. In the twenty preceding years the lot of almost all farmers had been a hard one. Some of them were chasing a rainbow; some of them thought they were getting "free land." And almost all of them had been subjected to a promotion and propaganda campaign of great proportions. Bonanzas, strikes, and booms have always attracted Americans, and this was a bonanza—at least it was billed as one— a land bonanza, a wheat bonanza.

In any event they came. By 1909 they had taken up more than 1,000,000 acres of Montana land. By the next year they had filed claims on close to 5,000,000 acres. Between 1910 and 1922 the honyocker had taken up over 40 per cent of the entire area of the state, about 93,000,000 acres. And lest it be assumed that he merely sat or that he was not much of a worker, it should be added that, in the year 1909, 250,000 acres were planted in wheat, and in the year 1919 nearly 3,500,000 acres were planted.

The jumping-off place for the honyocker was usually St. Paul. Most of them came to Montana by train, but some came by car or truck. They came on jammed sleepers and on freight cars, usually with all their worldly goods. And when they arrived, dirty and tired, at some new-sprung town in eastern Montana, they usually asked questions of neophytes like themselves; or, more likely, they were immediately approached by a "locator" who charged them twenty dollars and whirled them off over the flat country to look at the land.

They had, after locating their land, three immediate problems: to get shelter, to get water, and to get fuel. None of these problems would strike a humid-area farmer as being much to cope with. It is usually a simple matter to cut logs and find a stream. But there were no logs on the plains, and there were few streams.

An honest politician: Representative Joseph M. Dixon in 1904.

Bulwark of statehood: the capitol at Helena in the early
nineties.

The sod house, common to Nebraska, was not widely used in Montana, but it was not unknown. The sod house began as a hole scooped in a bank. The front wall consisted of blocks of sod, the roof of a few poles holding up a layer of sod and prairie grass. There was rarely glass for a window. The sod house, while it was warm enough in winter and cool enough in summer, was always dirty. As the sod dried, chunks of dust fell from the roof. When it rained, rivulets of mud ran down the walls. In the more elaborate houses, the walls were plastered with a mixture of clay and ashes; blankets were hung to mark off rooms, and chairs were made from crates.

But the usual dwelling of the Montana honyocker was a wood shack covered with tar paper on the outside and newspaper on the inside. Lumber, of course, was at a permium, and as little as possible was used. The shacks were usually poorly constructed so that they developed cracks that had to be filled with paper, mud, or rags. They were seldom located with any deference to wind, and if the shack itself was not blown down in the winter gales (which sometimes happened), it often emerged in the spring with its tar paper hanging in tatters about it.

As for water, few lived by streams. The fortunate few carried water to their dwellings in barrels. The majority relied on shallow buffalo wallows to catch rain water, or they made cisterns. In either case, "prairie fever," or typhoid, often ravaged whole families, and there was always the danger that it simply would not rain.

Not until the eighties was well-drilling machinery either efficient or common enough to be of much help, and often the honyocker had so little capital he simply could not afford to hire a drill. So he dug his own well. This was not so bad in low-lands, but often enough he had to go down two or three hundred feet with a pick and shovel while his wife hauled up the dirt with a windlass.

As for fuel, some carried it from stream beds many miles away. Most relied on cow dung. Many used hay or swamp grass, twisting it into "cats" so that it would burn longer. Many got coal from the railroads, but the price was high. Many a honyocker burned his fence posts or his "furniture" in an emergency.

Even the best of winters were cold and long with biting and sustained winds driving the snow. A great majority of the honyockers left to seek work in the towns during the winter or went to work for the railroad. The wife and children were left behind to sit out the bitterly cold days by the stove and to fend for themselves, except when the man of the house could journey long miles to be with them.

The honyocker built on the plains a different kind of town; or rather, those who came to serve him, or often to bilk him, built the towns. These communities were not marked by the saloons of the cow town or by riotous living. They were built around the grain elevator, the depot, and the bank. They usually had one street, one small school with the invariable bell, and one church. There were no trees, no hedges, and no grass. Sometimes there was a community hall, but usually the church served a dual purpose. These towns were grimly utilitarian. Their only character was the stuff of utility. They were neither bad nor good; they were merely useful. And between towns it was miles and miles across faceless country.

Why, in the face of these hardships at a minimum, were these people here? It all began, perhaps, with the government. The government had long sought to provide "free land" in the West, both as encouragement to the depressed Eastern industrial worker, to provide an "escape valve" for the Eastern

economy, and as an answer to the Westerner's constant demand for land. But the Homestead Act of 1862, which provided that a man could have 160 acres of land for a $10 filing
fee provided he took five years to "prove up," was conceived
by humid-area legislators. Nowhere west of the 98th meridian
was 160 acres a workable agricultural unit. The Homestead
Act was amended and augmented throughout the years. But
the Timber Culture Act of 1873, the Desert Land Act of 1877,
the Timber and Stone Act of 1878, the Dawes Severalty Act
of 1887, and still others led actually to land speculation and
to massive alienation of the public domain to railroads, large
stockmen, and other corporations. The Westerner at the turn
of the century was still bitterly agitating for free land in adequate amounts, and an Eastern-centered Congress still did
not understand the needs of the West. Their intentions were
good; their legislation was not.

In 1909 the Enlarged Homestead Act was passed. It expanded the acreage to 320 from 160. In 1912 this was augmented by legislation reducing the time necessary to prove
up from five years to three and permitting five months' absence from the claim each year.

These two acts constitute the first step in explaining why
the honyockers were to be found in their flimsy shacks in
Montana. But there was more to it than that.

In 1873, James J. Hill, taking advantage of the "railway
panic" of that year, won control of the St. Paul and Pacific
Railway. In 1879 he converted it into the Great Northern Railroad and started building toward the West Coast. Rails were
laid northward to Fargo and Grand Forks, and then the road
turned west to build slowly across Dakota. Devil's Lake was
reached in 1883, and Seattle in 1890.

The Great Northern, unlike the Northern Pacific, had no

land grant. It had to depend strictly on traffic for its revenue. Thus, Hill made every effort to develop the country as the road progressed. He built feeder lines, laid out model farms, brought immigrants from Europe, imported blooded cattle, loaned money to farmers, and offered free transportation to homeseekers. And he was tremendously effective with his whole "colonization" program.

The Great Northern poured out thousands and thousands of brochures and tracts telling of the richness of Montana's soil and the salubriousness of its climate. Professor Thomas Shaw, whose experience was all in eastern Canada, was Hill's "agricultural expert," and his analysis of eastern Montana as a farmer's paradise was glowing. Professor Shaw envisioned 1,400,000 acres divided up into 8,750 farms of 160 acres each. There was to be plenty of rich soil, plenty of rain, and plenty of profit.

There is no evidence that Hill himself was insincere. He hated more than anything else to see an empty boxcar headed east, but there is little question that he actually believed that northeastern Montana could become a land of small farms. He told an audience of honyockers in Havre, "You are now our children, but we are in the same boat with you." And he undoubtedly meant it. And that is the second reason that the honyockers were digging wells one hundred feet beneath the prairie floor. But again there was more to it than that.

Other railroads followed Hill's lead. The Northern Pacific wanted to sell its land to settlers and also wanted to benefit from their trade. So did the Milwaukee; so did the Burlington. So they set up dry-land demonstration and experimentation programs; they put on exhibits. The winter of 1910 and 1911 saw exhibit cars of the Great Northern, Northern Pacific, and Burlington all touring the Middle West and the East with

Montana products and propaganda. They even had agents in Europe soliciting settlers.

Land dealers, merchants, and the grain industry all joined the railroads in this campaign. So did local residents, merchants, and bankers, who had lived on the land for a long time. Indeed, the campaign became public policy in Montana. Here was the old cry for outside capital in a new guise, but it was the old cry just the same. But that is only the third reason why the honyocker was gathering cow dung for his stove; there was a fourth and final reason.

Between 1910 and 1917 nature was kind. It rained, and the war sent wheat to $2.00 a bushel. Land values skyrocketed, and the word spread. Land that had been worth $250,-000,000 in 1910 was worth more than twice that in 1918. Everyone expected wheat to go to $4.00 a bushel; hence the honyocker borrowed money and bought more land—and borrowed money and bought equipment. The banker was as optimistic as the honyocker. He loaned the honyocker money at 10 per cent which he himself had borrowed at 6 per cent. Towns mushroomed; the wheat wagons moved to the shipping points in a steady stream. The honyocker worked and borrowed and dreamed of getting rich. And between 1900 and 1916 the annual average yield of Montana wheatland was twenty-five bushels to the acre. It was the best wheat in the nation.

When the drought came, it did not come all at once or in all places at the same time. Drought is a little like cancer; it seems to spread outward until it encompasses everything.

In 1916, Shelby had 15.26 inches of rain. In 1917 it got only 9.96, and in 1918, 8.88. The next year only 6.86 inches fell at Shelby, 8.85 at Havre, and 7.74 at Glasgow. In the month of June 1919, only 0.09 inches of rain fell in the wet and fertile Gallatin Valley. The green little town of Bozeman was parched. Between 1900 and 1916, Montana land had averaged twenty-five bushels of wheat to the acre. In 1919 the average was two and four-tenths bushels. At the going price of wheat and land, this meant a $50,000,000 loss for Montana and the honyocker.

Dawn after dawn in the summer of 1919 came clear and hot. To the ravages of drought there was now added the scourge of fire and, as was inevitable, wind. Certain elements of nature have an affinity for each other. It begins with dryness, a lack of rain, and then comes wind and fire and, strange to say, hail and grasshoppers—and then dust. And all the while the honyocker looks out over the gray dust of his land, thinks of his debt and his long hours of work, and prays for rain.

The Montana Federation of Farm Bureaus met in Billings in June and again in Havre in July and, in frustration, could only request the Governor to call a meeting in Helena to deal with "a very serious situation . . . unusual and without precedent." The farmers stated their "absolute faith in the return of bountiful harvests" but requested the state Department of Agriculture to prepare information "with regard to the rainfall in various localities in Montana, so as to establish confidence in the *normal climatic conditions* . . . ." (Italics mine.)

The issue of the *Townsend Star* for July 14, 1919, carried on the front page the deliberations of the farmers and included an editorial on the necessity of summer fallowing.

But the crisis of the farmers was immediate. The politicians could not and did not help them. By August, Hill County alone had three thousand destitute, and elsewhere the great exodus had begun. They poured into the towns in rickety wagons, in Model-T Fords, or they simply walked with what they could carry on their backs. On the railroads that had brought them in they departed by the hundreds, only this time many of them rode the rods. There was neither federal nor state aid. The Salvation Army and the Red Cross could do little. The state Department of Agriculture sought at first to minimize the disaster by referring to conditions with peculiar inversion as "less than favorable." The Department sought to attribute the whole affair to the inexperience of the honyocker. "These clerks, barbers, factory hands, and others," reported the Department, simply did not know how to farm.

As bankruptcy followed bankruptcy and merchants, grain dealers, and bankers joined the cry for aid, the legislature convened in special session. They debated, but they did nothing else.

It was in 1920 that the winds came. Many an old-time stockman could have told the honyocker that this, far from being "unusual" or "abnormal," was right on schedule. First the drought and then the wind. Only this time there was a difference. There was no grass to hold the soil. The plow had destroyed it. The honyocker had plowed deep—ten inches and sometimes more—and now he watched his topsoil blowing into North Dakota. And then came the grasshoppers. As described in Rölvaag's *Giants in the Earth,* they:

> . . . gushed down with cruel force a living, pulsating stream, striking the backs of helpless folk like pebbles thrown by an unseen hand . . . . This substance had no sooner fallen than it popped up again, crackling and snapping—rose up and disappeared in the twinkling of an eye; it flared and flittered around them like light gone mad; it chirped and buzzed through the air; it snapped and hopped along the ground; the whole place was a weltering tur-

moil of raging little demons; if one looked for a moment into the wind, one saw nothing but glittering, lightning-like flashes—flashes that came and went, in the heart of a cloud made up of innumerable dark-brown clicking bodies. All the while the roaring sound continued . . . . They whizzed by in the air; they literally covered the ground; they lit on the heads of grain, on the stubble, on everything in sight—popping and glittering, millions on millions of them. The people watched it stricken with fear and awe.

Now it was 1921, another year of drought. There were more bankruptcies. In desperation the bankers had continued to lend, and the honyocker, or those who were left, continued to borrow, waiting for the rain. Neither drought, nor rain, nor insects were universal. And where crops could be grown, prices were high and labor cheap. But soon one out of every two farmers had lost his land. Between 1919 and 1925 there were twenty thousand foreclosures, the bulk of all the farm foreclosures in the history of the state. Eleven thousand farms blew away entirely or were eaten up. And of all the foreclosures one-fourth were by nonresidents.

And yet, incredibly enough, there were those who stuck it out. They were still on the land when the rain came again in the mid-twenties and when the drought came again in 1929 and when the rains came again in 1939. They are still there in some places today.

The honyocker's interlude was a strange and tragic one. He had not been welcomed by the stockmen when he came. They called him a "sod buster"; they were contemptuous of his grubby way of life. And when disaster befell him, it was the consensus among most Montanans that it was his own fault. He left behind him a wounded country and the skeletons of his towns—their deserted buildings banked with tumbleweeds, their windows staring bleakly off over the faceless country.

But there is a postscript to the story of the honyocker, because, as in the case of the cattle industry, something new rose from the ruins of the old. And, as with cattle, it was a process of adaptation. No human force can superimpose a theory over the facts of nature, nor, on any appreciable scale, can nature be made to fit a mold of human design. Land cannot be abused without consequence.

Neither drought nor rain is "normal" on the arid plains; both are. They are the outer reaches of the pendulum's swing. Between the extremities was the possibility of success if methods could be evolved to use the time of plenty to mitigate the time of ordeal. The country had to be dealt with on its terms not on man's terms.

During the catastrophic drought, specialists from the Montana Extension Service traveled to Canada and other northwestern states to study adaptation. They returned to preach the gospel. They urged diversification, summer fallowing, furrow drills, the planting of shelter belts, and strip farming. They ran demonstration trains, wrote pamphlets, made speeches, and toured the plains area inexhaustibly. They developed drought and rust-resistant wheat.

Increasingly the uneconomic 320-acre homesteads were replaced by farms of larger acreage. In Chouteau County the average farm in 1920 had been 586 acres. By 1950 it was 1,940 acres. And, in the meantime, the horse gave way to the tractor, and a mechanical revolution produced the combine and other labor-saving devices. There was a resurgence of optimism.

In all this there was a recognition that extremes were normal and that success could only be the consequence of adaptation. But adaption proved neither simple nor sure. No mechanical revolution and no scientific approach to dry-land farming could mitigate entirely an element of risk and the fact that the margins within which the plains farmer could produce were narrow. For instance, summer fallow had early been held up in Montana as a panacea. But it seemed to defeat itself. It was expensive, but, worse, when it began to be widely employed, it led to worse erosion than before. It conserved moisture, which was its aim, but it invited erosion on a massive scale. When only a few fields were fallow and surrounding fields were in stubble or plant, wind was not devastating, but when for miles and miles the land was nude, the wind was fatal. There was a contagion about it.

But if the strips of fallow land were narrowed and alternated closely with non-fallow land, the wind could not get a clean sweep, and there would not be contagion. Thus strip farming, born in Alberta, spread to Montana. Men like W. H. Reed were almost messianic in the spreading of this gospel, and it worked. It did not stop erosion—drought and wind were still devastating—but it arrested it. Combined with drought-resistant wheat, it gave the farmer a fighting chance. Montana is today the most "strip-farmed state in the Union." Nature was not defeated; it was merely fought more effectively.

After a revival in the mid-twenties, drought struck again in 1929. It lasted for ten years, although it was interspersed with a few wet seasons. Again, there was a difference between areas, but the annual average precipitation fell to 9.7 inches and the wheat yield to 6.6 bushels an acre. The depression brought low prices (wheat worth $100 in 1920 was worth only $19.23 in 1932), and Montana dry-land farmers were once again confronted with the devastating combination of the elements and the price structure. This time there was less panic. Most of these farmers were the tough survivors of the early twenties, but the situation was dire. All things conspired ta make the wheat farmer's cost about 60 cents a bushel and to make its market value 45 cents.

By 1935 one-fourth of all Montana's population was on relief. But at least there was relief. It has been estimated that the federal government poured $125,000,000 into Montana during the depression, much of it for agricultural relief.

Out of this second experience arose still more adaptation, now backed by federal funds and an increasingly active state Extension Service and agricultural experiment station. A new wet cycle coincided with the tremendous boom caused by World War II. In this cyclical picture, if the bad seems to compound the bad, the good seems to combine with the good. It is a business of extremes. Continued rain and good prices after World War II led to continued prosperity. Wheat farmers and cattle ranchers enjoyed rather spectacular success from 1941 until 1954 when a leveling off occurred.

How the concept of parity, the firm commitment of the government to a farm program of magnitude, will affect the Montana farmer in the long run is in the nature of speculation. Probably the direct political power of the farm element in the United States today is greater than ever before. What the Montana farmer never had in terms of power through his activities in the Grange, the Farmers Alliances, the Nonpartisan League, and the Farmer's Union, he now has simply because he is a farmer, and there is almost universal recognition that an agricultural decline or depression is devastating to the whole economy.

But of one thing the Montana farmer can rest assured. The wet years will end, and the dry will come. The wind will blow, and the land will parch. In every summer cloud there may be rain, but there may also be hail. The farmer who never experienced the bad years will inevitably have his mettle tested. Montana's wheat production averaged over 67,000,000 bushels in the decade from 1939 through 1948. It rose to a tremendous 93,958,000 bushels in 1950. But once again there is the element of boom in the picture. Motivated by quick profit, large areas of pasture lands have been cultivated; fallow fields are too often left in weeds; strip farming, except in the soil conservation districts, is being forsaken; and there has been a tendency to expand operations beyond the margin of long-term-yield expectancy. All these things weaken the solid front that scientific farming and intelligent planning can face toward the next attacks of nature, and if there is one thing the Montanan ought to have learned, it is to beware of the boom—too much too soon.

XII

THE MONTANA HERITAGE

Montanans often speak of being proud of their heritage. Perhaps no state in the West produces so many historical pageants, is more eager in support of historical societies, or is more given to celebrations and the erection of monuments in commemoration of some past event.

Yet strangely enough such commemoration is almost always a commemoration of myth and not of fact. Because the truth is that the average Montanan, even if he is perceptive and well read, knows very little about his real heritage. He has, rather, created one for himself. He idealizes the unfortunate Thomas Francis Meagher by placing a heroic equestrian statue of him on the Capitol lawn; as Walter Prescott Webb pointed out, he makes the cowboy into a noble knight of the prairies, and he makes a Titian out of Charles M. Russell. From the tragedy and hardship of the era of the open range he somehow makes romance. He makes a national monument of the Big Hole battlefield and somehow ignores the incompatibility in the fact that the descendants of Chief Joseph today huddle in misery on their reservation.

He makes a kind of god of George Armstrong Custer, whose foolish charge and demise at the Little Big Horn has inspired more writing than the Battle of Gettysburg.

In a way all this is understandable because his heritage confronts him with a dilemma. The past and the present in Montana merge uncomfortably for the liberal and the conservative alike. It is easier to ignore the past, or to deny that it has meaning for the present and the future, than to be confronted with the unclear composite in which an approximation of the truth shifts and moves in time. Everywhere the Montanan is surrounded by his real heritage. Almost nowhere will he recognize it.

Today Montana's daily press is still owned and controlled by the Anaconda Company. The day when such papers were used to fight fire with fire is long since gone. Today the papers are simply monuments to apathy and bad journalism. But the Anaconda Company, harking back to the time when one clever man and his vitriolic paper nearly drove them from the state, would think twice before it let them go. And so every morning, when the paper thumps on the front porch and when, having read it, they know no more than they did before about the real problems of their local community and the state, Montanans are looking the past in the face.

Today the influence of the Anaconda Company in the state legislature is unspectacular but very great. It has been a long time since the company showed the mailed fist. But no informed person denies its influence or the fact that the basic use to which it is put is to maintain the *status quo*—to keep taxes down, not to rock the boat. Few of the company personnel either in Butte or in New York remember F. Augustus Heinze or even, for that matter, Joseph M. Dixon, but it would be foolish for anyone to deny that the pervasive influence of the Anaconda Company in Montana politics is part and parcel of the Montana heritage.

The dilemma which confronts Montanans as a consequence of this is perhaps best demonstrated by the fact that neither the liberals nor the conservatives can take an unequivocal stand in state politics without discomfort. Part of what they stand for must be specious—a denial of the presence of the past. If a liberal attacks the company, personalizes the evil, and accuses it of pernicious and unwarranted control of the press and the machinery of government, the specter of past events rises up before him. Who first cried for outside capital? What would Butte and Montana have been without it? Who first bought votes in Montana and bribed the courts and corrupted the legislature? Dealing with corruption on all sides and with an almost fiendishly clever demagoguery in the person of F. Augustus Heinze, what choice did the company have? Was it not Montanans themselves who first invited the outsiders in and then forced them to fight fire with fire? The company as well as the state has a history. The company as well as the state had reason to be wary and fearful through the years. The company as well as the state learned a hard lesson early. And that is the liberal's dilemma. He cannot invoke history for the one and not for the other.

As for the conservative, his plight is similar, save that he stands in constant peril of captivity. How can he advocate conservative policies yet avoid the stigma of "wearing the copper collar"? How can he join the company forces on some issues and yet remain independent from them on others? His endorsement of them in most matters implies an endorsement in all. It is a wearying position, an uncomfortable position, and because company politicians are both clever and experienced, it is a dangerous position.

Today only 40 per cent of the Anaconda Company's total production of copper is in Montana. Sixty per cent of it is Chilean. What will the percentage be tomorrow? Today open-pit mining has replaced the elaborate deep mining in Butte that required thousands of men to cut the drifts, sink the shafts, blast, haul, and clear. With the levels down to five thousand feet, the old method was no longer profitable. How long will open-pit mining pay, and how many men, in comparison to the old system, will it employ? The answers to those questions mean a great deal to Butte and to Montana.

If Montanans think that the monotonous pattern of rush, boom, excitement, and collapse is a thing of the past or that surely the shrinking world has put an end to the exploitive aspect of our development, let them look to the recent re-emergence of the old story as it appears within the last decade with respect to oil.

Underlying the plains of southern Alberta, the western portion of the Dakotas, and the easternmost fourteen counties of Montana is what the geologists call the Williston Basin. The possibility that vast reservoirs of oil characterized the basin was first pointed out in 1921 by a Princeton geologist. But deep tests were discouraging.

However, in April, 1951, the Amerada Company struck oil at 11,955 feet in Williams County, North Dakota, and this lent impetus to further testing of the Montana portion of the Williston Basin. When in July, 1951, the Shell Oil Company completed a producing well in Dawson County with a potential of 1,656 barrels of 38-gravity crude, the leasing rush was on in Montana. By the end of the year an estimated sixty million acres were under lease in the Williston Basin. Deeptest drilling began all over the Montana portion of the area. By 1952 six different fields, spread over a 150-mile area, had been opened in Montana.

The city of Billings took on a new complexion. The lobby of the Northern Hotel was crammed with oilmen and lease men. There was intense excitement. In 1953, Shell Oil brought in a new well in Fallon County that had the immense calculated potential of 4,255 barrels a day. The excitement spread all over eastern Montana. Oilmen began to show up in the legislative corridors, and lobbyists began to work hard on favorable lease and royalty legislation with respect to state lands.

In one smoke-filled room in Helena's Placer Hotel an old-time legislator sat listening to a group of Texans expounding on what the oil boom would mean to Montana and why the state should liberalize its lease and royalty laws. "Why," said one Texan, "we can bail you out. It'll mean millions for your schools. It's the answer to your problems. You got to have our capital. You got to invite us in!" The old legislator squinted through the smoke. "I suppose so," he said, "but we done that once and it didn't work out so good. If it's all the same to you I'll just wait awhile. If the oil's there I reckon you'll get it soon enough." That was in the legislative session of 1953. Today, five years later, the excitement is gone. Companies that had moved their division headquarters to Billings have moved them out again. In the past two years, six such companies have left the state. The lobby of the Northern Hotel is frequented by few Texans, and the lease men have moved on.

What happened? For one thing, optimism simply outran the facts. There was oil. But marketing crude from Montana is expensive, and drilling costs are high. A well that probes to 10,000 feet costs much more than one that strikes oil at 7,000 feet. Drilling costs are about ten dollars a foot at 7,000 feet, but they rise to about one hundred dollars a foot at the 10,000-foot level.

Pipe lines, such as now exist between Billings and Spokane and Billings and Glendive, may one day be of importance in mitigating the economic disadvantage of Montana oil producers. But production will be held down far below potential until (if ever) Montana's product can meet the price of crude which costs less to produce and transport.

Montana did produce 21,401,000 barrels of oil in 1956 as compared to only 8,109,000 in 1950. It refines, at the present time, 30 per cent more gasoline than it consumes. The surplus is exported and sold at lower prices out of state than Montanans can buy it for. Here, once again, the extractive nature of another industry is clearly demonstrated. State taxes on gasoline do not account for this high cost. Billings, for instance, is a refining center and is very near the producing wells. A pipe line which originates there and terminates at Spokane carries gasoline through such Montana communities as Helena and Missoula. At both cities there are "tank farms," or terminals and storage tanks. Yet this gasoline sells more cheaply in Spokane than in Missoula. While the oil industry has involved explanations and statistical justification for this, the economics of it are quite simple.

During the course of a hearing before the Montana Trade Commission which was investigating the high price of gasoline in Montana, H. J. Kennedy, vice president of the Continental Oil Company, when asked why Montana's refineries produced more gasoline than the state could consume, replied, "Well, the explanation might be that we have all overbuilt the refining capacity in the state with ambitions to get more of the per cent—more of the available business in Montana than we have." But a short time later he remarked: "The

Yellowstone Pipeline [Billings to Spokane] was conceived and financed and built to promote the export of gasoline from Billings into eastern Washington. *That was the real purpose of it."* (Italics mine.) Having thus overbuilt (with both the cost of overbuilding and the cost of pipe-line construction included in the price of gasoline in Montana), Montana is in the position of subsidizing low gasoline prices for the citizens of Washington. The real explanation for Continental's lower Spokane prices is simply that Washington constitutes a market of real substance and Montana does not. For that hard economic fact Montana must pay the price.

So there you have it. One main current in the history of Montana, and perhaps the principal current, is to be found in the interaction of these facts. The land was far away from the main stream of American life. Its wealth, almost without exception, was of such a nature that it could only be converted into coin of the realm by devices and methods created and paid for outside of the region. The raw material could rarely be fabricated on the spot because of the simple economics of distance. And so the land—what was on it and in it—was given over to others. Distance meant cost, cost meant capital, capital meant absentee ownership, absentee ownership meant absentee control, and absentee control meant operation in the essential interest of outsiders with local interests a very secondary consideration. And so it was with beaver, beef, sheep, silver, copper, oil, and, to a lesser extent, even with lumber and wheat.

That is the core of the matter, but there were other factors that heightened the effect and set Montana apart from other areas which also were distant and shared its capricious climate.

In the first place, all of Montana's enormous wealth of copper was found in one place, in one great russet hill. This made it nearly inevitable, in the name of efficiency and economy, that one organization and not many would ultimately own and mine all the copper. Had this great wealth been physically dispersed, so, probably, would the wealth and power that came from extracting it have been dispersed. The physical concentration of the copper in one place led to a concentration of power also.

In the second place, while few states indeed are sensible economic units, the boundaries of Montana seem almost to have been drawn deliberately to frustrate economic unity and good sense. There is, of course, a historical explanation for this. Montanans in the seventies and eighties were accustomed to thinking almost exclusively in terms of the mountains and the west. As of 1880 the vast majority of the Territory's 89,159 persons lived in the west. In the decade that followed the population nearly doubled, but the increase was almost wholly, again, in the west. When it came, therefore, to drawing state boundaries, no one was conditioned to think much about the plains area. It was simply marked off and drawn in.

A cursory look at the map would indicate that eastern Montana has much in common with western North Dakota, and indeed it has. But it is important to note that the most influential portion of the whole of North Dakota's population lives in the humid Red River Valley and that the state's orientation is thus eastward toward the Twin Cities. Since Montana's population is western centered, the state is pulled asunder. Not only is there a kind of geographical pull within the state (a geographic incompatibility), but the state is pulled apart from the outside. Thus, as Carl Kraenzel noted in his recent book, *The Great Plains in Transition,* of the eighty-eight different federal governmental functions in Montana, "three agencies pull Montana to Spokane, eleven pipe it to Denver, one pulls it to Lincoln, five attract it to Minneapolis, four direct its attention to Salt Lake City, five siphon it to Portland, twenty-one attract it to San Francisco, one draws it to Kansas City, three pull it to Chicago, three siphon it to Seattle, two pull it in the direction of Omaha, one attracts it to Sacramento, one filters it down to St. Louis, and only seventeen have their headquarters in Montana itself." What can be said of federal agencies can also be said of insurance companies, banks, and many other private enterprises.

If factors conspire to separate Montana from its neighbors to the east and west, its isolation is more profound from a north-south point of view. Denver is six hundred miles south of Billings, yet the trip takes twenty-three to thirty-six hours by train. To get from the capital of Montana to the capital of Wyoming takes from twenty-six to thirty-two hours. While air travel has alleviated the situation somewhat, weather often makes schedules a farce. The outsider's concept of the air age's impact on remote regions such as Montana is usually profoundly erroneous. There are very few feeder airlines. To get from Helena to Boise, for instance, one must fly a sort of "great circle" route to Missoula, Kalispell, Spokane, Pendleton, Oregon, and Boise. A missed connection in Spokane means a twenty-four-hour layover.

While east-west transportation is much faster and better, its facility is overwhelmed by the cold fact of freight rates. Discriminatory freight rates do exist. The reasons are complex, and the justifications set forth are involved, but such students as Walter P. Webb in *Divided We Stand*, A. G. Mezerik in the *Revolt of the South and West*, Wendell Berge in *Economic Freedom for the West*, and many other scholars clearly and factually demonstrate that regional rate discrimination exists above and beyond the fact that distance and sparsity of population inevitably produce a higher basic transportation cost. Montana has frequently put the cart before the horse in endeavoring to build plants and attract industry to the area without attacking the problems of freight rates and transportation costs first. Neither power resources nor other local factors which might attract industry are sufficient to overcome the basic fact of this prejudicial cost. While it is unrealistic to assert that discriminatory freight rates are the sole cause of high transportation costs, it is also unrealistic for chambers of commerce, the state Planning Board, or other agencies to ignore the facts of discrimination in their endeavors to attract industry to Montana.

It is not only that costs for shipping goods outward are high and that goods shipped in have the high price of shipment tacked on them, it is also a basic fact that these prices, being determined outside Montana and being part of a rigid kind of system, bear no relationship to fluctuations in local conditions. Today there is no elasticity in the kind of things Montanans must buy or in what they must pay for them. The state's economy is rigid. Let drought be accompanied by a poor copper market and falling lumber prices, and the purchasing power of the average Montanan is suddenly and drastically reduced. Yet he must pay the same premium prices as always. There was a time when local self-sufficiency lent elasticity to this pattern. Retrenchment was possible. Today it is not, and as a consequence, even though Montanans participate in the high national standard of living, they do so with little margin of safety. Because they do not control any of the basic economic factors that affect them most directly, a lack of synchronization between local and national conditions

—a lack, in other words, of elasticity—can turn what might be merely a setback elsewhere into a calamity here.

Between 1920 and 1930, Montana suffered a 2 per cent loss in population. The bad years of this decade indicate the marginal nature of the economy. Between 1930 and 1940 there was a 4 per cent increase, and between 1940 and 1950, a 5.6 per cent increase. This gradual growth is hardly encouraging, especially when viewed on a comparative basis. In the same period (1930 to 1950) the state of Washington experienced a 52 per cent gain; Oregon, 60 per cent; Idaho, 32 per cent; and Wyoming, 28 per cent.

There has been a gradual urbanization in Montana, even though of the state's 591,024 people as of 1950, 332,990 persons or 56.3 per cent were listed as rural. It is still apparent that such centers as Great Falls, Billings, Missoula, and Kalispell are bleeding the surrounding counties, and the small towns in such areas are falling rather rapidly toward ultimate demise. There is little doubt but that the new interstate highway construction program, which will bypass many of these communities completely, will hasten their extinction.

Montana's tourist industry is looming larger and larger in its economy. Ranked now as the state's third largest industry, it brought an estimated $90,817,900 in revenue into the state in 1956. Tourist counts and estimated tourist expenditures would seem to be conservative. It is possible that the figure of $5.97 spent per day per tourist is low. This figure was obtained by questionnaires handed out at port-of-entry stations and sent by tourists to the state Advertising Department. In any event, tourist expenditures in Montana have jumped from about $25,000,000 in 1935 to nearly $100,000,000 in 1956. Naturally these dollars percolate through the whole economy, and the industry has become increasingly vital to the state. However, because the industry is more than usually sensitive to general business conditions (the luxury of the tour being one of the first items cut from the family budget), here, again, there is an instability which concerns every perceptive Montanan.

There has been a gradual diversification in the economy, however, which is heartening. Secondary industries are becoming increasingly important. Manufacturing and construction, for instance, made a gain of 47.5 per cent in the number of employees between 1940 and 1950. Fifty-seven per cent of the state's labor force is today at work in trade, service, finance, transportation, utilities, and government. Concomitantly, agriculture and mining dropped from 39.7 per cent of the total labor force in 1940 to 28.2 per cent in 1950. This trend does not indicate a burgeoning industrialism, but it does imply an encouraging though slow diversification.

Census figures projected to the year 1975 give Montana a population in that year of 767,414. Neither state nor federal statisticians see any basic factors calculated to bring about a swifter growth. That being the case, there is little immediate likelihood that the area's economy will develop a broader and hence healthier base.

No concentration on the specific ills that afflict Montana should obscure the overwhelming fact that the problems of isolation are problems of degree. The great trends that have shrunk the world and the nation have thoroughly permeated Montana. *The New York Times* for Sunday is on Montana newsstands by Wednesday. For those to whom the local captivity of the press is a bitter pill, there are the *Denver Post* and *Spokesman Review,* both of which cover Montana news, especially in their local or "bulldog" Sunday editions. Montana radio stations have CBS, NBC, and Mutual affiliations, and Montana television stations are rapidly becoming worthwhile. The great swaths cut across the plains and through the mountains by the tremendous interstate highway system now under construction put Montana cities closer both to the coast and to the urban centers in the Middle West.

A large portion of the Montana taxpayer's dollar goes for education, and the school system compares very favorably with the national average. The university system, while afflicted with too few instructors per pupil, is virile. Building programs both at Montana State University at Missoula and Montana State at Bozeman have kept pace with the inundation of students.

Missoula, in particular, has become a cultural center largely because of the university. The annual writers' conference held every summer at that institution has attracted such men as William Faulkner, Allan Nevins, Walter Prescott Webb, and many others. The music school is one of the best in the Northwest. The beauty of the country and the recreational facilities within a stone's throw of such centers as Missoula and Bozeman are increasingly attracting not only the visiting performer and scholar but also those who wish to stay. Tired of smog and the overwhelming problems of the mechanics of living in crowded urban centers, such people are appearing in increasing numbers on Montana's campuses. To some extent this is counterbalancing the loss of young talent which has so long characterized the scene.

The day when prominent Montanans felt that they had to send their children East to school "to have the rough edges knocked off" has not, unfortunately, passed. There is still a kind of complex about Eastern schools and Eastern experience which is more a part of family tradition and the echo of the day when Montana had no serviceable schools than it is an actual indictment of the educational institutions of Montana today. Irrespective of the merits of an out-of-state education, the trend is a bad one for Montana, especially as regards young men, because the contacts they make in Eastern colleges siphon the best of them out of Montana after graduation. The chance to capture the talented ones for Montana is lost.

For physicists, chemists, industrial engineers, and many others, Montana obviously has little to offer. But others who think there is no opportunity here have simply not been given the chance to see it.

If, in the last analysis, Montana's miseries have sprung from the land via the land's own nature and man's cupidity, one must still return to the land to understand what is good and satisfying about life in Montana. And there is much that is.

Nearly every Montanan, east or west, gives thought to the land because, late and soon, it is so much with him—in its beauty, its impersonal malevolence, and its productivity or the lack of it.

"Chauvinism" is a poor word to describe the strong emotion that one feels for a place. We understand what nationalism and patriotism mean, but we often fail to realize that the identical emotions apply to the smaller place—and perhaps in sharper measure because it is as close as the next step.

Montana is a land of space and beauty. Both commodities are increasingly in short supply in the nation. And in spite of the bitter aspects of his heritage, the average Montanan is open and friendly. There is a great bulk of testimony to this fact even in the works of the state's most bitter critics. There is a singular lack of class distinction and stratification. The Eastern expatriot who brings such notions with him must quickly lose them or be miserable.

Because Montanans are so few and the land is so large (each person having about one-quarter of a square mile to himself on the average), the Montanan is unusually mobile, unusually informed about what his neighbors are doing, and, in spite of close personal relationships, uncommonly tolerant.

Strangely enough, Montanans have a strong sense of belonging—a sense which grows, perhaps, out of their common necessities. They live, after all, in a place where nature can turn a face of cold inhospitality upon them in an hour's time. Without kindness, friendship, and co-operation they could not stand up in the face of it.

And perhaps Montanans feel that they belong, too, because of the kindredship of the old and the new. All around them are the old sights, old sounds, and old smells of the land itself. A stone's throw from any highway lies the wilderness. . . . The clear pool behind the beaver dam is the same today as it was in the time of the mountain man. There is the same tangle of brush, the same sibilant trees rise overhead, and the liquid bird song has not changed. The carrion magpie still flashes his black and white flag in the sky as he always did.

On a winter morning the cattle file down off the bluff and, lowing, move in a long line toward water, their nostrils steaming. It is an old sight and an old sound.

In many a gulch, clinging stubbornly to the hillside, is the ghost town, weathered, tumbled, and yet, somehow, with an aura of immediacy about it—as if a kind of camera trick might momentarily restore it to roaring life, as if by listening intently you could hear dim voices, the sound of a piano, and footsteps on the boardwalk.

In places along the highway the old Mullan Road is still visible—a healed scar along the hillside, a rotted cribbing where a bridge stood, and faint markings through the grass.

And whatever else has changed, the sky has not—its pale immensity in winter, its blue depth in summer, the great white fists of its clouds, and the fierce ecstasy of its sunsets.

Montana is still high, wide, handsome, and remote. There are many ways of looking at it and many ways of feeling about it. And there is room for all the ways.

SELECTED BIBLIOGRAPHY

This is a selective bibliography and is not intended as a guide to the historical literature of Montana.

1. *Unpublished Materials*

Albright, Robert E. The Relations of Montana with the Federal Government: 1864–1889. Unpublished Ph. D. dissertation, Stanford University, 1933.

Bates, J. Leonard. Senator Walsh of Montana, 1918–1924: A Liberal Under Pressure. Unpublished Ph. D. dissertation, University of North Carolina, 1952.

Close, J. A. Some Phases of the History of the Anaconda Copper Mining Company. Unpublished Ph. D. dissertation, University of Michigan, 1946.

Coon, Shirley J. Economic Development of Missoula, Montana. Unpublished Ph. D. dissertation, University of Chicago, 1926.

Farmers' Tax Conference, 1918. Typed transcript in Historical Society of Montana Library, Helena.

Farrington, Clayton. The Political Life of William Andrews Clark. Unpublished M. A. thesis, University of Montana, 1942.

Foor, Forrest L. The Senatorial Aspirations of William A. Clark. Unpublished Ph. D. dissertation, University of California, 1941.

Hauser, Samuel T. Samuel T. Hauser Papers. Historical Society of Montana Library, Helena.

Kennedy, Michael. From Beaver to Beef. Unpublished manuscript in author's possession, Helena, Montana.

McNeilis, Sarah. The Life of F. Augustus Heinze. Unpublished M. A. thesis, University of Montana, 1947.

Miller, J. K. Diary of Life in Virginia City, Montana Territory. Original in Bancroft Library.

Montana Council of Defense. Testimony at Hearings Held at the State Capitol, Helena, Montana, by the Montana Council of Defense, in Connection with the Arrest of Von Woldrau, 1918." Typed transcript, 2 vols., Historical Society of Montana Library, Helena.

Morley, James H. Diary of James Henry Morley in Montana, 1862-1865. Historical Society of Montana Library, Helena.

Sanders, Wilbur Fisk. Wilbur Fisk Sanders Papers. Historical Society of Montana Library, Helena.

Toole, K. Ross. Marcus Daly: A Study of Business in Politics. Unpublished M. A. thesis, University of Montana, 1948.

2. Documents

Annual Report of the Anaconda Copper Mining Company, 1926. Butte, 1926.

Annual Report of the General Land Office, 1885–1886 (49 Cong., 1 sess., *House Exec. Doc. No. 1,* Part V, vol. 1).

Harrington, Daniel. *Lessons From the Granite Mountain*

Shaft Fire, Butte. Bulletin 188, U. S. Bureau of Mines. Washington, Government Printing Office, 1917.

House Journal of the Eighth Regular and Extraordinary Sessions of the Legislative Assembly of the State of Montana, 1903. Helena, 1903.

House Journal of the Sixth Session of the Legislative Assembly of the Territory of Montana, 1869–1870. Helena, 1870.

Message of Governor Joseph M. Dixon to the Eighteenth Legislative Assembly of the State of Montana, January 1, 1923. Helena, 1923.

Message of Governor Joseph M. Dixon to the Seventeenth Legislative Assembly of the State of Montana, January 4, 1921. Helena, 1921.

Montana Department of Labor and Industry, First Biennial Report, 1913–1914. Helena, 1914.

Montana Department of Labor and Industry, Fourth Biennial Report, 1918–1919. Helena, 1919.

Montana Fifteenth Legislative Assembly, Senate. *Report of the Tax Investigating Committee.* Helena, 1917.

Perry, Eugene S. *Butte Mining District, Montana.* International Geological Congress, 16th session, United States, 1933, *Guide book 23*, Excursion C 2. Washington, Government Printing Office, 1932.

Proceedings and Debates of the Constitutional Convention Held in the City of Helena, July 4, 1889, to August 17, 1889. Helena, 1921.

Report of the Committee on Privileges and Elections of the United States Senate Relative to the Right and Title of William A. Clark to a Seat as Senator from the State of Montana (56 Cong., 1 sess., *Senate Report No. 1052.* 3 vols.).

Report of the Governor of Montana to the Secretary of the

Interior, 1885. Washington, Government Printing Office, 1885.

Report of the Governor of Montana to the Secretary of the Interior, 1889. Washington, Government Printing Office, 1889.

Senate Journal of the Eighth Regular and Extraordinary Sessions of the Legislative Assembly of the State of Montana, 1903. Helena, 1903.

Senate Journal of the Fifteenth Legislative Assembly of the State of Montana, 1917. Helena, 1917.

United States Department of Agriculture. *Yearbook, 1916.* Washington, Government Printing Office, 1916.

Warner, Frank W., ed. *Montana Territory History and Business Directory, 1879.* Helena, 1879.

3. *Newspapers*

Anaconda Weekly Review
Anaconda Standard
Billings Gazette
Bozeman Chronicle
Butte Bulletin
Butte Daily Inter-Mountain
Butte Daily Post
Butte Miner
Commercial and Financial Chronicle (New York)
Daily Missoulian
Engineering and Mining Journal (New York)
Great Falls Tribune
Helena Herald
Helena Independent
Livingston Enterprise
Lewistown Democrat

London Economist
Mining and Scientific Press (San Francisco)
Montana Free Press (Butte)
Montana Mining and Market Reporter (Butte)
Montana Socialist (Butte)
Montana Standard (Butte)
New Northwest (Deer Lodge)
People's Voice (Helena)
Reveille (Butte)
River Press (Fort Benton)
Rocky Mountain Husbandman (White Sulphur and Great Falls)
Townsend Star
Western Mining World (Butte)

4. Books

Athearn, Robert G. *Thomas Francis Meagher: An Irish Revolutionary in America.* Boulder, University of Colorado Press, 1949.

Bancroft, Hubert Howe. *History of Washington, Idaho, and Montana.* (Vol. XXXI in *Works.*) San Francisco, 1890.

Burlingame, Merrill G. *The Montana Frontier.* Helena, State Publishing Company, 1942.

———, and K. Ross Toole, eds. *A History of Montana.* 3 vols. New York, The Lewis Publishing Company, 1957.

Chittenden, H. M. *The American Fur Trade of the Far West.* 3 vols. New York, Francis P. Harper, 1902.

———. *History of Early Steamboat Navigation on the Missouri River.* 2 vols. New York, Francis P. Harper, 1903.

Connolly, Christopher P. *The Devil Learns To Vote.* New York, Covici Friede, 1938.

The Copper Handbook, I–IX. Houghton, Michigan, Horace J. Stevens, 1900–13.

Elliott, W. Y., and others. *International Control in the Non-ferrous Metals.* New York, Macmillan Company, 1937.

Ferris, W. A. *Life in the Rocky Mountains,* ed. by Paul C. Phillips. Denver, Old West Publishing Company, 1940.

Gerard, James W. *My First Eighty-three Years in America.* New York, Doubleday, 1951.

Glasscock, Carl B. *The War of the Copper Kings.* Indianapolis and New York, The Bobbs-Merrill Company, 1935.

Goodwin, Charles C. *As I Remember Them.* Salt Lake, 1913.

Hamilton, James M. *From Wilderness to Statehood: A History of Montana.* Ed. by Merrill G. Burlingame. Portland, Binfords and Mort, 1957.

Harris, Burton. *John Colter.* New York, Chas. Scribner's Sons, 1952.

Hibbard, Benjamin H. *History of the Public Land Policies.* New York, Macmillan Company, 1924.

Hill, Robert T. *The Public Domain and Democracy.* New York, Columbia University Press, 1910.

Howard, Joseph K. *Montana: High, Wide, and Handsome.* New Haven, Yale University Press, 1943.

Jensen, Vernon H. *Heritage of Conflict: Labor Relations in the Non-ferrous Metals Industry up to 1930.* Ithaca, Cornell University Press, 1950.

Kraenzel, Carl F. *The Great Plains In Transition.* Norman, University of Oklahoma Press, 1955.

Langford, Nathaniel P. *Vigilante Days and Ways.* Chicago, A. C. McClurg, 1912.

Laveille, E. *Life of Father DeSmet, S. J.* New York, P. J. Kenedy and Sons, 1915.

Lawson, Thomas W. *The Crime of Amalgamated,* Vol. I of *Frenzied Finance.* New York, The Ridgeway-Thayer Company, 1905.

Leeson, Michael (ed.). *History of Montana.* Chicago, Warner, Beers, and Company, 1885.

Levine, Louis. *The Taxation of Mines in Montana.* New York, W. B. Heubsch, 1919.

Lewis, Meriwether, and William Clark. *The Journals of Lewis and Clark.* Ed. by Bernard DeVoto. Boston, Houghton, Mifflin, 1953.

———. *Original Journals of the Lewis and Clark Expedition.* Ed. by Reuben G. Thwaites. 15 vols. New York, Dodd, Mead and Company, 1904.

Lindsay, John. *The Amazing Experiences of a Judge.* Philadelphia, Dorrance and Company, 1939.

MacKnight, James A. *The Mines of Montana: Their History and Development to Date.* Helena, C. K. Wells Co., Printers, 1892.

Mangam, William D. *The Clarks: An American Phenomenon.* New York, Silver Bow Press, 1941.

Miller, Joaquin. *An Illustrated History of the State of Montana.* 2 vols. Chicago, The Lewis Publishing Company, 1894.

The Mineral Industry: Its Statistics, Technology, and Trade. New York, McGraw-Hill Company, 1911.

Murdoch, Angus. *Boom Copper.* New York, Macmillan Company, 1943.

Murphy, Jerre C. *The Comical History of Montana.* San Diego, E. L. Scofield, 1912.

Older, Fremont and Cora. *The Life of George Hearst: California Pioneer.* San Francisco, privately printed, 1932.

Osgood, Ernest S. *The Day of the Cattleman.* Minneapolis, University of Minnesota Press, 1929.

Palladino, Lawrence B. *Indian and White in the Northwest: A History of Catholicity in Montana, 1831 to 1891.* Lancaster, Pennsylvania, Wickersham Publishing Company, 1922.

Progressive Men of Montana. Chicago, A. W. Bowen and Company, 1902.

Raymer, Robert G. *A History of Copper Mining in Montana.* Chicago, The American Historical Publishing Company, 1930.

———. *Montana: The Land and the People.* 3 vols. Chicago, The Lewis Publishing Company, 1930.

Renne, R. R. *A Preliminary Report of the Butte Economic Survey.* Butte, W. P. A. Writers' Program, 1939.

Roberts, Warren A. *State Taxation of Metallic Deposits.* Cambridge, Harvard University Press, 1944.

Ross, Alexander. *The Fur Hunters of the Far West.* London, Smith, Elder and Company, 1883; reprinted 1956 by the University of Oklahoma Press, Norman (ed. by Kenneth A. Spaulding).

Sanders, Helen F. *A History of Montana.* 3 vols. Chicago, The Lewis Publishing Company, 1913.

Sharp, Paul. *Whoop-up Country.* Minneapolis, University of Minnesota Press, 1955.

Stewart, Edgar I. *Custer's Luck.* Norman, University of Oklahoma Press, 1955.

Stuart, Granville. *Forty Years on the Frontier, as Seen in the Journals of Granville Stuart.* Ed. by Paul C. Phillips. 2 vols. Cleveland, Arthur H. Clark, 1925.

Trimble, William J. *The Mining Advance into the Inland Empire.* Madison, University of Wisconsin Press, 1914.

Webb, Walter Prescott. *The Great Plains.* Boston, Houghton Mifflin, 1936.

W. P. A. Writers' Program. *Copper Camp.* New York, Hastings House, 1943.

5. *Articles*

Anon. "Anaconda," *Fortune Magazine* (December, 1936–January, 1937).

———. "Anaconda Standard," *Time Magazine* (July 27, 1931).

———. "J. B. A. Haggin," *Pacific Coast Annual Mining Review* (1878–79).

Andrews, E. Benjamin. "The Late Copper Syndicate," *Quarterly Journal of Economics*, Vol. III (1888–89).

Athearn, Robert G. "Frontier Critics of the Western Army," *Montana: The Magazine of Western History*, Vol. V (Spring, 1955).

Connolly, Christopher P. "The Story of Montana," *McClure's Magazine*, Vols. XXVII–XXIX (August, 1906–July, 1907).

Fletcher, Robert S. "That Hard Winter in Montana, 1886–1887," *Agricultural History*, Vol. IV (October, 1930).

Forbis, Richard G. "The Flathead Apostasy," *Montana Magazine of History*, Vol. I (October, 1951).

———, and John D. Sperry. "An Early Man Site in Montana," *American Antiquity*, Vol. XVIII, No. 2 (1952).

Howard, Joseph K. "Butte," in *Our Fair City*, ed. by Robert S. Allen. New York, Vanguard Press, 1947.

———. "The Decline and Fall of Burton K. Wheeler," *Harper's Magazine* (March, 1947).

———. "The Montana Twins in Trouble," *Harper's Magazine* (September, 1944).

———. "What Happened in Butte," *Harper's Magazine* (August, 1948).

Ingalls, W. R. "Anaconda Financing," *Engineering and Mining Journal* (June 16, 1918).

Knapp, Henry R. "William Andrews Clark," *Cosmopolitan*, Vol. XXXIV (February, 1903).

Libby, Orrin G. "Some Verendrye Enigmas," *Mississippi Valley Historical Review,* Vol. III (September, 1916).

Mattison, Ray H. "The Hard Winter and the Range Cattle Business," *Montana Magazine of History,* Vol. I (October, 1951).

McElroy, Harold L. "Mercurial Military," *Montana Magazine of History,* Vol. IV (Fall, 1954).

Neuberger, Richard L. "Wheeler of Montana," *Harper's Magazine* (May, 1940).

Phillips, Paul C. "Marcus Daly," *Dictionary of American Biography,* V. New York, Charles Scribner's Sons, 1930.

———, and H. A. Trexler. "Notes on the Discovery of Gold in the Northwest," *Mississippi Valley Historical Review,* Vol. IV (June, 1917).

Plassman, Martha E. "Biographical Sketch of Hon. Sidney Edgerton," *Contributions* of the Historical Society of Montana, Vol. III (1900).

Rae, John B. "Commissioner Sparks and the Railroad Land Grants," *Mississippi Valley Historical Review,* Vol. XXV (September, 1938).

Rice, Claud T. "The Copper Syndicate," *Wall Street Journal* (July, 1932).

Richter, F. E. "The Amalgamated Copper Company: A Closed Chapter in Corporate Finance," *Quarterly Journal of Economics,* Vol. XXX (1915–16).

Sales, Reno. "Ore Deposits at Butte, Montana," *Transactions of the American Institute of Mining Engineers,* Vol. XLVI (1882).

Shamel, Charles H. "Should the Apex Law Be Now Repealed?" *Transactions of the Institute of Mining Engineers* (New York Meeting, February, 1914).

Shelton, Willard. "Anaconda's Big Steal," *The Nation* (January 5, 1952).

Smurr, John W. "The Montana Tax Conspiracy of 1889," *Montana: The Magazine of Western History*, Vol. V (Spring, 1955–Summer, 1955).

———. "A New Verendrye Theory," *Pacific Northwest Quarterly*, Vol. XLIII (1952).

Toole, K. Ross. "The Anaconda Copper Mining Company: A Price War and a Copper Corner," *Pacific Northwest Quarterly*, Vol. XLI (October, 1950).

———. "The Genesis of the Clark-Daly Feud," *The Montana Magazine of History*, Vol. I (April, 1951).

———. "When Big Money Came to Butte," *Pacific Northwest Quarterly*, Vol. XLIV (January, 1953).

Trimble, William J. "A Reconsideration of Gold Discoveries in the Northwest," *Mississippi Valley Historical Review*, Vol. V (June, 1918).

Villard, Oswald G. "The Press Today. Montana and the 'Company,'" *The Nation* (July 9, 1930).

Warren, Charles S. "Historical Address: The Territory of Montana," *Contributions* of the Historical Society of Montana, Vol. II (1896).

Wilber, C. W. "The Way of the Land Transgressor: How Montana was 'Done'," *Pacific Monthly* (January, 1908).

Woody, Frank H. "A Sketch of the Early History of Western Montana," *Contributions* of the Historical Society of Montana, Vol. II (1896).

INDEX

Index

273

MONTANA was set into type on the Linotype machine in eleven-point Caledonia with three points of spacing between the lines. This marks the first use of *Montanan,* the hand-drawn initial letters used in the chapter openings. *Montanan,* drawn by Richard Palmer of the Press staff especially for this book, is meant to convey something of the cleanness and sweep of the High Plains and mountains as well as some of the vigor of the frontier.

University of Oklahoma Press
Norman